T0283276

Praise for *Goodbye, Oakland*

"I am old enough to not only remember the American Football League—I still revere it. The Oakland Raiders of the late 1960s became a powerhouse and remained that way for many, many years thereafter as a team that knew how to 'just win, baby.'

"I am old enough to remember the arrival of the A's in Oakland to that brand-new stadium, which I thought was a beautiful place to watch a baseball game. Those green-and-gold uniforms, complete with white cleats, not only became a fashion statement, but they also became the attire worn by world champions for three straight years. Both the A's and Raiders were, in different ways, images of Oakland and East Bay grit, as well as Northern California coolness. Both had sizable national followings for good reason.

"Yes, I'm old enough to remember the National Hockey League's California Golden Seals skating in Oakland, which means I well remember the arrival of the Golden State Warriors from across the Bay. It all seemed so fresh and so promising. Times do change over a half-century. But with regard to Oakland sports, should they have changed so much? *Goodbye, Oakland* takes us through all of it, from when the sky was the limit to when the bottom fell out."

—Chris Berman,
original ESPN sportscaster, longtime NFL and baseball commentator, "heartfelt champion for the Bay Area"

"The saga of Oakland professional sports is an epic arc of political dealing, championship triumphs, misdirections, outright lies, a mule mascot, moving vans, naively loyal fans, and sad franchise evacuations. There are layers and layers (and more layers) to the story. No one knows those layers better than Dave Newhouse and Andy Dolich. Their take will go down as the definitive book on the subject."

—Mark Purdy,
retired *San Jose Mercury-News* sports columnist

"The Raiders, Warriors, and A's, those modern-day robber barons, captured the hearts of Oakland fans, and repaid that loyalty with callous disregard. Dave Newhouse and Andy Dolich chronicle the history of those teams run by colorful owners who eventually turned tail and slunk out of town."

—**John Porter,**
former *Oakland Tribune* and *USA TODAY* journalist

"This is a sad story, and Dave Newhouse is the writer to tell it. He's an eyewitness to the fleecing and bloodletting. Let's hope a new day will come, new franchises, and Newhouse is still around to tell us what's happening."

—**Barry Gifford,**
best-selling author, screenwriter, adventurer

"For 50 years, Oakland has been the center of professional sports in the Bay Area. Its story is best told by Dave Newhouse, who chronicled championships and Hall of Famers, and by Andy Dolich, an essential architect of the city's sports history."

—**Ted Robinson,**
Bay Area, national, and Olympic Games sportscaster

"Dave Newhouse knows more about Oakland sports than anyone, except maybe Andy Dolich, and they know *everybody*. Together, they'll show you things you've never seen or heard about the Raiders, A's, and Warriors, sharing the comings and—lately, sadly—goings of three championship franchises."

—**Pete Wevurski,**
former *Oakland Tribune* editor-in-chief,
current *San Francisco Chronicle* copy desk chief

"How did we get here? In *Goodbye, Oakland,* Andy Dolich and Dave Newhouse dive into the bowels of Oakland's colorful championship sports history to bring us a compelling, page-turning account of how Oakland has become the most scorned sports city on Earth despite producing so many legendary sports figures."

—**Dale Tafoya,**
Oakland sportswriter who covers the A's online

"I was born in Oakland in 1961. Little did I know what I would experience growing up: every time you turned around, *Oakland* and *winning* were in the same headlines. Oakland's glory years are now visible only in the rearview mirror. Such a shame."

—Mark Macrae,
Pacific Coast League Historical Society director

"If Dave Newhouse and Andy Dolich report it, then it is accurate. If Oakland and Alameda County officials, along with the Raiders, Warriors, and A's owners over the years, had half the knowledge of and commitment to Oakland as Newhouse and Dolich demonstrate in this book, then the three teams would be happily at home in Oakland today."

—Corey Busch,
San Francisco Giants executive emeritus

"*Goodbye, Oakland* is a story waiting anxiously to be told, a story of greed, corruption, and deception at the heart of the city's premier sports franchises. Dave Newhouse and Andy Dolich pull no punches in this hard-hitting account of how big-time sports has become big money and big business, looking for that pot of gold wherever they think they can find it. And fans be damned!"

—Michael C. Healy,
Oakland resident, retired Bay Area Rapid Transit executive

"Local teams are paramount to our sense of community. Dave Newhouse and Andy Dolich have brilliantly chronicled Oakland's loss of the Raiders and Warriors, and now possibly the A's. This fantastic read reveals many of the critical mistakes teams and municipalities make at the expense of their most fanatical supporters."

—Dennis Mannion,
Los Angeles Dodgers, Philadelphia Phillies, Detroit Pistons, Baltimore Ravens, and Colorado Avalanche executive

"Every time I drive past the Oakland Coliseum and Arena, I see my dad taking me to ball games for a look at Daryle Lamonica, Nate Thurmond, Reggie Jackson, Vida Blue, Catfish Hunter, etc. Losing two teams, and possibly a third, is a blow to Oakland. But memories are eternal in this smart tribute by ace scribes Dave Newhouse and Andy Dolich, and Oakland, as always, will survive."

—**Steve Lopez,**
ex-*Oakland Tribune* writer, current *Los Angeles Times* columnist,
author of *The Soloist*, which became a major motion picture

"Oakland is a special part of me. It's where I was born, and where my career experienced a rebirth. With the Oakland A's, we won the World Championship in 1989. I was the American League's Most Valuable Player and Cy Young Award recipient in 1992. Those years in Oakland paved the way for my induction into the Baseball Hall of Fame in 2004."

—**Dennis Eckersley,**
hometown hero and relief pitcher exemplar

"Some of my fondest memories are attending Oakland sporting events with my dad, including numerous Raiders comeback victories in the 1970s. I had a Dave Casper jersey that I wore almost every day. I played for the Dallas Cowboys in the Coliseum the first season the Raiders came back to Oakland [from Los Angeles], which was a huge thrill. The one common thread throughout the years has been Dave Newhouse's passionate support of Oakland professional sports."

—**Eric Bjornson,**
Oakland native and former Dallas Cowboys tight end

"When it comes to sportswriters, Dave Newhouse needs no introduction. He's written close to 20 books on sports—athletes and organizations. He's a fixture in Bay Area sports, so who better to write the history of Oakland sports than Dave and Andy Dolich, a former A's and Warriors executive?"

—**Delvin Williams,**
49ers and Dolphins 1,000-yard rusher,
two-time All-Pro, author

"Peerless and compelling, Bay Area sports deans Dave Newhouse and Andy Dolich chronicle the drama, anguish, and backstories behind Oakland possibly losing all three sports franchises. A highly recommended portrayal of owners' shifting priorities, with fans relegated to secondary status."

—**Christopher Weills,**
publisher of *The Ultimate Sports Guide* weekly e-zine

"Dave Newhouse and Andy Dolich have written a riveting and essential history of Oakland's sports losses."

—**Chris Westover,**
Oakland resident and retired attorney
who represented the Warriors and A's

"Oakland fans are the best in the world. Oakland will be home forever."

—**Stephen Vogt,**
A's catcher, after homering in his final career at-bat,
October 5, 2022

"Hey, you Hollywood screenwriters, listen up. There is a hilarious movie waiting to be made about Oakland sports—the heartless and greedy owners, the clueless and jock-sniffing politicians, the crazy-loyal fans, the infinitely entertaining athletes. All the right material for your screenplay is right here in this book. It's the definitive story of a gritty little town and the many teams that have f—d it over, an epic and eye-opening tale that can only be told by writers with boots on the ground and hearts in the game. So hats off to Dave Newhouse and Andy Dolich."

—**Scott Ostler,**
San Francisco Chronicle award-winning
sports columnist, author

"As someone who has been covering Oakland and Oakland sports for nearly 40 years, I thought I knew almost everything there was to know about our town. How wrong I was. This treasure of great stories, unforgettable characters, and an abiding affection for a city that has always loved its teams, but hasn't always received love in return, is a must read. But don't start late in the day. You'll be up until the next morning."

—Martin Snapp,
East Bay Times columnist

"An easy way to describe my reaction to Oakland's professional sports franchise problem is to share an unusual conversation my wife, Nancy, and I had in France with waiters at an upscale Paris restaurant.

"Our waiters spoke flawless English, and after learning of our San Francisco–area home, they asked if we were fans of American football. We replied that we had 49ers season tickets for 10 years, but why their interest in our game of football given their love of soccer? They said that they followed one NFL team very closely, the Green Bay Packers.

"Why the Packers? Because, the waiters said, they are city owned, individuals buying shares in a publicly owned team. No egomaniacal owners. What a breath of fresh air! Sooner or later, cities will learn they cannot trust those egoistic types to own and control sports franchises."

—Lawrence Ludgus,
retired Bay Area attorney now living in Delaware

Goodbye, Oakland

Goodbye, Oakland

Winning, Wanderlust,
and a Sports Town's Fight
for Survival

**Andy Dolich
and
Dave Newhouse**

TRIUMPH
B O O K S

No part of this publication may be reproduced, stored in a retrieval system, or transmitted in any form by any means, electronic, mechanical, photocopying, or otherwise, without the prior written permission of the publisher, Triumph Books LLC, 814 North Franklin Street, Chicago, Illinois 60610.

Library of Congress Cataloging-in-Publication Data available upon request.

This book is available in quantity at special discounts for your group or organization. For further information, contact:

Triumph Books LLC
814 North Franklin Street
Chicago, Illinois 60610
(312) 337-0747
www.triumphbooks.com

Printed in U.S.A.
ISBN: 978-1-63727-215-2
Design by Nord Compo
Photos courtesy of the Hayward Area Historical Society unless otherwise indicated

To the millions of Oakland sports fans who remained loyal when some owners didn't

—A.D.

To Callan and Campbell Newhouse, two shining stars in their grandparents' galaxy

—D.N.

Contents

Foreword

Oakland is tough, compassionate, fearless, and enlightened. I have tried to be all those things as a member of Congress and as a human being. Oakland has so many selling points that it would be hard to list them all, but start with its revolutionary spirit, which has put us on the front lines of the movements for civil rights and justice in this country, going back generations.

Oakland's diversity is at the heart of what makes it so unique. We have a multiplicity of cultures and social backgrounds. Nearly every ethnic group is represented, more than 125 languages are spoken within our borders, and we have cultural groups and centers for just about everyone. Our melting pot of cultures and communities creates more room for understanding and harmony and tends to lead to more empathy. We are a true city of the world and a great representation of our country at large.

Oakland often has been the subject of racist narratives that paint the entire community as out of control and dangerous. That has made it much more difficult for Oakland to present itself, and to move past its image as San Francisco's more rough-and-tumble neighbor.

However, Oakland often is ahead of its time. We have been out in front against police brutality and abuse. We have been ahead of the rest of the country on ending prohibition against cannabis, which was always rooted in racism. We are leading the state and the country in the fight for economic and racial and environmental justice. You need toughness to be ahead of your time, and one thing I love about Oakland is that we have the grit and resiliency to keep fighting for a more fair and just country, generation after generation, without ever losing sight of that goal.

Oakland also is a beautiful city in the heart of the most beautiful state in a country of beautiful states. We have the forests, the Bay, the lakes (Merritt and Temescal), the views of the San Francisco skyline and Mt. Tamalpais in Marin County. Yes, Oakland is a complex city, and we have many challenges, but these plusses are just some of reasons why people always have been drawn here. The city is diverse, but also dynamic.

Of course, too, I'm a fan of our sports teams, especially those remaining in Oakland, like the baseball A's. It was a personal highlight for me to throw out the first pitch at an A's home game on July 4, 2018, and to get the ball directly over the plate on only one bounce. And I still consider the basketball Warriors to be an Oakland team at heart, even if they're now across the Bay. That was a tough loss; nobody wanted the Warriors to leave. But it's also the nature of the professional sports business—these *teams are* businesses. The lesson here is that cities shouldn't base their entire economies or identities on private businesses, which may leave at any time if they think they can make more money elsewhere.

I think back to the 1960s when major league teams started coming to Oakland. First was the football Raiders, then came the A's, with the Warriors arriving in the 1970s. During that same period, Oakland had a plethora of issues. It was abandoned by industry, lacked major infrastructure projects, and was heavily segregated with a majority Black population that felt disenfranchised. Oakland was largely forgotten, but the reality is that the three major league teams helped to bring Oakland into note and contributed to the town's success. And, in return, Oakland helped to build those franchises and give them national prominence. So, of course, I want the A's to stay, but this city always has been more than its sports teams.

For Oakland isn't just about economics. Oakland also is an epicenter for culture and the arts, as embodied by the late Michael Morgan, the genius leader of the Oakland Symphony, which a few years ago was named the most diverse symphony in the country. Yes, we have real challenges, as do many other parts of the country, but there is a reason why so many people want to live and work here. If you define the entire complexity and vibrancy of a city by its most difficult problems, this creates a warped perception, and I think some of that, in terms of Oakland, is due to racist narratives going back decades.

Oakland is seen as a tale of two cities: one city that is booming economically for some people, and one city that has thousands of people living unsheltered in the streets because of a housing crisis. These two contrasting Oakland images often coexist in the same neighborhoods, on the same block.

Let's be clear: it has benefitted larger systems of oppression to portray Oakland as a troubled, hostile community. Over the years, Oakland has had highly aggressive policing in the Black and Brown communities. Our highways have cut off Black neighborhoods from our economic center and our waterfront. We have had dramatically unequal schools and unequal outcomes for students in different racial groups. And people in power make money by building or polluting or incarcerating without concern for the people who are being affected.

Though in readdressing Oakland's revolutionary spirit, the Black Panther Party comes to mind. But you can go back 100 years when the Pullman porters, under the leadership of C.L. Dellums, organized the first Black union in America right here in Oakland. You can't overstate how important those train porter jobs were for Black people at that time as a discovered pathway to economic security. And that long ago union activity was a precursor to the civil rights campaigns of the 1960s.

Like many big cities, we have too many people living in poverty. Gentrification has forced families out of their homes and out of the city. Too many people have been affected by crime and violence, but I believe that narrative is changing. It's about a city that has been fighting justice and equality for a century and is still leading the charge today in the era of Black Lives Matter and the struggle against poverty and exploitation.

Thus a new story about Oakland is emerging. I hope the A's and major league sports will continue to be a part of that story.

Barbara Lee, Congresswoman, 13ᵗʰ District, Oakland has served two decades in the United States House of Representatives, representing Oakland and neighboring Berkeley, after beginning her political career in the California State Assembly in 1991. The highest-ranking African American woman in Democratic leadership, she was the only member of Congress to vote against authorizing military force in Afghanistan following the terrorist attacks on September 11, 2001. Her fearless, heavily criticized vote proved accurate, as Afghanistan became American history's longest war.

Preface

I was raised in Newark, New Jersey, where the New York Yankees owned the Triple A Newark Bears, voted the greatest minor league franchise in history. In 1950, the Yankees folded the franchise simply because they wanted the ferociously loyal Bears fans to take the train to New York and pay to watch the Yankees instead.

That franchise loss turned Newark, then a city of 400,000, into a permanent athletic desert. The Hudson River separated it from New York City. At one end of the spectrum was the Big Apple, the glitz and glamour town of America, whose shadow smothered Newark.

Today, 2,890 miles to the west, across a Bay Bridge and locked into the massive shadow of San Francisco, the greed of big-time sports is in the process of turning Oakland into a far worse version of Newark West.

The Raiders are gone. The Golden State Warriors are gone. The Athletics are on the way out. The saddest sign in all of sports will be Oakland's municipal scoreboard: No GAME TODAY.

In this book, Andy Dolich and Dave Newhouse have written a brilliant insight into the athletic soul and spirit of Oakland's dispossessed fans, and the hard, cold truth of what greed did to them. When you read it, be aware that the same arrogance is on its way to another city, probably in a neighborhood like yours.

For references, check with Philadelphia, Boston, Milwaukee, Kansas City, Houston, and Washington, D.C. Continue checking with Syracuse,

Pittsburgh, Richmond, San Antonio, Teaneck, Birmingham, St. Louis, Brooklyn, Baltimore, Cleveland, Seattle, Buffalo, and a host of minor players large enough to stock another United Nations.

Those cities all lost teams. Some of them eventually got new teams as consolation prizes.

There are those in Oakland who still revere the memory of Al Davis. Amazing. This is a guy who abandoned them once for Los Angeles, then abandoned Los Angeles for Oakland, then tried to go back to Los Angeles, and now his son has the team in Las Vegas.

How can this be?

This isn't a franchise. It's a floating craps game.

In the words of the late H.L. Mencken, "No one ever went broke underestimating the intelligence of the American public."

Jerry Izenberg is a member of—count them—16 halls of fame. He was voted New Jersey Sportswriter of the Year five times, and he received the coveted Red Smith Award, the highest honor given by the Associated Press Sports Writers. He has produced or written for—start counting again—25 network television shows. He lives in Henderson, Nevada, with his wife, Aileen. At 92, he's still writing books, plus writing columns for the Newark Star-Ledger.

Authors' Note

This book went to press in late 2022 before the future of the A's—Oakland or Las Vegas—was resolved.

Introduction

O akland is America's most abused sports city, and there is no close second. For Oakland is the only city abandoned by the same team twice, the football Raiders, owned separately by the traitorous father and son duo, Al and Mark Davis, or Benedict Arnold and Benedict Arnold Jr.

However, the Raiders aren't the only team to raid Oakland and reap financial prosperity prior to fleeing town. The basketball Warriors, whom Oakland rescued from poverty in San Francisco in the early 1970s, returned to San Francisco immensely wealthy in 2019.

Now Oakland fears an unprecedented hat trick—all three of its teams departing. The baseball A's, who failed earlier to relocate in neighboring Fremont and San Jose, remain in Oakland, although temporarily on their time clock. Without a new ballpark in Oakland, the pushy A's likely will follow the Raiders to Las Vegas.

Oakland's image, then, would be cemented as a triple loser, albeit a gross misperception and an unfair characterization. For its three major tenants have won the Super Bowl (twice), the World Series (four times), and the NBA title (four times), even with Oakland's late start as a major league city in 1960. A loser? Hardly.

And fan passion in Oakland is unmatched anywhere. Raider Nation resembled Mardi Gras on a hallucinatory drug at home games in "Oaktown." The Davises' dual betrayals scarcely altered that fanaticism. Stomped on twice, Raider Nation remains blindly loyal, even while staring forlornly at its Black Hole gravesite inside the Oakland Coliseum.

Equally passionate, though less costumed, were Warriors fanatics in Oakland. San Francisco's Warriors rooters finish a distant second to Oakland in hoops fervor, then and now. But that fierce loyalty was lost upon ungrateful, avaricious sports owners who didn't find Oakland sexy enough, and so its arena became a basketball entombment.

The A's various owners, excepting the holy-like Haas family, have abused Oakland ever since the team's arrival in 1968. And that abuse has greatly affected A's attendance, largely through dismantled team rosters, a slipping-away tactic used in Charles O. Finley's ownership and replicated in John Fisher's current ownership a half-century later.

And, to think, Oakland spoiled its three tenants by building what was hailed in the mid-1960s as America's finest sports complex. But team owners generally reside in their own universe, beseeching: What have you done for me lately? Thus, Oakland renovated its Coliseum and Arena for $200 million in the 1990s to lure the Raiders home from Los Angeles and to retain the Warriors, alas, with bad outcomes. And Oakland's three franchise ingrates put up no money to stay or to return.

The A's, unlike the Raiders and Warriors, weren't pampered in terms of upgraded edifices. And so Oakland's grip on the irate A's will loosen permanently if a new ballpark isn't built—soonest. Ownership roulette is a deadly game—and played no more deadly than in the City of Oakland.

Oakland's potential hat trick of lost sports franchises is, truthfully, a twelve-gallon hat. For Oakland has witnessed 12 of its teams with leaving on their minds. Besides the A's, should they move, the Pacific Coast League's Oakland Oaks and the Negro League's Oakland Larks were other baseball teams that moved or dissolved. The United States Football League's Oakland Invaders, the Oakland Panthers of the Indoor Football League, the National Hockey League's California Golden Seals, the American Basketball League's Oakland Oaks, pro soccer's Oakland Clippers and Oakland Stompers, pro tennis' Oakland Aces and Oakland

Breakers, and Roller Hockey's Oakland Skates either folded in Oakland or fled and folded, not the best track record, regardless, for Oaktown.

If the A's do depart, then the top four professional sports—football, basketball, baseball, and hockey—will have waved Oakland goodbye, some of these sports repeatedly. Charles O. Finley once owned the puckish Seals, but then sold them to the NHL before they perished in Cleveland. The carpetbagging Finley also attempted to peddle his A's to Denver and might have succeeded if the locally treasured Haas family hadn't stepped in and saved the franchise for Oakland.

Barry Van Gerbig, a millionaire socialite who became the NHL owner in Oakland in 1967, summed up Oaktown: "The Bay Bridge is 10 miles from Oakland to San Francisco. From San Francisco to Oakland, it's 1,000 miles." Translated: Oakland lives universally in San Francisco's immense shadow. As proof, after San Francisco billionaire Mel Swig and crooner Bing Crosby bought the Seals, the advertising budget for the franchise's last season in Oakland, 1975–76, was $5,000, a measly figure still remembered by the team's public relations director, Len Shapiro. The resulting perception: Oakland is either beyond promoting or not worth saving.

"The Seals never drew well," recalled John Porter, the team's beat writer for the *Oakland Tribune*, "except when Montreal, Boston, and the New York Rangers came to town. Later, when Philadelphia's Broad Street Bullies showed up, there would be a sellout. The big problem with attendance was the team wasn't that good over the years. But the NHL took advantage of Oakland, just as the other leagues did."

Some pertinent road map history: the Raiders' roots were planted in Oakland, whereas the Warriors, by way of Philadelphia and San Francisco, and the A's, via Philadelphia and Kansas City, were imports. Sports facilities do age, but one positive cannot be refuted about Oakland's sports complex: its ideal location.

The unwieldy-named Oakland Alameda County Coliseum Complex was built at a most suitable spot, smack dab in the middle of five counties: Contra Costa to the north, Santa Clara to the east, San Mateo to the south, and San Francisco and Marin to the west. Plus, the Bay Area

Rapid Transit (BART) system would frame one side of the complex, with a 10-lane freeway located on a second side, and railroad tracks overlooking a third side. This perfect architectural plan included two giant parking lots and an airport five minutes away. No sports complex in the USA, in fact, had more thoughtful spectator access.

Now check out the Warriors' state-of-the-art $1.4-billion-dollar palace in San Francisco—the Chase Center—that doesn't abut a freeway or rapid transit. Its parking is limited, its arena is largely accessed by foot, and the closest airport is a $30 cab ride. And relocation doesn't always make teams play better. The Warriors, coming off five consecutive NBA Finals in Oakland, finished dead last in the NBA in their San Francisco return, although it was a truncated season due to COVID–19. The Warriors resurged during the ensuing 2021–22 season to defeat Boston for the NBA championship, but to emulate their parting five-year dominance in Oakland is pure fantasy.

The wanderlust Raiders play in the sparkling, $2 billion, taxpayer-supported Allegiant Stadium in Las Vegas—at 3333 Al Davis Way no less. Only there is no adjoining railroad or rapid transit there, and general parking is a bus ride from the stadium. The Davises, it can be said with validity, excel at bolting, not blueprinting.

Home attendance isn't yet a problem in Las Vegas, but major internal issues arose in the team's second year in the desert. Team president Marc Badain resigned along with chief financial officer Ed Villanueva, controller Araxie Grant, and vice president of strategy and business development Brandon Doll, all four disenchanted, reportedly, with owner Mark Davis, a perpetual loose cannon.

Then, explosively, coach Jon Gruden exited after emailing racist, misogynistic, and homophobic comments from 2011 to 2018 to former Washington Commanders executive Bruce Allen, who was the Raiders general manager during Gruden's previous coaching run in Oakland.

The situation worsened as Raiders wide receiver Henry Ruggs III was involved in a fatal pre-dawn Las Vegas crash. Ruggs was accused of driving his Chevrolet Corvette at 156 mph with a blood level of 0.16 percent—twice the legal DUI limit in Nevada—when he slammed into the rear of Tina Tintor's Toyota Rav4 SUV, killing Tintor, 23, and her dog, Max. The Raiders cut Ruggs after earlier overlooking, or perhaps denying, his character issues at the University of Alabama.

Also in 2021, the Raiders released cornerback Damon Arnette, a 2020 first-round draft pick, following a social media post showing him brandishing a gun and threatening to kill someone. Then in early 2022, Raiders rookie cornerback Nate Hobbs pleaded guilty to DUI and reckless driving charges, speeding 110 mph in a 65 mph zone.

As further proof the storm doors had blown off the team's Las Vegas offices, Dan Ventrelle was fired as Raiders team president just four months after replacing Badain. Ventrelle had addressed a "hostile working environment" inside the Raiders organization, voicing complaints of female employees. Ventrelle presented those issues to Mark Davis, who was "dismissive and did not address the warranted level of concerns," said Ventrelle, who next complained to the NFL of "Mark's unacceptable response," and was quickly fired by Davis.

Davis then sought to quell this front-office upheaval and workplace dysfunction by hiring Sandra Douglass Morgan in July 2022 as the team's third president within a year, but in doing so made pro football history. Morgan, former chairperson of the Nevada Gaming Control Board, is the first Black woman to hold the position of team president for an NFL franchise. Whether her hiring will change Raiders mismanagement is uncertain.

Despite all that discord, the 2021 NFL season delivered yet another haymaker to poor Oakland. The Raiders demonstrated Vegas-like sleight-of-hand mastery to somehow squeeze into the postseason. They won their last four league games to finish 10–7, all due to the late-game accuracy of placekicker Daniel Carlson, the league's top scorer. The Raiders lost their first-round playoff game 26–19 to the host Cincinnati Bengals. Mark Davis then showed his gratitude by firing general manager Mike Mayock and interim head coach Rich Bisaccia. Josh McDaniels replaced Bisaccia, and McDaniels' New England Patriots colleague, Dave Ziegler, took over for Mayock.

What is it about the City of Oakland that makes it teams so wanderlust, and itself so gut-punched, even though Oakland is currently
viewed as a happening USA city? Oakland, in fact, hasn't ever experienced such a "boom"—in the late Raiders coach John Madden's
broadcast phrasing—as presently. New buildings are touching the clouds
in Oakland's skyline and new businesses are growing in droves. With
its bejeweled lake downtown, its breathtaking view from its lovely hills,
and its tree-lined hiking trails, Oakland has transformed itself from an
ugly duckling into a lovely swan.

Nevertheless, critics continue to view Oakland through a negative
lens. Author Gertrude Stein grew up in Oakland, but upon her return
from Paris years later, the Oakland she knew didn't exist. It hadn't
grown ugly; her neighborhood had changed, and that was the genesis
of her quote, "There is no there there." Her comment, though, was
interpreted as a knock on Oakland, and that knock keeps on knocking.
Thus Oakland has the highest level of low esteem found anywhere.

That's a sad commentary, for Oakland has more beauty marks than
warts. Its sports teams, for instance, thrived at the Coliseum Complex,
known as the "House of Champions." Oakland is proud of its great
teams and marquee athletes—basketball products Bill Russell, Jason
Kidd, Gary Payton, Paul Silas, Jim Pollard, and Damian Lillard, plus
Warriors imports Rick Barry, Nate Thurmond, Chris Mullin, Mitch
Richmond, Tim Hardaway, Stephen Curry, and Klay Thompson.
Oakland's baseball homegrown include Frank Robinson, Joe Morgan,
Rickey Henderson, Dave "Smoke" Stewart, Dennis Eckersley, Jackie
Jensen, Bill Rigney, and Vada Pinson, plus these outsider A's: Catfish
Hunter, Rollie Fingers, Vida Blue, and Tony La Russa. Oakland foot-
ball natives include John Brodie, Chris Burford, Wendell Hayes, and
MacArthur Lane. The Raiders' Pro Football Hall of Fame inductees:
Jim Otto, Willie Brown, Ted Hendricks, Gene Upshaw, Art Shell, Dave
Casper, Ray Guy, Ken Stabler, Cliff Branch, Al Davis, John Madden,
and Tom Flores. Tennis legend Don Budge is an Oaklander. Undefeated
boxing champion Andre Ward lived and trained in Oaktown.

The above represent a Who's Who of sports celebrity. Name another city that can match Oakland's athleticism or, for that matter, its colorful sports nicknames: The Tooz, Assassin, Dr. Death, Mr. October, Mr. Mean, Ghost, Snake, Chicken, Rooster, Grasshopper, Mad Stork, Mad Bomber, Sleepy, Hoot, Catfish, Wrong Way, and the Bash Brothers. Translated in order: John Matuzsak, Jack Tatum, Skip Thomas, Reggie Jackson, Larry Smith, Dave Casper, Ken Stabler, Fred Stanley, Pete Banaszak, Charles Dudley, Ted Hendricks, Daryle Lamonica, Eric Floyd, Claude Gibson, Jim Hunter, Roy Riegels, and Jose Canseco and Mark McGwire.

And no American city can approach Oakland's weirdest trifecta of sports owners: devious Al Davis of the Raiders, huckster Charles O. Finley of the A's, and hipster Franklin Mieuli of the Warriors.

"Oakland had three owners who marched to their own drummers," said Billy North, an A's outfielder during Oakland's charmed era, "but who had personalities that could grate on you."

Oh, how they could grate. But standing alone among Oakland's sports owners was Walter A. Haas Jr. of the A's—the finest, kindest, and most accomplished of men, either inside baseball or inside the community. He was a deacon of decency compared to the Davises in football or the A's other owners—Finley, Steve Schott and Ken Hofmann, Lew Wolff, and John Fisher—or the Warriors' owners—Mieuli, Dan Finnane and Jim Fitzgerald, Chris Cohan, and Joe Lacob and Peter Guber. They all had "Goodbye, Oakland" on their minds from the time they assumed ownership. Oaklanders saw snakes dressed in thousand-dollar suits.

But just as reptilian were NFL owners, who came within one vote (Tampa Bay's) of unanimously allowing the Raiders to escape a second time after Oakland had rebuilt the Coliseum with the Raiders, not the A's, in mind. Davis the younger moved to Las Vegas anyway as the NFL reconfirmed that it's one body with no heart.

The USFL's Invaders tried, unsuccessfully, to replace the Raiders in Oakland's broken hearts. The Invaders ascended to the league's championship game in their third year, 1985, but lost to the Baltimore Stars 28–24 before folding along with the springtime league afterward.

The USFL had been the vision of New Orleans businessman David Dixon, with franchise owners including actor Burt Reynolds and a future president named Donald Trump. The USFL focused on cities lacking NFL franchises, such as barren Oakland. The Invaders' primary owner was Polish immigrant Tad Taube, a successful businessman and respected San Francisco Bay Area philanthropist, but who viewed coaches as quick turnaround write-offs.

Joe Starkey was the Invaders' play-by-play broadcaster all three seasons, while also announcing San Francisco 49ers and University of California games in the fall. Thus, he worked football nearly year-round.

Starkey relived those USFL days vividly 40 years later. "The Invaders won their first regular season game 24–0 over the Arizona Wranglers before a crowd of 45,000 in Oakland," he said. "The Invaders made the playoffs, losing to the host Michigan Panthers 37–24 before 60,000 fans, while the ABC telecast drew eye-popping ratings. The USFL projected a great future with an average home attendance of 31,000.

"The Invaders struggled in their second year, finishing 7–11 as home attendance dropped to a 23,000 average. Head coach John Ralston was fired in midseason, replaced by Chuck Hutchinson. Then with their third head coach in three years, Charlie Sumner, the Invaders finished 13–4–1 as attendance fell to an 18,000 average. The USFL then sued the NFL, won its anti-trust case, but was awarded one dollar."

The USFL, seeing no future, called it quits. Starkey, who retired from announcing in 2022, didn't duck the big what-if question.

"The best USFL teams would probably struggle in the NFL," he projected. "Some big-league talent, but not much depth."

The USFL fired up again in April 2022 with just eight teams, and every game to be played in Birmingham, Alabama. Oakland wasn't part of this recurring USFL clown show, though gratefully uninvited.

Revealing another side of Oakland is its elite list of non-sports notables: authors Jack London and Stein; actors Clint Eastwood, Buster ("Tarzan") Crabbe, and Tom Hanks; singers Tony Martin, Tower of Power, The Pointer Sisters, Sly Stone, Zendaya, and rapper M.C. Hammer; Governor and Supreme Court Justice Earl Warren; lead biker Sonny Barger of the Hells Angels; Black Panthers co-founders Bobby Seale and Huey Newton, and our first woman vice president, Kamala Harris. What other city can match such diversity?

The true Oakland is gritty, gutsy, and self-preserving, with a feisty blue-collar mentality, though it's guilty of messing with a pirate's booty on sports' high seas. Davis the father was a user, while Davis the son is a loser, and Oakland has walked that same pirate ship's plank twice. But pirates do die by their own sword, thus the eye-patched scamp on the Raiders' logo should beware: it's common to blow fortunes in Las Vegas.

Warriors, too, lose battles by invading lands they coveted in the past before encountering the very same enemy, themselves. The treasure-hunting A's consistently cast off elite players while doubling ticket prices, devaluing fan support, and shopping their franchise around. And instead of finding buried treasure in 2022, the A's were buried: 102 losses.

Oakland is left, cruelly, with the forfeiture of championship sports teams, the memories of legendary athleticism, and the potential loss of hundreds of millions of dollars of irreplaceable commerce and jobs if the Port of Oakland, the city's most vital resource, is victimized by a bold, but foolish, ballpark proposal.

Founded in 2018, the Oakland Roots of the professional National Independent Soccer Association draw capacity crowds of 5,500 at Laney Community College in town. Selling out, not bailing out.

Dave Newhouse became involved with Oakland sports in 1964 and co-author Andy Dolich in 1980, a combined 102-year perspective. Dolich conceived of this book project, quickly recruiting Newhouse. With a vast understanding of the subject matter, they embarked on a 30-month project to present the most accurate detailing yet of how this exodus occurred, including how Oakland's elected officials were played as political fools by disingenuous sports owners and league commissioners, thus sharing the guilt of Oakland's fleeing franchises.

A perfect epitaph on Oakland's sports tombstone: FANS GAVE UNSELFISHLY, OWNERS ACCEPTED GREEDILY, AND FRANCHISES MOVED HEARTLESSLY.

Now Oakland, for the first time in literary form, defends itself against these pillaging deserters in a duel of principle.

Swordsmen, assume your positions.

En garde, looters!

Chapter 1

Al Davis:
Charming Rogue

Al Davis going into the Pro Football Hall of Fame is like John Dillinger going into the banking hall of fame.
—Vito Stellino,
Pro Football Hall of Fame sportswriter

Al Davis, king of the underhanded, revealed his scurrilous nature by burying a knife in the back of his primary benefactor in Oakland.

"Ed, did you read the contract before you signed it?" *Oakland Tribune* sports editor George Ross spoke sharply into the telephone.

Ed McGah, co-owner of the Oakland Raiders, was on the opposite end of the line, choking on his words after being caught off guard.

"Ed, I'm going to ask you again," Ross persisted. "Did you read the contract before you signed it?"

Ross was at his desk inside the *Tribune* sports department. Since it was pushing 7 AM, a tongue-tied McGah most likely was in his pajamas.

"Ed, for the third time," said Ross, feeding paper into the typewriter, "did you read the contract before you signed it?"

Ross finally got the response he wanted, even though McGah muttered something nonsensical. Ross hung up the phone and typed the truth: Al Davis had gone behind the back of Wayne Valley, the Raiders' principal owner who had given Davis the power he so craved—head

1

coach and general manager of a professional football team—and coaxed the pliable McGah into giving Davis a new 20-year contract with unlimited franchise power and limited ownership interference.

Valley wouldn't be the first, or last, person Davis ever hoodwinked.

Davis and Ross had a solid working relationship up to that pivotal point. Davis sought football dominance, Ross was pushing Oakland onto the national sports map, and they needed each other. They even dined together after Raiders home games, before Ross returned to his office to write his game column for the next afternoon's *Tribune*. But, Ross, after speaking with McGah, phoned Davis to inform him of what he was about to put into print. Davis replied, coldly, "Then I can never trust you again." That ended their close bond, and they never spoke again. Only sycophants were admitted into Davis' coterie of friends. Everyone else was perceived as disloyal and subsequently dismissed by Davis forever.

The world of football, as well as the City of Oakland, learned at that critical juncture—Ross' accurate reporting—that Davis was a cunning demigod who knew no boundaries in gaining power, even legally, although unethically, knifing the man, Valley, who hired him without ever sensing this Brooklyn pirate's concealed cutlery.

"The only mistake I've made in character judgment on a human being in my life," Valley, a shrewd millionaire contractor, said later of Davis. Defiantly, Valley sued Davis, but a contract is a contract, regardless of which owner signed it, and so Valley was adjudged a beaten man in the court of law. He stepped away as owner, enabling Davis to become the Raiders managing general partner, with total control of the franchise and no misgivings about his back-alley tactics.

"The words 'cunning, shrewd, devious' don't have a bad connotation to me," Davis strategized. "Look at the history of people in positions of leadership. They've said of everyone of my time that he's devious—from Roosevelt to Churchill to Eisenhower, Kissinger, and Mao."

Davis, a Jew, added, "Hitler was a cocksucker who had to be stopped, but he was one of the greatest men who ever lived, because he knew how to get power."

And Al Davis thirsted for power, while ingesting the innocents.

"I think I can charm anybody," he boasted. "But in order to run an efficient organization, there has to be a dictator. And I'm going to dominate."

But even con men of Davis' caliber possess some virtuous qualities. He was the first NFL owner to hire a Black man, Art Shell, and later a Hispanic man, Tom Flores, as pro head coaches in the modern era. (Fritz Pollard was a Black head coach during the league's infancy in the 1920s.) Davis was also the first football owner to name a woman, Amy Trask, as chief executive. Unlike Shell and Flores, she wasn't fired, but exited, Raider-like, regardless.

Among his other firsts, Davis relocated his football team—from Oakland to Los Angeles in 1984—without a unanimous vote of fellow owners. He moved regardless, and his relocation held up in court, where the clever Davis dominated as he had on the gridiron. NFL Commissioner Pete Rozelle sized up Davis perfectly, labeling him a "charming rogue." Rozelle became yet another adversary of Davis, who kept his enemies in sight—including the face in his bathroom mirror.

The calculating Davis, in his brief commissionership of the American Football League, was primarily responsible for the merger with the NFL, by his clever attempts to steal the NFL's premier quarterbacks. The two leagues quickly reached an agreement. Davis' adversaries then began to watch him warily, fearing his next deceptive move.

While forging his own guileful entrance into the Pro Football Hall of Fame, Davis occasionally acted within the rules, though mostly executing his will outside them. Yet his profound impact on the game cannot be denied. He also won three Super Bowls with the Raiders, in Oakland and Los Angeles, while courting dangerous company en route.

The Corleones, anyone?

When Davis' relationship with Ross was positive, he told the veteran newsman this story: as a teenage lifeguard, Davis saved a kid from drowning—the son of a Mafioso. Ross believed Davis, from that point forward, had the Mafia on his side. That act of heroism wouldn't be Davis' last interaction with the Mafia, he noted in a banquet speech years later. When the Raiders arrived in Miami the week before playing

Green Bay in Super Bowl II, Davis received a call in his hotel room from a representative of a national undertakers group, informing Davis that Meyer Lansky—yes, that Meyer Lansky—requested his serving as keynote speaker at the group's dinner the night before the game. Davis begged off, noting the importance of facing Vince Lombardi's Packers. Then on Friday, the phone rang again in Davis' room, with the same undertakers' representative telling Davis that Lansky insisted on his speaking before the group, and that a limousine would be at the team's hotel to pick him up. Davis caught the limo to the gravediggers' dinner.

Then there was Eastmont Mall, an Oakland shopping center that listed Davis as a partner along with Allen R. Glick, a person described by the FBI as a "straw party controlled by the organized crime syndicate." Shortly after Glick acquired the mall in 1974, Davis received a 25 percent interest for a $5,000 investment. After their relationship became public, Davis issued a statement through a spokesman denying "any implication of wrong-doing. Mr. Davis is a limited partner in an Oakland shopping center in which Mr. Glick is a general partner. And that is the extent of their association, and that association is winding down." Davis then divested himself from all ties to the mall and refused to discuss his Glick connection publicly. Like other accusations against Davis, rumored or real, they ran their course, disappeared, and were followed by new accusations. Slippery as an eel, Davis nearly was impossible to reel in legally.

As a young man, Davis was a decent athlete himself, though not as talented as the Raiders media guide later suggested. For Davis listed himself in that guide as a three-sport letterman—football, basketball, and baseball—at Syracuse University. This ruse was eventually exposed; he lettered in none of the three but was involved long enough to appear in team pictures, and then he was gone. His résumé was part myth, and the three-sport letterman lie was omitted from future Raider guides.

Davis' early coaching stops included The Citadel, whose president was a famous general, Mark Clark. Davis named his son, and only child, Mark Clark Davis in tribute, but also as a sly means of seeking advancement at the academy. The wise general rejected the father, who showed up next as an assistant coach at the University of Southern California after coaxing a Citadel player, Angelo Coia, into transferring to USC, which landed the latter institution on NCAA probation. Davis' shady moves were gaining attention; thus his strategy was to keep moving. He joined the Los Angeles Chargers in 1960, the first year of the AFL, as an offensive end coach. The Chargers, who eventually moved to San Diego, won two division titles in the AFL's first three years, providing the impetus that propelled Davis north to Oakland in 1963.

Speaking of San Diego, Chargers owner Gene Klein accused Davis of resorting to "the big lie" to achieve whatever goal he desired.

"I've always been aggressive," Davis admitted, "not to hurt anyone, but to get things done, to speed it up, to have the feeling I can dominate."

Speeding up things in Oakland was imperative as the Raiders were AFL vagabonds their first two seasons, playing in San Francisco because Oakland lacked a football stadium. Those early, inept Raiders lost 19 straight games playing for three head coaches—Eddie Erdelatz, Red Cochran and Marty Feldman—while losing a million dollars. The eight original owners whittled down quickly to Valley and McGah, the latter also a wealthy builder, though not in Valley's league financially. But a million dollars spent still was a million dollars gone.

Valley and McGah were viewed as rough-hewed men who built their separate fortunes with tenacity and smarts. The only difference: Valley wasn't the type of businessman to be played in the same manner that Davis played McGah, like a violin. But, in the end, the cagey Davis played both men like a Stradivarius.

Decades before engaging Davis, Valley was a fullback and javelin thrower at Oregon State, which tied and also defeated USC's mighty "Thundering Herd" in football in the 1930s, with Valley scoring the winning touchdown in the major upset. His toughness reputation grew with adulthood. In 1959, he crash-landed as a passenger in a twin-engine plane in Pleasanton, California. The plane's right wing hit the ground first, spinning the craft around and skidding 100 feet. Remarkably, neither the pilot nor Valley was injured. But it's no wonder that Valley became the "strong man" of the Raiders' two owners.

Davis arrived in Oakland in 1963 during the franchise's fourth season, and its second year at Frank Youell Field, an upgraded junior college campus facility with 21,000-seat capacity. Davis took over a franchise with a dismal 9–33 record. "I have sole and complete control of the operations of this football team," he announced. Valley detected slickness from the start but felt he could control it. "You don't have to love Davis," he said, "you just have to turn him loose." Valley discovered, too late, that Davis was an untethered wild stallion without any reins.

Those early Raiders were attired in black, gold, and white, akin to the Chicago Bears, until Davis redesigned them, sharply, in silver and black. The Raiders responded to his coaching, finishing 10–4 in 1963. Davis was named AFL Coach of the Year and Oakland's Young Man of the Year by the Junior Chamber of Commerce. But the City of Oakland wasn't equipped to deal with this sudden turnaround, and so a postseason downtown parade was a flop, with 10 antique cars and a high school band. "I think it stuck a little bit in Al's craw," Ross remembered.

Unbeknownst publicly, Ralph Wilson, the Buffalo Bills owner, bought a 25-percent interest in the struggling Raiders in 1963. Such crossover-owner chicanery was needed in the AFL's fly-by-night operation, which wasn't flying all that high in '63. The ego-driven Davis floated the idea of being called "The Genius" through Ross, a willing partner. Valley, gleefully, called Davis "The Genius" to his face, even right after Davis' early failures to win conference championship games. Valley's sarcasm only widened the schism between the two men.

Nonetheless, Valley considered Davis a wise investment, because he instantly made the Raiders respectable, with nine more wins in '63 than the year before. Future Pro Hall of Fame center Jim Otto, an original Raider in 1960, was stunned by the team's quick turnaround.

"When Al took control of the team," Otto recalled, "he said he didn't care about anything but winning. 'Just win, baby' was his motto even then, although he never said it publicly. He told us we were going to work hard, all of us, and that we were going to win. He said it so often that we started to believe him. In training camp, we hit, hit, hit in the morning, then we hit, hit, hit in the afternoon. Day after day, we hit. Al stressed that the Raiders would be a team of hitters, and there would be no slacking off, even if we were injured. He told me that he never wanted to see me come off the field."

Otto never came off, playing in 210 consecutive league games, a franchise record, despite repeated physical challenges. The Raiders began the ensuing 1964 season poorly but rallied for a 5–7–2 record. Davis had righted the ship through his unerring eye for talent—and where that talent would be best utilized. He traded for running back Billy Cannon and made him a tight end. He traded for tight end Hewritt Dixon and made him a running back. Both men prospered. Willie Brown was a nonentity in Houston and Denver before Davis groomed him into a Pro Football Hall of Fame cornerback. Daryle Lamonica was a backup quarterback in Buffalo before becoming Oakland's "Mad Bomber."

Matt Millen was a standout defensive lineman at Penn State, but Davis converted him into a middle linebacker. In Millen's rookie season, 1980, the Raiders became Super Bowl champions. Millen was an instant believer in Davis, though friction would divide them at times.

"Al and I had a good relationship, but we'd get into arguments," Millen recalled. "He didn't talk to me for two years, because, well, you're not right all the time. Then we finally talked, but to understand the Raiders, you have to understand the man who ran the team. He was brilliant, he loved to fight—it was an outlaw thing—and the team took on his personality. Our motto was, 'We're not given anything; we take what we want.' We had two rules listed at training camp in Santa Rosa: 'No. 1: Cheating is encouraged. No. 2: See No. 1.'"

Millen spent nine seasons with the Raiders, appearing in the postseason five times and winning a second Super Bowl in 1984.

"Those were phenomenal years," he said, "with some of the smartest bunch of guys I've played with. They studied the game, and then would come off a three-day drunk and play well. Al really liked his players; he took care of his guys. There were very few complaints about that. I made $35,000 my first year. When I tried to buy a house. I asked Al for a loan, and he gave me $50,000. [Repayment] never came up again. He did a lot of stuff like that quietly. I'm a big Al fan."

The NFL wasn't a Davis fan, and vice versa. Davis was the only NFL owner who didn't support NFL Charities, a pet project of Rozelle's. But Davis supported his players. He paid for defensive tackle Dan Birdwell's funeral and the funerals of other Raiders. Dr. Samuel Johnson, the 18th Century British wit, though, would have seen through Davis' veneer as a team personnel patriot. "Patriotism," Dr. Johnson mused, "is the last refuge of a scoundrel." And scoundrel was a softened image of Al Davis.

But Millen gives Davis a pass, even forgiving Davis' bolting the city that gave him the opportunity to become somebody.

"I loved Oakland," said Millen, a Pennsylvanian. "Oakland grounded you. It had a little guy feel in a metro area, an earthy feeling. Oakland had great football fans, and they understood the game. But here is the problem: Oakland didn't have any money. If it did, Al would've stayed."

Millen knows how money works in the NFL, for he later became the Detroit Lions president. Like the Raiders, the Lions left their home in Detroit and moved to Pontiac, Michigan, before moving back to Detroit. But the Lions never left Detroit again, while the Raiders fled Oakland a second time. Los Angeles, unlike Oakland, reeked of money, but it couldn't keep the Raiders. Sometimes, it's the ownership, not the money.

Davis' coaching swan song was 1965, the Raiders forging a bounce-back 8–5–1 winning record. Davis' life was about to change, dramatically. The AFL's original commissioner, Joe Foss, a Marine fighter ace in World War II and a Congressional Medal of Honor recipient, resigned after the '65 season, just when merger talks with the NFL heated up. Who would replace Foss? Wayne Valley had an idea: Al Davis. Valley's idea carried by one vote among AFL owners, thereby giving Davis the power he so craved, which he unleashed on the NFL. Unsuspecting owners, even Valley, never saw this sucker-punch coming.

"Wayne had nothing against Al except that he was a liar and a cheat and a despicable cad," said Valley's widow, Gladys. "Nobody wanted the [commissioner's] job, and Wayne said, 'Well, Al's a dirty fighter, and he comes from New York, and he'll only be a figurehead—we'll do the dickering with the NFL.' So, finally, everybody said all right, and they gave him a limo, and let him use the title of commissioner."

No sports commissioner ever played dirty like Davis, who instantly pursued the NFL's marquee quarterbacks. Oakland signed the Los Angeles Rams' Roman Gabriel to a three-year contract with an option year, effective the 1967 season. The Houston Oilers then signed the San Francisco 49ers' John Brodie to a quarter-million-dollar deal, commencing also in '67. NFL and AFL owners already were negotiating a merger, but there is no denying that Davis' plot to raid NFL quarterbacks hurried the merger, which occurred on June 8, 1967. Davis' commissionership lasted all of five months, for there would be only one unified commissioner, Pete Rozelle. That was a slight Davis never got over; Rozelle became his mortal enemy thereafter.

Davis returned to Oakland miffed, but rewarded with a new contract, upgrading him to part owner and general manager. He also attained unlimited power, ruling every phase of the franchise's operation except ownership, which he then worked, sneakily, on seizing. His return was timed perfectly with Oakland's brand new outdoor-indoor sports complex. John Rauch was elevated from Raiders assistant coach to head coach in Davis' absence, but after Davis' return, Rauch felt his breath on his neck day and night. "Al wouldn't let me be myself," he said.

Even with Rauch as a figurehead coach, the Raiders became AFL champions in 1967, finishing 13–1 during the regular season before pounding Houston 40–7 in the title game in Oakland. The Raiders demonstrated "Pride and Poise," the little brother to "Commitment to Excellence," Davis having stolen the latter motto from Vince Lombardi, whose Packers then roughed up the Raiders 33–14 in Super Bowl II.

The Raiders resurged in 1968 with a 12–2 record before dismantling visiting Kansas City 41–6 in the postseason opener. Then facing the Jets in New York for the AFL title, a Jets defensive recovery of a Raiders backward lateral secured a 27–23 win for Joe Namath's team. Rauch then shuffled off to Buffalo to become the Bills coach under that hidden ex-Raiders mini-owner, Ralph Wilson.

"Al, I'm leaving," Rauch informed Davis.

"You can't do that," Davis replied. "You're under contract."

"Al, if you stand in my way," Rauch warned, "I'll tell everybody what I know about you."

Davis paused, looked at Rauch, and quickly granted him permission to leave. What was it, though, that Rauch had on Davis?

"I don't even want to reveal it," Rauch said years later. "But so many things he did back in those days, like business stuff, make Watergate seem like child's play."

Watergate? Well, Wayne Valley did resign his presidency in Oakland. Art Thoms, a Raiders defensive tackle from 1969 to '76, said the team's players had limited interest in the Valley–Davis break up.

"I wasn't involved at all," said Thoms. "I knew about the lawsuit, but I was just happy to get a paycheck. We hit 'em high, hit 'em low, hit 'em any way we could. Our defensive backs hit receivers all the time. George [Atkinson], The Assassin [Jack Tatum], Dr. Death [Skip Thomas]—there were no rules back then. It was fun to be called the 'criminal element.'

"The only rules we had: be at practice and show up on time. Everything else was cool. John Madden wasn't much of a disciplinarian, though at training camp, he worked us hard—28 straight days of two practices a day. The coaches beat the hell out of us."

The players still managed to turn drudgery into fun.

"With those Raiders, if you weren't cheating, you weren't trying," said Thoms. "There wasn't a [mandatory] weight-training program back then. Half the team smoked before games and even at halftime.... Fred Biletnikoff was a chain-smoker. Otis Sistrunk and I were 'Salt and Pepper.' We'd take a limo to home games. Otis is Black, I'm white, but he wore a white hat, I wore a black hat, and we smoked cigars in the limo."

The party-hearty Raiders continued winning, making the playoffs in seven of Thoms' eight seasons working for Al Davis. "My relationship with Al was always good," he said. "I was drafted during Madden's first year as head coach. John didn't like rookies, and for two years, he was rough on me. Finally, I went in and asked him about it. He laughed, and we got along well after that. But when it was the Raiders' turn to draft, eight guys in their draft room might have wanted one guy, and one guy in the draft room wanted another guy. That one guy was Al."

Davis always got what he wanted, including Madden. Davis saw that Madden was dedicated to the bone, plus he had great rapport with the players. Madden was less rigid than Rauch, thus open to Davis' hands-on approach. With Madden as a rookie head coach in 1969, the Raiders kept on rolling with a 12–1–1 record and a 56–7 playoff trouncing of Houston. Oakland had beaten Kansas City twice during the regular season, but the visiting Chiefs sprung a 17–7 surprise on the Silver and Black in the AFL championship game. Like Namath and the Jets shocking Baltimore 16–7 the previous season, the Chiefs then toppled Minnesota 23–7, enabling the upstart AFL to end its 10-year "junior league" existence with stunning back-to-back Super Bowl victories.

The 1970s continued as a triumphant, albeit turbulent, time for the Raiders. The decade began with the right-handed Lamonica at quarterback and ended with southpaw Kenny Stabler taking snaps. The decade also started with Valley as the principal owner, but somewhere in the middle Davis wrested control in a legal, yet unprincipled, manner. Stabler was the Snake and Davis, the Sneak, but both prevailed.

The Raiders made the playoffs seven of ten seasons during the '70s, losing six times, five of those losses coming in the American Football Conference title game. They finally won their first Super Bowl during the 1976 season, stomping Minnesota 32–14 at the Rose Bowl in Pasadena. Those Raiders teams produced a lifetime of memorably named thrills in just one decade: the Immaculate Reception, the Sea of Hands Catch, the Holy Roller Play, Ghost to the Post, and the Ice Bowl. No NFL team created more high drama than the Raiders.

There was added Raiders drama in the courtroom after Davis and his chosen puppet, McGah, filched the franchise from Valley. McGah played his part in the filching by suffering a convenient brain lock.

Contacted by Ross that morning on April 5, 1973, the muttering McGah finally admitted that he hadn't read the contract before signing over unlimited power to Davis without Valley's knowledge.

"Did you tell Wayne that you hadn't read it?" Ross asked McGah.

"No, I don't think anybody read it," McGah replied.

"Wayne says you told him you hadn't read it," Ross pressed on.

"I never told Wayne anything," McGah said, weakly.

"Ed, you just told me you did."

"Yeah, I just told you."

Ross then told McGah their conversation would appear in print.

"I don't give a damn. Do anything you want."

Ross informed McGah, and then Davis, that it was his journalistic duty to get the facts and report them, although he knew about but never wrote that Davis had facilitated McGah's extramarital affairs. Regardless, Davis' currying favor with McGah, the lesser owner, just couldn't turn out well for Valley, and it didn't. His suit to remove Davis from the Raiders was heard in Alameda Superior Court in June 1975.

McGah swore to tell the truth, but after taking the stand, he said he "misunderstood" Ross' questions over the phone, even though Ross had repeated them. McGah seemed confused, contending he had actually read the contract that Davis handed him before he signed it. McGah then altered his testimony, saying he first read the contract in the office of team attorney Herman Cook and once more at home. Then he called that testimony a "misstatement" by saying that he hadn't taken the contract home. Courtroom observers wondered how the mixed-up McGah ever became a millionaire.

But Valley dug his own legal grave. He testified that when Davis told him about the contract extension right after it was signed, Valley deemed it a "trial balloon" created to "apply pressure" for a new contract, and not evidence of the contract itself. Regardless of Davis' intentions, and McGah's confusion, Valley came across weakly in his own defense, thus providing Davis all the legal leverage he needed.

Davis also captivated the courtroom with his smooth mannerisms and crisp memorization of details. Then a surprise witness tilted the suit in Davis' direction. Philadelphia Eagles owner Leonard Tose testified that he offered Davis "10 to 15 percent of the club" in 1971 and 1972, when Davis was between Raiders contracts. McGah informed the court that he had to sign Davis or lose him, and that testimony won over the presiding judge, Redmond C. Staats Jr., who determined, "The court feels Mr. Davis' testimony [is] more creditable." Staats then chastised Valley for not taking "some action [earlier than he did]," thus, "by his conduct of silence or acquiescence, [he] had ratified the...contract."

Touchdown, Davis!

Valley, to his detriment, had fallen asleep at the legal switch, thereby enabling Davis to seize control of the Raiders, and that control held up in court. However, Davis wasn't a winner in the court of human dignity.

"He's just petty and small," said Gladys Valley. "He's like a rat under your house." Only the newly empowered Davis had become King Rat.

Valley didn't vanish immediately from the pro football landscape. The San Francisco 49ers, directly across the Bay Bridge, sought new ownership. The Morabito sisters-in-law, widows of the franchise's co-founders, wanted to sell the franchise, but had difficulty finding an owner. Valley decided to put in a bid. That's when a new set of circumstances, with Davis' fingerprints all over them, unfolded.

Follow the bouncing football, folks.

Before the 49ers could be sold contractually, they first had to be offered to their minority ownerships, which narrowed down to Franklin Mieuli, principal owner of the NBA's Golden State Warriors. Mieuli had a small piece of the 49ers, "but my money's just as good as Valley's," he boasted. Mieuli then partnered with former San Francisco Mayor Joe Alioto to buy the 49ers, which forced Valley to drop out of the NFL picture again—and all because of, yes, Al Davis.

The Mieuli–Alioto bid merely was a smokescreen to block Valley. Even with their combined finances, Mieuli and Alioto lacked the necessary capital to purchase the team. The DeBartolo family from Youngstown, Ohio, then entered the scene by buying the 49ers. And guess who received a "finder's fee" of a reported $100,000 to swing that deal? Why, none other than Davis. King Rat, indeed.

Now guess who legally represented Davis when he moved the Raiders to Los Angeles? That's right—attorney Joe Alioto. What goes around comes around in Davis' scheming world. Valley had a 15 percent ownership share of the Raiders, but he generously gave Davis a 16 percent share upon the latter's return to Oakland from his brief commissionership. After Valley departed the Raiders, Davis' share rose to 25 percent compared to a paltry 2.3 percent for McGah, a measly reward for his complicity.

And while Valley contemplated buying the 49ers in 1976, the Raiders reached the zenith that season by winning their first Super Bowl. The conniving, conquering Davis was on top of his element. "Just win, baby" echoed throughout the NFL. Rozelle presented Davis the postgame NFL championship trophy with grace, even though Davis had been the only owner to vote against Rozelle's receiving a contract extension. But Rozelle, gracefully, said of the trophy, "I'm sorry it's not silver and black, but it's close. Al, your victory was one of the most impressive in football history." That trophy exchange was done with minimal eye contact and without the two adversaries shaking hands.

Victory was sweet, but short-lived. The Raiders were riding high— the highest—but would not scale that same summit the remainder of the decade. But, because they were the Raiders, further conflicting issues, including domestic, muddied their ascent.

Madden had guided the Raiders expertly, complete with sideline histrionics, while recording the highest regular season winning percentage ever, .759, among pro coaches with 100 victories. But he was just 9–7 in the playoffs after a 20–17 AFC title game defeat at Denver during the 1977 season, including yet another postseason controversial call involving Oakland. Broncos running back Rob Lytle fumbled the ball away at the visitors' goal line, but the officials claimed they never saw the ball slide down Lytle's body and blew the play dead. Denver scored on the next play, and the "Phantom Fumble" marked Madden's final playoff appearance as Davis fumed again at the NFL—and Rozelle, believing he had been purposely cheated out of victory.

Also in 1977, Madden testified in the George Atkinson slander suit that went to trial in July. Madden contended Atkinson's forearm to the back of Pittsburgh's Lynn Swann's helmet was "an instinctive reaction by a safety, not a premeditated cheap shot." Madden clearly was protecting one of his players, reflecting the coach's loyality. Pittsburgh coach Chuck Noll admitted, finally, that his Steelers also were guilty of a "criminal element" behavior, an accusation he had charged the Raiders with initially. But Noll and the Steelers were cleared of all charges, a bitter defeat for Davis that he felt, once more, was NFL orchestrated.

The 1978 season, with the Raiders missing the playoffs for only the second time since 1966, took a heavy toll on Madden. Besides battling an ulcer, he stopped speaking to Davis late in the season. And so Madden retired from coaching altogether before launching a second career as a megastar NFL television analyst. Tom Flores was promoted from assistant coach to replace Madden in 1979.

The biggest Raiders story that year was internal, involving Davis' wife Carol, or Carolee to her husband. Davis' supporters and critics alike were convinced he was married to football. Ross recalled having a postgame dinner with the Davises, when the husband announced he had to return immediately to training camp. His wife spoke up: "I've been sitting home all week smoking cigarettes. You're coming home tonight and be a husband." Ross blanched; Davis went home.

The chain-smoking Carol Davis' heart stopped beating at home on the morning of October 19, 1979. Her husband found her on the floor, eyes glazed, unable to speak, gasping for breath. Stricken with both a heart attack and stroke, she was hospitalized. Davis forgot about the Raiders and moved into the hospital, where his Carolee remained in a coma for 17 days. Then, miraculously, she awoke and asked, "What happened?" Her husband said, "You were sick, baby." Following extensive therapy, amazingly, she made a full recovery. She's now the NFL's oldest woman limited franchise owner at 91.

The Raiders were 9–7 again in 1979, with their majority owner only partly available as he balanced football with his interpretation of love. "I only want to be loved by certain people—my players, the people I live with," he said. "No, not by humanity. I push it away because I don't need it. Maybe everyone else should work at it, but we need a few people to lead and dominate and get things done. I feel the role of love belongs to other people."

As for the people he lived with, besides Carol, there was teenage son Mark, who ran away from home one summer with his father at training camp in Santa Rosa. Carol, in a panic, called her husband. He responded that with an upcoming roster cut down, his hands were tied. "Al," she shot back angrily, "this is your son!" He said he would call her right back. When he did, he said, "I'll send down a limousine to go look for him." A limousine? Mark returned home, but not with a limo driver.

Life was back in order in 1980, at least on the home front. But not inside the Raiders' offices or on the practice field in nearby Alameda, where quarterbacks were going and coming. Davis traded Stabler to Houston for Dan Pastorini, who flopped before breaking an ankle in the early season. Waiting in the wings was Jim Plunkett, the Rose Bowl hero and Heisman Trophy winner at Stanford, who was dumped by both New England and San Francisco before the wily Davis rescued him.

After losing three of their first five games, the Raiders, led by Plunkett, caught fire and steamrolled their way into the playoffs with an 11–5 record. They then knocked off visiting Houston—and Stabler—27–7 before winning in freezing Cleveland 14–12 after Mike "Bad Hands" Davis intercepted Brian Sipe, the NFL's Most Valuable Player in '80, in the icy end zone with time running out. The road Raiders won again in San Diego, stunning the Chargers 34–27 for the AFC title. And the Raiders then dominated Philadelphia 27–10 in Super Bowl XV in New Orleans. The comeback kid, Plunkett, was voted the game's MVP, even though Raiders linebacker Rod Martin had three interceptions to set a Super Bowl single-game individual record.

In off-field NFL news, the Rams fled Los Angeles for a more affluent land deal in nearby Anaheim, leaving Memorial Coliseum vacant. With the Olympic Games coming there in 1984, Los Angeles was elevated to the No. 1 sports city in the nation, hosting the baseball Dodgers, the basketball Lakers and Clippers, the hockey Kings—and the Raiders. With USC and UCLA, two powerhouse colleges, Los Angeles was red hot.

Wayne Valley was hot, too, under the collar. "I feel it's outrageous," he said of the move to the southland. "The Raiders have been supported by the fans in a great way. The team has been successful and attended. There's no reason for the team not to stay in Oakland."

No reason at all, but the Raiders debuted in Los Angeles in 1982. And within three years, both of their original co-owners had passed away. McGah died first in 1983 at 84, eulogized by the Raiders as the man "who added stability and credibility to the franchise for three decades." When Valley, 72, died of cancer in 1986, the Raiders offered no eulogy. But Rozelle called Valley "a tenacious owner. Without Wayne, there would have been no Raiders in Oakland and no stadium."

Pallbearers at Valley's funeral, while Al Davis looked away, were former Raiders Jim Otto, Fred Biletnikoff, Tom Keating, and Tony Cline. Gladys Valley explicitly told police that Davis wasn't to enter the church. He didn't show up, but Carol Davis came. "She threw her arms around me," said Gladys, "and I stood like a pole until she got away from me."

The Raiders flourished in Los Angeles on the playing field, but it wasn't ever in Al Davis' DNA to be totally pleased with stadium management. He felt the Los Angeles Coliseum hadn't followed through with all its promises, and so he searched for a new stadium site in, of all places, nearby nondescript Irwindale, which handed Davis $10 million in good faith. That agreement fell through, and Irwindale was out the $10 million, having found out too late that negotiating with Davis was pure lunacy. Los Angeles Coliseum officials filed a $58 million breach of contract suit against Davis, who filed a countersuit against them. Litigation was endless with Davis; he was either suing or being sued. Of course, in his jaded mind, it wasn't ever his fault.

He continued winning, unfazed, from 1982 through 1985, making the playoffs each year, and capturing his third Super Bowl in 1983, a 38–9 whipping of Washington in Super Bowl XVIII in Tampa. Then the Los Angeles glow faded because of lawsuits, unsuccessful drafts, and even unruly fans. Raider players hesitated before walking to their cars after games, for an aggressive crowd awaited them in the lots. Something else had been lost in leaving Oakland: safe, undying fan love.

That fact became obvious even to Davis' most loyal servant, Al LoCasale, who ran the Raiders' front office with dictatorial authority. He worked so hard to make things function correctly in Los Angeles that he was hospitalized with pneumonia. He also lacked a driver's license and would ask the team's public relations aide, Bill Glazier, to take him to booster club events, including in suburbia one rainy evening. During the drive, LoCasale suddenly blurted, "This isn't working out. We should never have left Oakland." Glazier was so stunned, he lost control of the wheel and crashed the car, breaking LoCasale's arm.

Beginning with the 1986 season, "Commitment to Excellence" had lost its commitment. The Raiders strung together nine successive non-playoff seasons, sandwiched around their heralded return to Oakland in 1996. The Oakland Coliseum was renovated to welcome home its wayward lads, and the move injected new life into a flat franchise. The Raiders began a three-year postseason run, highlighted by their fourth Super Bowl appearance, unfortunately a 48–21 thrashing by the Tampa Bay Buccaneers in San Diego. That setback marked the termination of Al Davis' dominance. He then morphed into a disoriented football figure.

Davis had run off Jon Gruden as his head coach, and Gruden resurfaced in Tampa Bay, coaching Tampa to its Super Bowl slaughter of the Raiders, who were coached by Bill Callahan, who also would be run off by Davis. But, by then, it didn't matter who was coaching the Raiders, or playing for the Raiders, because Davis had misplaced his winning edge for good. The enemy that he lived to dominate had become himself.

His once unerring eye for draft picks failed him repeatedly. Beginning with Bob Buczkowski in 1986, then adding John Clay, Anthony Smith, Todd Marinovich, Chester McGlockton, Patrick Bates, Rob Fredrickson, Rickey Dudley, Darrell Russell, Matt Stinchcomb, Derrick Gibson, Phillip Buchanon, Robert Gallery, Fabian Washington, and Michael Huff, they were all No. 1 draft picks, and mostly outright busts. And these were Al Davis' picks, because he had the final say. Super scout Ron Wolf, who had discovered fiuture Pro Football Hall of Famers, was gone, and nobody could—or even tried to—convince Davis to back off. Thus, the Raiders became irrelevant. A shell of his former genius, Davis sat on his self-appointed throne, a disoriented ruler, with his worst move coming.

In 2007, with the first overall pick of the NFL draft, Davis selected quarterback JaMarcus Russell from Louisiana State University. Russell had a strong arm, but no aim, and the kid imploded in so many ways. He was huge in size, fat and getting fatter. He refused to put in the extra work to become even a decent quarterback. The Raiders played him anyway, but Davis could barely watch the films. And if Russell's performance wasn't bad enough, late at night he drove to a supermarket and bought cases of cough syrup possessing a certain kick that might "enhance" his mind, but not his football ability. The Raiders, in 2009, let him go as the worst No. 1 overall draftee by any NFL team this century. And nobody wanted him, further tarnishing Davis' legacy.

There won't ever be another Al Davis in pro football because there wasn't anyone like him before. His negatives aside, he is the only NFL figure to be an assistant coach, head coach, general manager, owner, and commissioner. His impact on the game is unquestioned and unequaled. He changed the way pro football is regarded, because of his unique style and the renegade manner of his Raiders teams. Davis was the NFL's greatest individualist, manipulating the league, yet insisting against all known evidence, "I am the establishment. I always have been." He was, indeed, a charming rogue, but also an eternal enigma.

He died October 8, 2011, at 82. The Raiders erected a tribute in his honor: a tall, garish, gas-operated torch, featuring the letters AL, to be lit by a former Raider before home games. Davis' son, Mark, never a functioning part of the Raiders front office prior to his father's passing, then assumed ownership controls, with predictable chaos forthcoming.

The son had his father's same compassion for Oakland, which is zilch despite unparalleled fan fidelity. Jon Gruden returned as Raiders head coach with less pleasing results, both on the field and in his own character. The Raiders discarded their greatness in Oakland long ago. Thus, the odds of that dominance reoccurring in a gambling town is a long shot at best.

The Davises, father and son, became a risky gamble that ceased paying off—wherever.

Chapter 2

House of Champions: Hometown Memories

Oakland was the sports capital of the United States.
—Warriors basketball great Rick Barry

As late as America's entrance into World War II, major league sports divided the country. The East Coast and Midwest were the haves, the Rockies and West Coast the have-nots. That's why minor league baseball and colleges filled the sports entertainment gap out west. And Oakland was no exception.

The Oakland Oaks baseball team put Oakland on the sports map in 1903 as a charter member of the AAA Pacific Coast League. The Oaks started off bumpily with a string of losing seasons before winning the PCL championship in 1912. The Oaks were a force from the onset of that year, as evidenced by this April 11, 1912, article in the *Oakland Association News:*

> The Oaks certainly treated Danny Long's trained Seals shamefully the past week. Six out of seven was an awful beating for the Seals' highly touted aggregation. And it was lucky for the latter that the Oaks mercifully handed the opening contest to them.

Of course, it was principally luck that caused the Seals to drop those six games in a row. The Oaks deserve no credit for better stick-work, better base running, better pitching, and better inside work. To hear the San Francisco apologists talk, all the luck broke in favor of Bud Sharpe's men, who played the unwieldy Seals off their feet, and made them slip back into the puddle of defeat. Looks like the new infield of the Oaks is a big improvement over that of last season....

Those Oaks infielders were as smooth as the infield itself at Freeman's Park, located at the corner of 59th Street and San Pablo Avenue. The following year, 1913, the Oaks were housed in a brand-new $80,000 ballpark, Oaks Park, in neighboring Emeryville. "The grandstand was close to the field," recalled one critic, "and when you walked in, there was the smell of hot dogs boiling. The stands creaked a lot. It had wooden walkways that gave when you walked on them."

Baseball, itself, treaded poorly in 1916 when Oakland broke the sport's color line. The Oaks signed pitcher Jimmy Claxton, who contended that he was Native American. He pitched both ends of a doubleheader before it was discovered that he was actually African American. He was promptly released—31 years before Jackie Robinson integrated the major leagues.

The Oaks didn't repeat as PCL champions until 1927, the same year Babe Ruth hit a record 60 home runs. Buzz Arlett, the "Babe Ruth of the Minor Leagues," was given a day in his honor in Oakland that year. The honoree hit two home runs and pitched late in the game, a 12–6 win over the rival Seals.

Russell Loris Arlett was called "Buzz" for his proclivity in cutting down hitters as a spitball pitcher. His overall pitching record: 108 victories, 93 defeats, 3.42 earned-run average.

Like Ruth, Arlett started his career as a pitcher before switching to the outfield to utilize his prodigious power. He played for Oakland from 1918 through 1930. Over 13 PCL seasons, he amassed 215 homers and 1,135 runs batted in.

He only sniffed the major leagues, playing one season with the Philadelphia Phillies, 1931, batting .313 with 18 homers, utilized mainly as a pinch-hitter as he was a defensive risk.

The 6'4", 230-pound Arlett returned to the minors. His totals of 432 homers and 1,786 RBI were minor league records that lasted into this century. He also batted .341 in the minors, and three times he hit four homers in one game. Born in Elmhurst, California in 1899, he died at 65 in Minneapolis in 1964.

Oakland's first homegrown hero emerged not on a baseball diamond, but on a football field in Adolphe "Ade" Schwammel, a 6'2", 225-pound Oregon State tackle. He was first-team All-America in 1933 after the 6–2–2 Beavers beat powerhouse Fordham and held another force, USC, to a scoreless tie.

A Fremont High School of Oakland product, Schwammel was a three-year letterman at Oregon State before appearing in the 1934 College All-Star Game. He then was chosen All-NFL twice with Green Bay, in 1935 and 1936, and played on two championship teams with the Packers, 1936 and 1944. His NFL career lasted five years, with a seven-year gap in between, un-retiring in 1943 because of a wartime player shortage.

His time at Oregon State included a national rules change. Schwammel and Harry Schields, also 6'2", hoisted 6'7" Clyde Devine on their shoulders to block a place kick against rival Oregon. The NCAA quickly banned that maneuver.

Schwammel, capable with his fists, was heavyweight champ on a southern California naval base, and briefly considered fighting professionally. He was inducted in the Oregon State University Hall of Fame and the Oregon Athletic Hall of Fame. He manufactured plastic goods in Hawaii for several decades before passing away at 71 in Honolulu in 1979.

In 1949, the University of California's All-American fullback Jackie Jensen, another Oakland native, signed a baseball contract with the Oakland Oaks, thereby forfeiting his senior year on the gridiron. He later became the American League's MVP as a Boston Red Sox outfielder in

1958. And he holds the distinction of being the first athlete to appear in a Rose Bowl, World Series, and baseball's All-Star Game.

The Oaks won additional PCL titles in 1948, 1950, and 1954. Then, in 1956, the franchise moved to Vancouver, British Columbia. The ramshackle Oaks Park was razed soon after.

"I attended the last game at Oaks Park, a very sad occasion," said John Simmonds, then a teenage Oakland resident and a future *Oakland Tribune* sportswriter. "After the last pitch was thrown, I walked across the field as fans down the left field line started tearing down the fence to get souvenirs. Oaks Park was a wonderful place to watch a game and then go home with your pants full of slivers."

Oakland became big league in 1960 with the founding of the homeless Raiders, who played two seasons in San Francisco before their first game in Oakland. With the A's moving west from Kansas City in 1968, and the Warriors crossing the Bay Bridge from San Francisco in 1972, Oakland had three major league franchises. Oaktown hit the heights in the mid-1970s when all three of its teams won league championships, and the wordy Oakland Alameda County Coliseum Complex then received the justified distinction of "House of Champions."

The A's got the ball rolling with a flourish in winning three successive World Series in 1972, 1973, and 1974. The Warriors were NBA champions in 1975, and the Raiders won the Super Bowl during the 1976 NFL season. One American city—five national titles in three sports in a two-year span, in Oakland, California.

"We were putting Oakland on the national map," recalled Vida Blue, a Cy Young Award pitcher for those dominant A's. "When you win a baseball, football, and basketball championship in a short span, that says a lot about your city. Oakland was looked at as San Francisco's stepchild…the little city that was trying to get recognized. The A's winning three in a row put us over the top.

"We had all those great players on the A's. The Warriors had Rick Barry, and Al Attles was no slouch as a player or coach. The Raiders had a multitude of stars on their team. Oakland was a blue-collar city, and the Oakland Alameda Coliseum Complex meant a lot to the players' lives and the fans' lives."

The House of Champions, indeed. The A's added another World Series title in 1989, the Raiders won another Super Bowl in 1983, and the Warriors strung together five consecutive NBA championship series appearances, 2015 through 2019, winning the title three times. Oakland ruled.

Sadly, the House of Champions became a house divided as the Coliseum and Arena turned into an unhappy duplex. Two of their three championship tenants, the Raiders and Warriors, fled to Las Vegas and San Francisco, respectively. Only the A's remain, but unhappily, as their field of dreams concept in Oakland could be a potential nightmare. Team president Dave Kaval repeatedly has said the franchise is on "parallel paths," either pursuing a ballpark at Oakland's Howard Terminal or becoming the Raiders' neighbor near the Las Vegas casinos.

Oakland is left, mostly, with memories and mementos in referencing its sports heritage. Yet it's quite a heritage. The A's and New York Yankees, 1998 through 2000, are the only Major League Baseball teams in a half-century to win three straight World Series. Both teams had demonstrative owners: Charles O. Finley and George Steinbrenner. A's players were stuck with Finley until 1976, when baseball free agency commenced. A bunch of A's stars signed elsewhere, and a dynasty imploded. But it was quite the show while it lasted.

The '70s A's featured Baseball Hall of Fame players in pitchers Catfish Hunter and Rollie Fingers, and outfielder Reggie Jackson. The team was deep in proven talent, winning four ways: clutch offense, solid defense, superb pitching, and mistake-free execution. Their chief obstacle was, oddly, their owner, Finley, who focused attention on himself with continual harangues against his players and the baseball world itself.

The A's also had a Hall of Fame manager in Dick Williams, at least for their first two World Series, 1972 and 1973. Then he could no longer stomach Finley's interference, bolting for the California Angels. Finley routinely phoned in lineups from his farm in La Porte, Indiana, constantly making roster moves that were occasionally beneficial, while he battled with baseball's power structure on a yearly, monthly, or weekly basis.

Not once during that A's dynasty did they win 100 games; it was 93, 94, 90 victories, claiming division titles by 5½ , 6, and 5 games. Their leading hitter, statistically, was Joe Rudi, who batted .305 in 1972. And despite their dominance, they drew one million fans just once, 1973, during those three World Series championship runs.

The postseason odds were stacked against those A's from the very start. They needed all five games to eliminate Detroit in the 1972 AL Division Series, but lost their slugger, Jackson, to a pulled hamstring in the process. His absence loomed large, for Cincinnati's "Big Red Machine" was their World Series foe. Up stepped Gene Tenace, a sometimes catcher, sometimes first baseman, who batted .225 with five home runs during the regular season. Then, spectacularly, he homered his first two times at bat, and the visiting A's won the opener 3–2.

Hunter followed up Ken Holtzman's quality start in Game 1 with an equally impressive 2–1 victory. Once again, the A's relied on the spectacular, Rudi's leaping catch against the left field wall to rob Denis Menke with a runner on base.

The Series shifted to Oakland, where the Reds won two of three games, and then evened the Series at 3–3 in Cincinnati with an 8–1 drubbing of the A's. Finally, it all came down to Hunter, who combined brilliantly with Fingers for a 3–2 clinching victory, a World Series stunner of stunners.

Cincinnati scored 21 runs in seven games, or three runs per, as A's pitching muzzled the Big Red Machine's vaunted lineup. Fingers relieved six times, including one incredible strikeout. Johnny Bench thought he was being walked intentionally, but Fingers froze him with a 3–2 fastball for strike three. Tenace finished with four homers and nine runs batted in, plus the MVP award, as the underdog A's won their first World Series championship since 1930 in Philadelphia.

Outfielder Billy North joined the A's in 1973 and learned immediately why a dynasty was materializing in Oakland.

"It was Dick Williams," he emphasized, "and the competitiveness of those players. Dick taught them how to play baseball without mistakes, and the players had the ability to see what he was talking about: Don't give up extra outs. And that's how we played the game, to fundamentally buy in."

Buying in was vital because those A's had baseball's strongest pitching staff, starters, and relievers, from the first inning through the ninth. Williams used that staff strategically.

"We would get the lead," North said, "and then stop them from scoring late."

The stingy A's, who seldom breezed in October, needed another fifth-game victory, Hunter's 3–0 shutout of Baltimore in the AL Division Series, to reach the 1973 World Series against the New York Mets. And, once again, the Series came down to Game 7, only this time ladled with controversy.

The Mets, after eliminating Cincinnati in seven games in the NL Division Series, were favored to beat the A's. Unlike the regular season, Oakland's pitchers again were forced to take their at-bats in a World Series—ah, but with positive results. Winning pitcher Holtzman doubled in the third inning and scored on a fielding error. Rudi singled in another run in the same inning as the A's won the opener 2–1 in Oakland.

Game 2 would be the longest game in World Series history, 4:13, although that's not why it's remembered. Mike Andrews, anyone? Oakland rallied from a 6–4 deficit in the ninth inning with run-scoring singles by Jackson and Tenace. In the 12th, Willie Mays put the Mets ahead 7–6 with a single, the last hit of his glorious career. A's second baseman Andrews followed by letting John Milner's grounder skip through his legs for a two-run error. Jerry Grote's ensuing grounder to Andrews was thrown wide to first for another run-scoring error as the Mets won 10–7.

The Mike Andrews' horror show was just beginning. Finley reacted by "firing" Andrews, deactivating him after citing a bogus shoulder injury.

Commissioner Bowie Kuhn, seeing through this ruse, re-instated Andrews, much to the delight of the Oakland squad and manager Williams.

The Series shifted to New York, where the A's won Game 3 on shortstop Bert "Campy" Campaneris' 11th-inning single 3–2. But the Mets won the next two games 6–1 and 2-0 to lead the Series 3–2 as the teams headed back to Oakland. Then one Hall of Fame pitcher, Hunter, defeated another, Tom Seaver, 3–1 as Jackson had a pair of run-scoring doubles before singling to score the third run.

Then in the deciding Game 7, Campaneris and Jackson each hit two-run homers in the third inning as the A's rolled to a 5–2 victory. Holtzman got the win, but the A's bullpen was once again heroic. Fingers appeared in six games, while workhorse Darold Knowles relieved in all seven games. But since it was the A's, the drama was only beginning. Williams, tired of Finley's interference, fled as manager. The Andrews' incident, Williams intimated, was the final straw. Alvin Dark was named as his replacement, and Andrews was sent packing.

Oakland opposed the Los Angeles Dodgers in the '74 World Series, but before the opening pitch was thrown, the A's opposed each other. Fingers and John "Blue Moon" Odom got into a fistfight in the visiting clubhouse. But not even team discord fazed those A's, who won the opener 3–2 as Jackson homered and Holtzman doubled and scored on a Campaneris squeeze bunt. Dark's imaginative managing included Hunter relieving Fingers, who got the win and Hunter, oddly, the save.

North hasn't forgotten the Fingers–Odom fisticuffs, but as he pointed out, "Every team I've been on has had fistfights. We just happened to be the world champion, but with peculiar personalities. We had some arrogant people, and some who were not, but it was one of the most interesting locker rooms you could ever imagine. We won championships, but we had a lot of tension, and push and pull. Reggie and I would go a couple of weeks without talking. Nobody ran that locker room, but Sal Bando oversaw it, one of the greatest leaders I ever saw. We called him Captain Sal, and he was solid.

"We had unity. When we got between those white lines, we played as one, and we played the game right, a cerebral team. Everyone knew what he had to do as a 25-man team. There never was any question about our grit and character."

But how difficult was it playing for a compulsive, hands-on owner like Finley?

"It wasn't like that for me. I got along with Charlie. He liked me," North replied. "But Dick Williams wouldn't let that b.s. from Finley get down to us. Charlie wanted him to do things, but whether he did them or not, Dick was a shield who protected us. At the same time, when it came down to playing the game right, you didn't want Dick to go south on you."

Williams bristled over judgment failure, but the Dodgers evened the series with a 3–2 win as A's "designated runner" Herb Washington was picked off base after replacing Rudi, who had just ripped a two-run single. Washington, a former track sprinter, was a Finley discovery who appeared in 105 regular season games without ever batting. Following that boneheaded play, the series shifted to Oakland, where more theatrics awaited, although this time favoring the A's.

Hunter and Fingers combined to win Game 3, 3–2, as the A's benefitted from two unearned runs. Then pitcher Holtzman was the man at the plate again, homering off Andy Messersmith in Game 4, while also working 7⅔ innings and getting the win as Fingers finished up a 5–2 victory.

"Before that World Series started, Bill Buckner of the Dodgers was quoted as saying that only two A's players, Catfish Hunter and Reggie Jackson, could make the Dodgers roster," Rudi remembered. "But in Game 5, Buckner tried to stretch a double into a triple and was thrown out on a perfect relay from Reggie in right to second baseman Dick Green to Sal Bando at third. When Buckner went out to left field, the fans there gave him grief and started throwing things on the field.

"The game was held up for 15 minutes as the trash was cleaned up. I was getting ready to face reliever Mike Marshall, who had won 15 games that season while making a record 106 relief appearances. Well, Marshall had a big ego, and a different way of pitching, believing in mental concentration. He was on a different planet from us, and while play was stopped, he was talking to the shortstop and throwing no practice pitches. He had a great screwball, but I knew he wouldn't throw one after doing nothing for 15 minutes. So, I was sitting on a fastball, which wasn't his best pitch, and that's what he threw. I hit it over the left field fence in the bottom of the seventh, and Rollic Fingers then closed out a 3–2 win."

Rudi's home run concluded a third consecutive World Series title for Oakland. Then, after Williams departed for Anaheim, A's players also took flight—possibly also because of acrimonious relationships with owner Finley?

"I believe it was," Rudi said. "He wouldn't even offer us a raise after we had won three consecutive World Series. We sent in contract requests, and he didn't even respond. He traded Reggie and Holtzman to Baltimore for outfielder Don Baylor, pitcher Mike Perez and a young player. But Baylor and I signed instead with the California Angels. Campaneris then went to Texas, Fingers and Tenace to San Diego, Bando to Milwaukee, and catcher Ray Fosse to Cleveland.

"I'm sure if we had held that team together, although you can't always tell with injuries, we would have been in the championship mix for another five years. Because most of us were in our middle twenties."

Managing who was left in Oakland fell to Dark, who didn't have the best timing, although it wasn't altogether his fault.

"The manager who came after Dick Williams, all he had to do was get out of the way," said North. "We knew what we had to do, and Alvin was more like a lightning rod between us and Charlie. It was Dick Williams' team, then [with Dark] it became Charlie's team."

In 1975, Hunter pitched for the New York Yankees, winning 24 games while Oakland stepped off its dynastic throne. The A's were swept in three games by Boston in the 1975 Division Series and didn't return to the postseason until 1981.

North played 11 big-league seasons with five teams, including the A's from 1973 to 1978. He batted .261 over his career but still won games with his speed, offensively and defensively. After baseball, he finished his degree at Central Washington University and became a financial planner.

North had a long-concealed confession he needed to make. "When I was 18, I got hit in the right eye with a baseball and lost the sight in that eye," he said. "I played my whole career that way, and nobody knew it because I never told anybody. But if I lost sight in the other eye, I'd need a cane."

Vida Blue was stunned years later to learn that he had a partially blind teammate in Oakland. "What? No way," he reacted in disbelief. "Well, I'll be damned."

The Coliseum's other tenant, the Raiders, also reached for the stars in the 1970s, but didn't land in orbit until the 1976 season, when they finally reached the Super Bowl after three straight American Conference title game defeats.

The Raiders were nearly perfect that season at 13–1, the best record in football. They had taken down Super Bowl champion Pittsburgh in the opener 31–28, then dominated everyone else but host New England in Week 4, losing 48–17. Tom Flores, a former Raiders quarterback who became the head coach of two Raiders Super Bowl champions, was an Oakland assistant coach during that 1976 season. He hasn't forgotten that one-sided loss to the Patriots.

"The Patriots just killed us," he said. "But we were a great team that year because everyone had peaked—Ken Stabler, Fred Biletnikoff, everyone! Look at the Hall of Famers on that team. That 1976 team, and my 1983 team were two of the greatest teams in Raider history."

Coaching those Raiders teams were two Pro Football Hall of Fame inductees: Madden and Flores, both Al Davis hires.

Oakland was perfectly balanced that 1976 season. Fullback Mark van Eeghen had the first of three consecutive 1,000-yard rushing seasons (1,012), quarterback Ken "the Snake" Stabler had his most productive autumn with 27 touchdown passes, tight end Dave Casper came into his own with 53 receptions and 10 touchdowns, and wide receiver Cliff Branch had 12 touchdowns and 1,111 receiving yards. Ray Guy had a below-normal 41.6 yards average with his sky-high punts, but he still was voted All-Pro with Casper and Branch.

The Raiders filled up a hall themselves at the Pro Football Hall of Fame. The equally talented Steelers had their own hall in Canton, Ohio. Those two storied franchises clashed five times in the postseason in the 1970s, with historic flair.

"We had gotten close so many times," Biletnikoff reflected, "but I'm not one to say it would have been different if this or that had happened. We were the same team in '76, but guys were making plays. Guys just got better, and we were maturing. I will say this: there was a real closeness on that team."

The '76 Raiders sought payback against New England in a first-round playoff game in Oakland, a give-and-take contest with a classic ending. The Patriots felt they had sealed the victory when Stabler threw an incomplete pass on fourth down. However, the Patriots' Ray Hamilton received a roughing-the-passer penalty, giving the Raiders new life. Reaching the 1-yard line with 14 seconds left, Kenny the Snake rolled to his left and side-winded into the end zone. Linebacker Monte Johnson then intercepted Steve Grogan to complete an exciting, though controversial, 31–28 win.

The Patriots felt robbed by a bogus call, and their coaches assailed the officiating crew under the stadium afterward. The Raiders laughed at those Patriots complaints, for Oakland lost to Pittsburgh in 1972 on the more controversial Immaculate Reception postseason touchdown catch by Franco Harris.

"I was upstairs in the coaches' box during that [1976] game," said Flores, "and we knew that if the game was tight, we'd turn it over to Snake, and he would get it done. Those were the days when quarterbacks called their own plays, and Snake was a big-time guy in big games."

The Raiders then faced, of course, Pittsburgh for the AFC crown. The Steelers, 10–4 that season, trounced Baltimore 40–14 in the first round of the playoffs, but lacked injured running backs Harris and Rocky Bleier this time around. That mattered little to Stabler, who flipped short touchdown passes to halfback Pete Banaszak and backup tight end Warren Bankston as the Raiders romped 24–7. After a nine-year gap, Oakland was once again Super Bowl bound.

Minnesota and its stifling Purple Gang defense presented the opposition, but the Raiders took the field at the Rose Bowl Stadium in Pasadena brimming with confidence, believing they were considerably better overall than the Vikings.

"That was our absolute feeling," Flores remembered. "The night before the game, we finished our quarterback meeting and John [Madden] asked the assistant coaches what they thought would happen the next day. Lew Erber said, 'We're going to win 42–0.' John just about choked on his cigarette. Then John looked at me, and I said, 'I don't think the score will be like that, but there's no way they can beat us, unless our special teams screw up.'"

And that's exactly what happened immediately as the Vikings' Fred McNeill blocked Guy's punt and recovered it at the Raiders' 3-yard line. No harm was done, though, as Oakland linebacker Phil Villapiano stripped running back Brent McClanahan, with linebacker Willie Hall recovering the fumble. The Raiders then buried the Purple Gang, gaining 429 yards, 266 coming yards on the ground, both Super Bowl records.

"We were really focused," said Biletnikoff, "and we just got stronger as the game went on."

Clarence Davis rushed for 137 yards on 16 carries, Errol Mann kicked field goals of 24 and 40 yards, Banaszak scored on two short runs, Casper caught a one-yard touchdown lob from Stabler, and Willie Brown returned a Fran Tarkenton interception 75 yards for a final six-pointer as Raiders broadcaster Bill King shouted "Old Man Willie" into the mic.

"We just played with such confidence that day," said Flores.

Oakland won in a breeze, 32–14. How dominant were the Raiders? The Vikings' stalwart defensive end Jim Marshall failed to make one tackle as massive Art Shell overpowered him. The game's MVP was Biletnikoff, with four catches for 79 yards, setting up one touchdown. But in accepting that award, Biletnikoff felt nostalgic.

"I thought of Billy Cannon, Daryle Lamonica, Wayne Hawkins, Cotton Davidson and Jim Otto, teammates who never got a chance to play in a Super Bowl," he said. "When I was a young kid on the Raiders, starting off slowly, those guys offered me encouragement. But my Super Bowl MVP choice would have been Kenny. He was our general."

Villapiano summed up that Super Bowl rout perfectly. "If the Vikings feel they just had a bad game today, I'll tell you what we'll do," he said in the victorious locker room. "We'll take Monday off and play them again on Tuesday."

There would have been no takers among the Purple Gang.

But the most improbable champion of the three Oakland franchises was the 1975 Warriors, who were supposed to be swept by the Washington Bullets, but then swept the Bullets in the most astonishing of NBA championship series upsets.

The Bullets won 60 games to the Warriors' 48 during the regular season. But Warriors coach Al Attles, operating with only one All-NBA star in Rick Barry, devised a unique rotation system for those times, utilizing 10 players. The Warriors overwhelmed teams with rotation and hustle, providing them an edge against the Bullets, who stayed with their main stars.

Yet it wasn't an easy road for either team in reaching the NBA Finals. Seattle, coached by Bill Russell, proved a tough match for the Warriors, who needed six games to advance out of the first round. Then they required seven games to eliminate gritty Chicago, though the Warriors proved grittier, erasing 13-point deficits in five of those games. Washington outlasted Buffalo, and the NBA's top scorer, Bob McAdoo (34.5), in seven games before next ousting a potent Boston team in six games.

Coach K.C. Jones' Bullets had standout players in guards Kevin Porter and Phil Chenier, center Wes Unseld, and forward Elvin Hayes. Crazily, the Warriors' postseason home games would be played in San Francisco, from whence they came, at the antiquated Cow Palace. The conflicting issue: an Ice Follies scheduling at the Oakland Arena, whose management, feeling the Warriors weren't playoff caliber, had earlier slotted an ice show at the same time.

The heavily favored Bullets ran into a buzz saw from the beginning as the host Warriors swarmed all over them with tight defense and manpower. With Barry getting scoring help from his bench, the Bullets were iced 101–95 in the opener.

If Washington felt Game 1 was a fluke, the Warriors followed up with a squeaker 92–91 win in San Francisco. Back home in Landover, Maryland, the Bullets tried to mount a comeback, but the Warriors dashed their hopes with a 109–101 victory to go up 3–0.

Game 4 brought out the host Bullets' growing frustrations. After Barry scored 38 points in Game 3, the Bullets resorted to back-alley tactics. Three minutes into the contest, Washington forward Mike Riordan picked up his third foul by roughhousing Barry. When Attles saw Riordan with a wrestling hold on Barry, he charged onto the court to defend his star player and had to be restrained. Attles was ejected and assistant Joe Roberts then took over, splendidly, as the Warriors won 96–95 to complete their amazing sweep.

"We never panicked, and we just kept doing what we knew we had to do," said Barry, who had 20 points and five assists in the Final. "Even when we fell behind by eight points near the end, we just knew we were going to come on and win. We could see they were tired."

Frustrated, too, were the Bullets, but they reacted nobly. "We tried," said Jones, "but they played better." Unseld added, "They simply played sounder basketball than we did."

Roberts, at 83, was still an Oakland resident in 2020 when he was contacted about that special Warriors team.

"The organization's mind-set at the start of the season was that the team looked like 50–50 in its division," he said. "What happened was that we had five or six new players, with Phil Smith and Keith Wilkes having spent four years in college, so they knew how to play."

Roberts then dissected the individual skills of those Warriors that blended into a winning recipe.

"Some All-Americans have a reputation, but they don't know how to play the game," he said. "Wilkes just knew how to play. Charles Johnson brought toughness. Teammates called him 'Jack,' like Jack Armstrong, the old radio hero, because of his toughness. He was really strong for his (6'1") size. We didn't have scorers like the Warriors have now with [Stephen] Curry and [Klay] Thompson, but guys like C.J., Butch Beard, Wilkes, and Smith could hit their shots.

"The Warriors traded Nate Thurmond for Clifford Ray before the season. Nate was getting old, when you can't play any more at top efficiency. So they brought in Clifford for toughness and rebounding. And they matched him at center with George Johnson, a tremendous shot-blocker with long arms and great timing. They became a great tandem.

"Butch was a team leader, but a quiet leader at guard," Roberts continued. "When the team was doing some running, and some guys didn't want to run, Butch would say, "C'mon, it's a party. Let's keep the party going.' They would follow Butch.

"Phil Smith had know-how, energy, and tremendous athletic skills. He never said a word, a good kid, but at the end of his rookie year, he was one of the top two '2' guards in the league, and he later became the top '2' guard. Derrek Dickey didn't really like to practice; he always had an excuse. So Wilkes passed him to become the starting forward. But Dickey could shoot, and he didn't miss against the Bullets.

"Charles Dudley was called 'The Grasshopper.' He and C.J. were really good defenders. Earl Monroe and Walt Frazier didn't want to play against them, because Dudley and C.J. would pick them up at half court and just dog them. Dudley had a tremendous amount of energy, and the attitude to play hard, because he had been cut before [by Seattle].

"But we wouldn't have won the title if we didn't have Bill Bridges," Roberts noted. "In that Chicago series, Bob Love and Chet Walker weren't getting much pressure until Bill Bridges entered the game. And they said, 'Damn!' There were no more easy shots when Bill was on the court."

Jeff Mullins filled out the Warriors bench. Once a consistent 20-point scorer, he was at the tail end of a stalwart career. But—no doubt in Roberts' mind—the Atlas-like figure that carried this team on his shoulders was Rick Barry.

"He's the only player who has led the NCAA, NBA, and ABA in scoring," Roberts stressed. "He was a scorer, but he had a bad reputation when he joined the Warriors as being selfish. That wasn't true when I was there; he was a team player. He'd tell George and Clifford, 'Get open and I'll get you the ball.' He'd keep them active. He was a tough competitor."

Roberts had his one moment in the NBA spotlight: Game 4 against Washington after Attles was thrown out.

"It was too late to do anything [different], just do it to the best of your efficiency," he said. "What I tried to do was keep three shooters on the court at all times. I did have this hair-brained idea of putting George on the Big E [Hayes]. And that was a turning point, because [Hayes] wouldn't leave the basket, so he got no easy shots with George's long arms."

Those gritty Warriors wouldn't give up, falling behind regularly, then battling their way back into the lead.

"That was Phil Smith," Roberts stressed. "He brought that toughness and shooting ability [off the bench]. And with all those players we ran at teams, that was the difference. That team isn't appreciated at all. Down the stretch of that season, these guys caught on to fundamentals, and that's what beat Washington. Jerry Sloan, the Bulls guard, had this great statement: 'Our first team was better than the Warriors' first team, but their second team made the difference.' They were energy guys who could play and shoot."

Roberts, 86, died of cancer on October 10, 2022.

Oakland's three-team championship "parlay" in the mid-1970s was utterly fantastic, but the city's sports history also is rich in fabulous homegrown athletes who starred elsewhere.

Jim Pollard came out of Oakland to win an NCAA title at Stanford in 1942 before achieving five NBA titles with the Minneapolis Lakers. Pollard, known as the Kangaroo Kid for his jumping ability as a 6'3½ forward, was picked among the NBA's top 50 players at the league's 50th birthday.

Oakland native John Brodie was an All-American quarterback at Stanford in 1956 before spending 17 seasons with the San Francisco 49ers, leading the NFL in passing twice, and selected as the league's MVP in 1970. He's in the College Football Hall of Fame, but not in the Pro Football Hall of Fame, even though his statistics surpass some inducted quarterbacks.

Brodie suffered a massive stroke in 2001 that could have killed him. But with the same mental resolve and toughness that typified his NFL career, he fought his way back, even with limited speech, to an ambulatory life, still functioning ably in his late eighties. Sue Brodie contributed to this book after speaking with her husband about his Oakland roots:

"When John grew up in Oakland, it was a vibrant sports area. He lived on Golden Gate Avenue, and 'lived' at Montclair Park. No super-organized sports—just kids doing their thing. At Oakland Tech, he played football, baseball, and basketball against many superstars—Curt Flood, Bill Russell, etc. John and his brother, Bill, played American Legion baseball, which was before 'travel' sports. John and I discussed [professional teams leaving Oakland], and we agree that the teams follow the money. The Chargers left San Diego, the Rams left St. Louis, etc., etc. Oakland has never been considered a wealthy area."

Oakland's greatest athlete is the very same Bill Russell, who led the University of San Francisco to its only NCAA basketball championships, in 1955 and 1956, before winning an Olympic gold medal in '56 and then leading the Boston Celtics to 11 NBA titles in 13 seasons, the last two titles also with Russell as the NBA's first Black coach. Basketball—nor any other contact sport—hasn't produced a bigger winner than Bill Russell.

Frank Robinson, an Oakland product, was a Baseball Hall of Fame inductee as a Triple Crown–winning player—batting average, home runs, runs batted in—at Baltimore (1966), before becoming baseball's first African American manager (Cleveland). Oaklander Joe Morgan, twice a league MVP (Cincinnati), joined him in Cooperstown, where Oakland's own Rickey Henderson, the all-time base stealer, also is enshrined.

Zoe Ann Olsen was an Oakland-grown diver who won 24 AAU championships before earning a silver medal at the 1948 Olympics in London and a bronze medal at the 1952 Olympiad at Helsinki. She wed football-baseball great Jackie Jensen, a union of golden-haired stars, although the marriage didn't last.

Don Budge was born in Oakland, honed his racquet skills at the neighboring Berkeley Tennis Club, and was then the first man or woman to win tennis' Grand Slam—Australia, France, Wimbledon, and the U.S. Open—in the same year, 1938. He won 10 grand slam matches overall and the annual Sullivan Award as the nation's finest amateur athlete.

Helen Wills Moody, women's tennis' greatest player pre–Martina Navratilova, also played on Oakland courts. She won 31 Grand Slam tournaments, including 19 singles titles. Born in neighboring Berkeley, she was voted the top international female player eight times in the 1920s and 1930s.

Jason Kidd grew up in Oakland, won two state high school basketball titles at St. Joseph Notre Dame in abutting Alameda, was a first-team All-American at the University of California, and then launched a 17-year NBA career as a definitive point guard, with superb passing and ball-hawking skills, plus unmatched stamina. He's now a successful NBA head coach.

Marshawn Lynch attended Oakland Technical High School and was an All-American running back at Cal and a punishing runner with Buffalo, Seattle, and Oakland in the NFL, winning a Super Bowl with the Seahawks. Ever loyal to Oakland, he unretired to play for his hometown Raiders prior to their move to Las Vegas before becoming an Oakland businessman.

Damian Lillard is the latest Oakland-groomed basketball talent to become a marquee NBA player, with the Portland Trailblazers. This backcourt star ranks among the game's finest clutch marksmen, hitting big-time shots from all distances.

There's a coolness and toughness to Oakland-based hoopsters, though none more definitively than Gary Payton. Known as the Glove for his defensive tenacity, Payton was an all-around gamer whose stone-faced glare reflected his tough Oakland playground training. He spent 17 seasons in the NBA, 13 with the Seattle Supersonics as a perennial All-Star. His son, Gary Payton II, was a key reserve on Golden State's 2022 NBA championship squad and now plays in Portland.

Then there are Oakland A's pitchers Dennis Eckersley and Dave Stewart, both Oakland born though Eckersley grew up in nearby Fremont before becoming a Baseball Hall of Famer as a dominant reliever. Stewart won 20 games four consecutive years during the A's World Series run of the late 1980s. The A's have retired both their numbers.

But Oakland's greatest ballplayer, bar none, is Rickey Henderson, one of the top 10 position players of all time. He is the only man in history with 3,000 hits, 2,000 runs, 2,000 walks, and 1,000 stolen bases. Add 297 home runs, the most ever by a leadoff hitter, and Henderson was a Baseball Hall of Fame shoo-in. It's a reasonable prediction: there will never be another Rickey Henderson.

Future sports stars are growing up in Oakland. We don't know all their names yet, but we will in time, because Oakland always turns out superb athletes, Hall of Famers and milestone figures such as Curt Flood, the father of free agency in baseball.

No other city has left such a wide imprint on the American sports landscape as Oakland, although its triumphant history has been tarnished by abandonment, with sparse sympathy felt elsewhere. For professional sports leagues, and even legal bodies, blame Oakland for the loss of its franchises. Oakland always is portrayed as the perpetrator, never the victim.

The unaccepted truth: it's all one big lie.

Chapter 3

Charles O. Finley:
Donkey to Dynasty

Charlie [Finley] instructed me to run any promotion
I wanted to, "as long as you don't spend any money."
—Ted Robinson,
global sportscaster and former A's gofer

In 1990, the Bay Area Sports Hall of Fame, or BASHOF, inducted Oakland A's pitcher Jim "Catfish" Hunter; the San Francisco 49ers' greatest cornerback, Jimmy Johnson; golfer "Champagne" Tony Lema; and San Francisco Giants first baseman Orlando "Baby Bull" Cepeda.

As a BASHOF board member, I, Andy Dolich, was invited to the VIP cocktail party in the penthouse of the St. Francis Hotel in downtown San Francisco. I hadn't spent one-on-one time with A's force of nature Charles O. Finley. Finley was easy to pick out holding court in the sports star-studded ball room. Both men were dressed in their teams' colors—Finley was wearing a lime green sports coat and gold tie. Davis wore a black suit and silver tie.

Finley was the inductor for Hunter. I noticed that Finley was tightly holding onto a football, which seemed a bit different for a former baseball owner. The visually enhanced pigskin featured bright yellow stripes from nose to nose instead of the traditional white stripes near the ends. Finley had personally designed this luminously striped football. I

41

immediately thought about Finley's "Alert Orange Baseball" that was tested in spring training games before its rejection by Major League Baseball owners in the mid-1970s.

Since I was vice president of business operations for the A's franchise, I figured why not be friendly and introduce myself to these power brokers. After I had his attention, Finley nodded my way and continued talking to those huddled around him. "Gentlemen, this is the football of the future," I heard him say. "In 95 percent of high school football stadiums in the country, the lighting is inadequate. My new football will benefit the players, officials, and spectators at these games, along with millions of TV viewers in the future. People will be able to follow the flight of the ball at all times. It will also benefit the players and officials, who can see the ball easier."

Finley further informed the group that he had received an invitation to make a presentation about his new football in Kansas City to a combined meeting of the NCAA and National Federation of State High School Associations rules committees in November. About that time, a photographer for a local newspaper walked into the group and asked Finley if he could borrow the ball as a prop to take a few shots with a football player. Finley brusquely told the cameraman, "No!" When he smiled and asked again, Finley raised his voice. "No, I invented this ball last year," he replied. "If you want a damn picture, I'm right here!" The lensman snapped a few shots of Finley and scuttled off.

Clearly, Charles O. Finley wasn't big on sharing anything other than what was on his mind. But as I drove home from the dinner, I kept thinking that while Finley was viewed as a fantastic self-promoter, his world championship teams of 1972, 1973, and 1974, led by multiple stars, failed to draw big crowds in Oakland.

Calvin Griffith, then owner of the Minnesota Twins, referred to Finley as the "P.T. Barnum of Baseball." But prior to baseball, Finley was the "Einstein of Medical Insurance." While in his thirties, Finley was hospitalized for two and a half years with tuberculosis. During his prolonged recovery, he learned from doctors that they didn't have medical coverage, which he subsequently provided in becoming a millionaire before he was 40. This acquired wealth led to his purchase of an MLB franchise in Kansas City. But his ownership never gained traction in that community, only enemies, and so he moved the team to Oakland in 1968. Finley ran both the A's baseball and business operations on a shoestring budget as an absentee owner, while tending to his thriving insurance business, either from his office in Chicago or from his farm in La Porte, Indiana.

Shoestring? The listing of Finley's front office staff in the A's media guide had only 10 full-time employees in 1968. They were as follows:

1. Charles O. Finley, President
2. Charles O. Finley Jr., Secretary-Treasurer
3. Chuck Cottonaro, Controller
4. Carl Finley, Director of Public Relations and Promotions
5. Norm Koselke, Minor League Director
6. Bob Hofman, Traveling Secretary
7. Lorraine Paulus, Ticket Manager
8. Frank Ciensczyk, Equipment Manager
9. Joe Romo, Trainer
10. Steve Vucinich, Visiting Clubhouse Manager

(Vucinich continued working for the A's for 53 years, mainly as the home team's clubhouse manager prior to retiring in 2021.)

In smaller print among staff members: Accounting: Janelle Schrad; Minor League Scouting: Toni Russo; Switchboard: Jeanine DeSalles; Ticket Office: Julie Delk, Ann Vargas.

This was, far and away, the smallest business operation in all of Major League Baseball. How in the heck did the A's, under the direction of baseball's P.T. Barnum, win three World Series in a row? Three in a row, or even four World Series titles consecutively, has been done by two teams in the modern era: the New York Yankees in 1936–39, 1949–53—the only team to win five consecutive October Classics—and 1998–2000, and by the A's in 1972–74, who also won five straight division titles. Finley, despite his penuriousness, was an absolute whiz in figuring out who could play and who could not.

In 1969, Oakland finished at 88–74, the most wins by the A's since 1932. Under Manager Dick Williams, the A's won the Western Division in 1971 with 101 victories. Reggie Jackson had become the leading power hitter in the game. Campy Campaneris made the team a threat to run at all times. The pitching staff, with Hunter, Vida Blue, John "Blue Moon" Odom, and Ken Holtzman and with Rollie Fingers cleaning up games out of the bullpen, kept other teams off the basepaths. Finley's A's were poised to make their historic runs through the postseason for seasons to come.

Finley was a legendary self-promoter who brought a number of marketing and promotional breakthroughs to the "National Pastime." He ruled with an iron hand and a loud mouth. He understood that the world of sports was changing from a ballgame to a mass entertainment event. He always pushed the envelope, but even with his flair for promotion, much of it was directed at marketing his own image. Thus, anti-Finley fans stayed away in droves from the Oakland Coliseum, often referred to as the "Oakland Mausoleum" by A's captain and third baseman Sal Bando for its utter lack of attendance.

To me and many others, Finley was a mystery. He clearly knew how to sell, but he chose not to channel his skills toward a franchise that had experienced tremendous success on the field. He pushed, instead, for innovation: the designated hitter, designated runner, mid-week World Series games played at night—which became a television ratings bonanza—and orange baseballs, which failed to replace white baseballs. He wasn't done innovating, regardless.

In 1972, he decided that real men—i.e., his A's players—should proudly grow and display facial hair. Baseball, in the modern age, had been clean shaven. Finley offered a $300 bonus to any player who grew a mustache. The poster child for this program was Rollie Fingers, whose waxed-and-curled villianous stash became his trademark. Other teams eventually followed the A's hairy example.

Finley also rocked baseball's establishment by introducing ultra-bright green-and-gold (or yellow) uniforms. And, once again, baseball followed his example by slowly moving ahead from white (home) and gray (away) uniforms to all colors of the rainbow.

Finley wasn't done yet. He hired a teenager, Stanley Burrell Jr., as the team's executive vice president, though he was basically Finley's in-house spy on the players. Burrell would later become rap star MC Hammer with initial financial support from A's players.

More Finley creativity: Harvey the mechanical rabbit, who popped out of the ground behind home plate whenever umpires needed more baseballs, plus a ball girl in each bullpen, cow-milking contests, Hot Pants Day, and sack races with A's players between doubleheaders. There was Charlie O. the mule and team mascot, whom Finley was advised to leave in Kansas City as Oakland was deemed more "sophisticated." Typically, he chose otherwise.

For Finley believed in showmanship above all else. He nicknamed pitcher John Odom "Blue Moon." Pitcher Jim Hunter became "Catfish." Third baseman Sal Bando became "Captain Sal." Finley asked pitcher Vida Rochelle Blue Jr. to legally change his middle name to "True." But Vida, mercifully, said no to becoming "True Blue."

The Oakland A's World Series victory in 1972 over the Cincinnati Reds was the first major sports championship in Northern California history (excluding soccer—the Oakland Clippers were national champions in 1967). The 49ers, San Francisco Giants, Golden State Warriors, and Raiders had been on the trail to the Holy Grail of a world championship, and only the Giants would fail over the next 10 years. But the Chicago insurance man beat those four to a title.

Unfortunately, Finley, a noted protector of the dollar, had the skimpiest front office in baseball. In 1980, the A's player payroll was a Major League Baseball low of $1.3 million dollars. His cousin, Carl Finley, essentially did the work of 30 employees. There was no marketing, no advertising, and radio broadcasts of A's games were spotty at best.

How could Charles O. Finley, one of the most unabashed self-promoters in sports history, do such a terrible job in marketing one of the greatest teams in baseball history, and with iconic stars? I don't know the answer. Was it commision or omission? Critics feel it was Finley's not spending enough time in Oakland, thus not becoming an integral part of the community. But we will never know why he didn't.

Finley finally reached the point of refusing to challenge the new multimillionaire owners in Major League Baseball. "I just couldn't compete," he said, faking sincerity, "with the idiotic, astronomical, and unjustified salaries of today's players. Baseball is now realizing what I said five years ago—just like they are usually five years behind me—that a team should be compensated for its free-agent losses."

Finley, that same month, sold the team to the Haas family, owners of the ultra-successful Levi Strauss jeans company, for a reported $12.7 million. No other MLB owner regretted his departure.

When I, Andy Dolich, was hired by the A's in November 1980, it was an indication that the Haas family was building a front office with industry professionals. I arrived from the East Coast the next month, and was told by my new bosses, Roy Eisenhardt and Wally Haas, to spend time with Carl Finley. Carl was involved in every detail of the A's operation, all because Charlie was the ultimate absentee owner who utilized Carl as his on-site administrator—a one-man front office.

Arriving for my first day of work on December 3, I met the staff and then sat down with Carl for an introductory chat. Later, after I visited a most unique front-office bathroom, I asked Carl, "Is that a phone over the urinal?" I had never seen anything like that before. What purpose was it serving? Well, Carl always was on the phone with Charlie, who called from the Midwest during games. This was before stations picked up games, so Carl—long before cell phones and ESPN—was broadcasting to Finley over the phone from, um, wherever.

The overworked Carl was in charge of creating each game's financial statement, which was sent to Major League Baseball immediately afterward. When Carl ran down from the press box to the A's offices to work with box office director Lorraine Paulus on final totals from the game, he had to make sure that, if nature called in the middle of his multiple jobs, Charlie could connect with him in the bathroom. Think of this as an early experiment in streaming before digital streaming even existed.

For a full overview of the amazing multitasking abilities of Carl Finley, I'd advise readers to check out *Finley Ball* by Carl's daughter, Nancy. The A's, under Charles O. Finley's largely absentee status and penny-pinching ways, lacked any strategic marketing plan. Thus, the team's ticket-selling efforts were elementary at best. So, for me, even with Carl Finley's valuable help, it was like starting from scratch.

In one week's time in May 2020, the Oakland A's lost two in-house Hall of Famers. Public address announcer Roy Steele, aka the "Voice of God," died at 87 in Auburn, California. His partner in the Oakland Coliseum operations booth, Chester "Chet" Farrow, had died four days earlier in Walnut Creek, California, at 77. These two men were a major part of the A's public image from the day Finley hired them until their retirements years later.

Steele worked the PA mic for more than 3,000 A's games at the Coliseum, from 1969 to 2007. Farrow was hired by Finley in 1969. I talked to Farrow at the 30th anniversary of the A's 1989 World Series team, held at Massimo's Restaurant in neighboring Fremont. Every 10 years, a group of A's alumni holds an event to celebrate the sweep of the San Francisco Giants in the 1989 earthquake-related World Series.

At that event, I asked Farrow, "How did you get the job as scoreboard operator for the A's?" He said, "I heard about the job through Don Warner, who was assistant general manager of the Coliseum. I was put in touch with Finley's secretary, Carolyn Kaufman. I wanted to get paid $250 to be trained on the scoreboard equipment. She told me that only Mr. Finley could approve that request. 'OK,' I said, 'please give me his phone number.' I still remember that it was (312) 467-0442.

"I called and Charlie answered. I quickly spat out, 'My name is Chester Farrow. I'm your new scoreboard operator for the IBM 1131. Mr. Finley, we trained hard during five days of Easter vacation. I'm a high school teacher. I'd like to be paid $250 for the time I spent getting ready for the season.' 'Or what?' Finley responded. 'Or I can't work.' He finally said, 'All right.' On my first day on the job, there were two envelopes, one for me and another for my co-worker Ray Crawford, with checks for $250. That's how I was introduced to Charles O. Finley."

Chet Farrow and Charles O. Finley became friends, to the point that Finley called Farrow "Ace." According to Farrow, it was based on Finley's not knowing his real name. Plenty of people, it turned out, were called "Ace" by Finley.

Mickey Morabito has been the A's traveling secretary since coming to the team from the New York Yankees in 1980. In a recent interview with me, he explained that Billy Martin, who he had bonded with on the Yankees, wanted him in Oakland. Morabito resigned his position with the Yankees and joined the A's at our spring training site in Scottsdale, Arizona.

Finley, who hired Mickey over the phone, was concerned that he would be accused of tampering by Yankees owner George Steinbrenner. Morabito told Finley he had resigned, but Mickey wanted to make sure Carl Finley wasn't going to get financially dinged. Mickey was paid $20,000 a year by the Yanks, which Finley was willing to match. But he wanted Mickey to handle the team's public relations, one of Carl's many responsibilities, in addition to the traveling secretary role. Mickey did both for a short time until the A's, under the new ownership of the Haas family, bulked up the front office with separate public relations and marketing departments.

Mickey had minimal contact with Charles O. Finley, taking his orders mostly from Billy Martin and, sometimes, Carl Finley. According to Mickey, Charlie referred to him as the "Italian guy, Billy's friend from the Yankees." By the time Mickey Morabito joined the A's, Charlie already was focused on completing his deal with Marvin Davis to move the team to Denver, a deal which never happened.

In 1965, Finley received a Missouri mule from Governor Warren Hearnes to serve as a mascot for his Kansas City A's. Finley named the mule "Charlie O" after himself, joking—proudly—that he was naming the mule "after an ass." The mule spent more time with Finley than, oddly, most of his employees and players. When the A's moved to Oakland, Charlie decided to bring his ass along, though *Oakland*

Tribune sports editor George Ross advised him not to, saying Oakland was too cultured for such gimmicks. Finley went with his instincts, but, in the long run, Ross' advice was correct. And when the A's departed Kansas City, Missouri senator Stuart Symington called Oakland "the luckiest city since Hiroshima." Ouch!

Ted Robinson joined the A's in 1980, beginning a distinguished career as one of the most accomplished multisports broadcasters, working in professional football, basketball, and baseball, plus major tennis matches and the Olympic Games. Robinson luckily was hired by Finley when he was 23. Eagerly, he became a trusted member of the Carl Finley team, doing whatever was needed to get whichever job accomplished ASAP. That included "Billy Martin Day."

As Finley completed the sale of the A's to the Haas family, he wanted to display his "generosity" by honoring Billy's role in the team's on-field resurgence. And so I was assigned with soliciting local businesses to "donate" gifts for Billy. That included a Cadillac, although Carl Finley, thankfully, took on that task. We compiled a great list of gifts, all of which were stockpiled on the Coliseum field for a pregame ceremony—except, that is, for the Cadillac. That was behind the center field fence, to be driven onto the field with special "Friends of Billy" as passengers.

Charlie worked to get New York Yankees stars Mickey Mantle, Whitey Ford, and Hank Bauer to Oakland for Billy's day. Amazingly, Charlie gave Mickey Morabito his credit card to treat the Yankee greats to a dinner at Francesco's in Oakland. And the next day, Charlie's plan went off perfectly. Billy received a hero's salute, and the Cadillac came onto the field with Mantle, Ford, Bauer...and even Joe DiMaggio. The driver: the A's young promotions director, Ted Robinson, an assigned chauffeur of baseball royalty.

Charles O. Finley wasn't exactly a matinee idol, but his cash and cache had a magical way of attracting youthful beauty. You can fill in the blanks on how this magic worked, but in many instances, money can serve as honey. In 1971, Charlie hired fetching young women as Ball Girls. Their job was to retrieve foul balls and return them to the dugout. One of those lovelies was Debbi Sivyer. After her Ball Girl days, she became "Mrs. Fields," the chocolate chip cookie chief of a very successful national company.

In 1975, Finley was selected as one of the "Bay Area's Sexiest Bachelors" by the *Oakland Tribune*, even though he wasn't from the Bay Area. He was, however, a divorced bachelor, squiring women who looked more like Ball Girls than an age-appropriate date for an MLB owner in his sixties.

But why own just an MLB team when you can own a few other pro franchises? Finley purchased the Oakland Seals of the National Hockey League in 1970, renaming them the California Golden Seals. Mimicking the A's, Finley changed the team colors to green and gold and had the Seals wear white skates instead of the traditional black, a move unpopular with players and fans and deeply unpopular with hockey's old-school establishment.

Also in 1970, Finley purchased the Memphis franchise of the American Basketball Association, changing the team's nickname to the Memphis Tams, the name being an acronym for Tennessee, Arkansas, and Mississippi. As was the case with the A's, he changed the Tams' colors to green and gold. He hired legendary Kentucky Wildcats basketball coach Adolph Rupp as team president. Finley ran it on a shoestring budget. After the first season, he sold the two teams and returned his focus to baseball.

The downhill slide for Finley began after the 1976 season, when he became involved in a messy divorce, or divorces: Finley's own marriage plus the Finley vs. (baseball commissioner Bowie) Kuhn lawsuit, Finley's battles with Oakland officials, the collapse of the A's sale to Marvin Davis, and, finally, Finley's trading away most of his stars who regularly took the A's to the postseason.

Finley had used his incredible eye for talent to bring in the likes of Rickey Henderson, Tony Armas, Dwayne Murphy, Rick Langford, Mike Norris, Brian Kingman, Mike Morgan, Matt Keough, Steve McCatty, and Bob Lacey. Finley then realized that free agency was pricing him out of the baseball business. And along came Billy Martin.

Martin became the Minesota Twins manager eight years after retiring as a player. He then traveled a rocky road in the skipper's seat to Detroit, Texas, and the New York Yankees multiple times. Here was the perfect, yet imperfect, combination: the creator of chaos, Martin, and the master of mayhem, Finley. In 1980, Finley hired Martin to perform the dual roles of general manager and field manager. That same season, the A's became the embodiment of their manager through the scrappy way they played, i.e., "Billy Ball." Even though the wording of Billy Ball came from *Oakland Tribune* sports columnist Ralph Wiley, the concept was the final act for Finley after his 12 years as owner of the Oakland A's.

The night before the sale of the Oakland A's from Charles O. Finley to the Haas family was announced at a press conference in Oakland, Roy Eisenhardt and Wally Haas, who had negotiated the deal on behalf of Walter A. Haas, invited Finley to dinner in San Francisco that same evening. To prevent the media from breaking the news early, they decided to take Finley to a private dining club.

A very private dining club, as it turned out, for the only three people in the club for dinner that evening were Finley, team president Eisenhardt, and executive vice president Wally Haas, son of the A's owner. They settled in at the table, and after a celebratory cocktail, Finley smiled at the A's new owners. Then, with his usual bravado, he said, "Roy, Wally, I'm very impressed with the fact that you had to buy the restaurant out, so it would just be the three of us. Well done!

That was Charles O. Finley, a man who created his own script for every day of his unscripted life.

Chapter 4

Dick Spees,
Ignacio De La Fuente:
A Political View

If you don't put your ass on the line to preserve those teams, they will be gone, which, unfortunately, has happened.

—Ignacio De La Fuente,
former Oakland politician

Politically speaking, Dick Spees is a campfire and Ignacio De La Fuente a forest fire. Spees speaks calmly and respectfully, using the King's English, while De La Fuente is explosive with sparks dancing on his words, fueling occasional expletives.

However, both men fully understand the inside and outside of Oakland's ongoing sports drama, thus joining together to articulate its heyday and the parade that is passing it by today.

Spees proudly wore the title Mr. Oakland, based on his five terms as councilman, totaling 24 years, and his paternalistic approach to the city at 90, his age when interviewed in February 2020. Even in retirement, he kept a close eye on Oakland, visually and mentally, from his third-floor lodging in a senior citizen residence across the Oakland Estuary in Alameda, affording him a clear view of the city he embraces.

"I *love* Oakland," he offered with unabashed emphasis.

De La Fuente, conversely, is Mr. Oakland Sports. Aged 72 when interviewed in January 2021, he was 21 and a Mexican immigrant upon arriving in California, then building himself into a labor union representative and an Oakland City Councilman, 1992–2012, rising to Council president, though failing thrice at becoming Oakland's mayor. As a member of the Joint Powers Authority, Alameda County's governing body of Oakland's stadium-arena complex, he remains the longest and most powerful political influence in the city's sports history, while consulting during daytime hours to pay the bills.

"Back in the 1990s, we managed to remodel the Coliseum and the Arena and to retain our three sports franchises," De La Fuente said. "But, sorry to say, in my opinion, we are going to be a city with zero sports teams."

The Warriors have left, the Raiders left again, and the A's may yet leave, creating an empty feeling within an embattled city. Las Vegas, which shanghaied the Raiders, may also pirate away the A's, whose Triple-A team already plays in Sin City.

"The A's have picked a site for a new stadium here that has no hope," De La Fuente stressed. "When Libby Schaaf was elected [Oakland] mayor, I tried to impress on her the importance of Oakland's sports teams, the jobs they create, and [Oakland] being on national television 250 days a year. But none of the politicians in Oakland had the backbone to do the work in retaining our teams."

While the reserved Spees relies on calm, diplomatic observations, the fiery De La Fuente spews arsenic-laced political barbs. But both men, regardless of disposition, have monitored closely Oakland's crumbling sports scene, and each of them makes sense, even with diverse tones.

"It's tough with a public agency, because we don't have a lot of money," Spees noted. "We can't meet all those private demands, and we can't use public money indiscriminately. On the other hand, I don't think the people of Oakland truly understood or appreciated their sports teams in terms of what an asset they were to the city. They were truly important. But I found Al Davis trustworthy, although I didn't see him all that often, just at special events or in negotiations."

Ah, Al Davis, the earl of exodus, a greedy man most absorbed by the wallet, his and yours. Spees and De La Fuente were asked, separately, to describe their negotiations with Davis.

"Actually, I enjoyed it," Spees said, laughing, "but it was trying. We were unsuccessful the first time, and the reason we were unsuccessful was that we felt we had buttoned up all the issues. Then at 3 o'clock in the morning, I got a call from Al, who wanted another five million dollars. At 3 o'clock in the morning, where was I going to find it? Certainly not public money. So it fell apart."

The Raiders, shortly thereafter, bolted for Los Angeles, but then later returned to Oakland, chagrined yet again with Davis making further huge monetary demands, though without Spees' involvement the second time around.

"I wasn't interested in doing it again," he said, "though I had a good relationship with Al. He called me Richie. I went to every game. He presented me with a full uniform with 'Spees' on it, and No. 1 on the jersey. I'd wear it at Halloween parties."

Davis sweet-talked Spees the way connivers do when they want to steal something from you. Reliving those days, Spees shifted uncomfortably in a stuffed chair at Cardinal Point, his retirement home, grinning to hide any physical discomfort.

"Al was an interesting personality," he continued. "To people who were close to him, he was incredibly kind, considerate, a pretty fine human being, though there weren't too many who were that close. I believed in collaboration, as a politician and as a person, for that's the only way to get things done. I tried to deal with Al on a friendly basis. He was susceptible to that, and very amenable. I thought he was straightforward and honest. He didn't try to play me, although he did at the end because he wanted more money. But that's part of negotiations."

Give and take, steal and run: Davis' negotiating tactics.

"I had the opportunity to sit at the table and negotiate with Al Davis," said De La Fuente, "and I can tell you from the get-go, he was a tough cookie, a tough negotiator. As a labor negotiator, I learned that the person on the other side of the table is going to do the best he can for his side. And one thing about Al Davis, you might not like the guy, but his word was his bond, his word was always good."

But while others slept, Davis was awake and plotting. Spees agreed with De La Fuente that Oakland had, indeed, dropped the ball on the Raiders' two departures.

"I'd hate to put it in those terms, but there was guilt on the part of Oakland and the public," Spees said. "It's just that they didn't value—a better word—the importance of the Raiders. Because they were, worldwide, the most recognizable [American] sports team. Raider uniforms were all over the world. The Raiders really put us on the map."

An Oakland map, for sure, though with changing boundaries.

"There were people on the Oakland City Council and the Alameda County Board of Supervisors who didn't think it was a good idea," De La Fuente said of Oakland's holding onto the Raiders in either takeaway situation, Los Angeles or Las Vegas. "I put my ass on the line along with others to hold onto those three teams…but now the A's have one foot out the door."

What would Oakland be like without all three franchises?

"It's happening now," De La Fuente noted. "I've never seen it so bad, and I don't mean the pandemic. The people elected now for political office in Oakland don't have the history of what Oakland used to be, and I blame these officials for not getting into the trenches and negotiating with the Raiders. The Warriors were impossible. Millionaires and super-millionaires wanted the prestige of being in San Francisco. Nobody could have stopped that, but Oakland could have kept the Raiders. Oakland just needed a champion to make that happen."

De La Fuente meant someone like himself, who played the champion's role in luring the Raiders back from Los Angeles. If he had been elected mayor on his first try, 2012, would Oakland be looking at a different sports scenario today?

"Absolutely, unequivocally," he said. "I would have managed to put a deal together with the Raiders to stay…to build a new stadium or put together a deal that was livable. Right now, there is no one person for [Oakland] sports teams to go to, to work together, to benefit the team and the people of Oakland."

Spees agreed wholeheartedly with his former council colleague that Oakland fumbled away the Raiders.

"It's cumbersome, but it should have been done more skillfully," he said of that process. "The Raiders were revered here with the Black Hole and all that occurred. The Raiders didn't have that kind of loyalty in L.A., they just didn't. But the Raiders are always looking for money. Al Davis thought he was going to make a lot of money in L.A., and it didn't happen."

Nonetheless, from father down to son, Al Davis to Mark Davis, loyalty was missing in the family's gene pool.

"It's really unfortunate that the Raiders have left Oakland again," said Spees. "I'm very, very disappointed that it came to that. On the other hand, I do understand that when you play football on a baseball field...the recobbled Coliseum was a mess, and really ruined it for baseball. The city and county didn't really do a good job either time in working that out."

But isn't Oakland enjoying a commercial turn-around as a go-to municipality, regardless of its sports departures?

"These last six years have been a boom for Oakland," De La Fuente agreed. "We are the most progressive, most liberal city in America. But we are mismanaged. They're talking now about cutting back on police and fire protection. Are they crazy? Things are going to get a helluva lot worse before they get better. Oakland is its own worst enemy."

Still, why didn't Mark Davis, unlike his father, embrace the financial growth that currently is bettering Oakland?

"It just didn't translate," Spees responded. "It's the major corporate people who supply the money, like the Chase Center in San Francisco, where the Warriors now play. The Warriors had tremendous fans in Oakland, but it's all about the money."

Yes, but nobody cashed in like the Davises.

"I knew Mark briefly," said De La Fuente. "It's obvious that he's not his father."

Maybe not cerebrally, but he's still an NFL owner.

Truthfully, Oakland is stigmatized simply because it is…Oakland. The Warriors never had "Oakland" on their game shirts in nearly a half-century stay in Oaktown. But as soon as they moved across the Bay, "San Francisco" appeared on their jerseys, although the team is still officially the "Golden State" Warriors. Then, on occasion, they will don "Oakland" jerseys, sticking it to their most-recent deserted city unmercifully. Heartless harpies.

But didn't those double putdowns of Oakland rile Spees?

"Absolutely," he said. "It's sad. I have not watched a Warriors game since they moved, except when [Stephen] Curry came back from an injury. I just wanted to see how he'd play. But they still owe Oakland 40 million bucks. They owe it, really."

(A state appeals court ruled later that the Warriors were, indeed, responsible for that amount.)

De La Fuente emphasized that the dismantling of Oakland's sports scene has damaged its expansion chances irreparably.

"It's huge," he stated. "No Raiders, no Warriors, and probably no A's, yet you hear people say, 'We're going to get another franchise.' That's bullshit, pie in the sky."

When other sports cities were abandoned, such as Baltimore, Cleveland, and Los Angeles, they were made whole again through expansion or relocation. Yet Oakland hasn't ever been made whole, either by the NFL or the NBA. And if an A's departure comes to pass, MLB will make it a snub trifecta for Oaktown.

The franchise that remained in Oakland, at least temporarily, was the baseball A's, who then got a raw deal when the Raiders came back from Los Angeles. The Oakland Coliseum was reconfigured to benefit the vagabond Raiders, thereby removing all aspects of a baseball stadium, although architecturally inferior to begin with in the 1960s.

"I think the A's will stay," predicted Spees, even though the franchise failed in earlier attempted moves to Fremont and San Jose. "But for the life of me, I can't figure out why the A's have chosen the site they have [for a new ballpark in Oakland]."

Current A's ownership selected a waterfront site for a stadium that, unlike the Coliseum property, does not abut rapid transit and a freeway, lacks abundant parking, and is a logistical issue for Oakland's valued shipping industry. So why move rather than rebuild at the more ideal Coliseum site?

"The people in charge of Oakland, politically, are out of touch and have no clue," answered De La Fuente. "They just don't have the willingness or backbone in recognizing the value of sports franchises to a city."

Then what about De La Fuente, a politician and a force of nature, tossing his hat in the ring for a third try at mayor?

"I'm thinking about it," he replied.

De La Fuente then, indeed, declared his candidacy in June 2022, saying, "We need a mayor with a proven track record for getting things done." But could his third attempt at becoming mayor prove successful?

It did not, and De La Fuente disappeared into the political twilight—Oakland's loss, not his, truthfully.

"The Haas family [A's] ownership was our high point," Spees said, remembering the good times. "It was terrific. The son-in-law [Roy Eisenhardt] running the team was great.

"With the next A's ownership [Steve Schott, Ken Hofmann], we weren't quite sure what they might do. They didn't play square. A downtown ballpark looked great, but Jerry Brown, then mayor, said to me, 'Over my dead body will there ever be a f—ing ballpark downtown.' With the next A's owner [Lew Wolff], I became disillusioned about him. Now the ballpark that the current A's ownership [John Fisher] wants [by Jack London Square] is undoable."

De La Fuente sided with Spees about the Haas family representing the Mount Everest of Oakland sports ownerships.

"The Haases absolutely cared about Oakland," De La Fuente said. "In fact, when they sold the team [to Schott and Hofmann], it was to make sure the team stayed in Oakland."

With nary an ownership around comparable to the benevolent Haases, Oakland could become a sports orphan.

"It's a very difficult situation," Spees agreed, "but it's all about money and image. I took Gertrude Stein's comment about her native Oakland—'There is no there there'—very hard. No. 1, Oakland is a very beautiful city; you just have to get acquainted with it. No. 2, it's the center of the Bay Area, a very fascinating city, one of the most diverse in America."

Now a nonagenarian, Spees reflected on his dedicated, but possibly dead-end, role in saving Oakland's athletic landscape.

"I loved the teams, all of them," he said. "I went to all the Raiders games, as I said, and many of the A's games, even after I left the council. And I went to spring training. I'm an authentic fan. Do I think the Raiders will come back again? No. People who've seen that Las Vegas stadium say it's unbelievable."

Could Oakland, in retrospect, have done anything differently to retain all three of its teams—the Raiders, Warriors and A's?

"No," Spees said, flatly. "Things could have been done, but you have to know how to do it. I'm a basic optimist. I genuinely care about Oakland. I came up with four things needed for the future of Oakland. No. 1, we're a port city, and you build on the port. No. 2, we're the transportation hub of the Bay Area; everything crosses us, so you have to build on that. No. 3, it is housing or residences. We've housed everything for a long period of time, but we're too spread out; there's got to be a center. No. 4, we're the government center locally, though San Francisco has sucked some of that back."

It's odd that Spees, the numbers man, became Mr. Oakland, for he isn't a native son. Born in Oregon, he met his late wife, Jean, at Oregon State University. They came to Oakland when Spees was hired to work for Kaiser Aluminum and Chemical Corporation, which employed him for 32 years. Wanting something more out of life, he ran for District 4 city council after George Vukasin vacated that seat in 1979.

Spees succeeded, fulfilling Vukasin's remaining two years, then was reelected over and over, even though he was the only Republican on a strictly Democratic council. He jogged five miles daily to stay in condition for the political infighting.

But Oakland was, Spees became convinced, worth fighting for "because it's a place where the cultural mosaic and progressive industry find a home." The *Oakland Tribune* endorsed him for a fourth term because of "his get-it-done business perspective and a history as a coalition builder."

Spees even looked after his Democrat councilmates in 1995 by proposing a 10 percent pay raise that passed, pushing annual salaries from $35,330 to $38,951. He rose to vice mayor, but never sought the position of mayor, explaining, "That's not just me. I'll push more as a No. 2 than if I were a No. 1. I didn't want to get my head above water. I didn't need that."

After entering politics, Spees' council terms coincided with the triple-header of oddball sports ownerships.

"I loved Franklin Mieuli, a funny cat; I thought he really fit our city," said Spees. "We supported his Warriors, and tried hard, while remodeling the arena, to get them to become the 'Oakland' Warriors. But the city wouldn't insist on it. I had no dealings with Charles O. Finley."

De La Fuente's half-century of living in Oakland has given him a pragmatic view of what this complex city is all about.

"Like I said before, it's the most diverse city I know of," he reiterated. "Although diversity is beautiful, it is very difficult to manage. A city has to be run as a business in order to survive and to provide. Oakland still shoots itself in the foot by not making decisions in the interest of the majority, and all because of its internal infighting. We're always on the verge, but we manage to screw it up. Imagine what we would become if we were facilitators instead of obstructionists."

So what, then, is Oakland's future, with or without sports?

"Oakland can't miss," Spees insisted. "It's dead center in the [local] market, it's starting to thrive, and it's going to grow."

But can Oakland truly prosper without its sports teams?

"Absolutely," said Spees, Mr. Oakland incarnate.

De La Fuente, Mr. Oakland Sports, has a contrarian's view.

"I told Libby, our mayor, that when she leaves office, all three of our teams will be gone," he said, "for Howard Terminal [Oakland's proposed ballpark site] will never happen.

"It's a sad thing. Nobody wanted to lead the march to save our teams, nobody wanted to be blamed, and nobody wanted to take the risk to do anything."

When De La Fuente launched his third try at becoming Oakland's mayor, he said, "We need a mayor with the political backbone and experience to make the tough decisions to get this city back on track."

On track, he meant, with a sports identity, but he lost—again.

And so Oakland's only true political fighter for sports takes off the gloves after a third mayoral rejection. Goodbye, Oakland indeed.

Chapter 5

Heavenly Haases: Ownership Paradise

"We have to create the mood of a team that's part of the community rather than as a private or personal activity of the owner."

—Roy Eisenhardt,
Oakland A's chief executive, speaking in 1980

On April 17, 1979, the A's drew a crowd of 653—if you could use the word "crowd"—to a game at the Oakland Coliseum against the Seattle Mariners. One night after that franchise attendance low point, the less-than-magnetic A's drew 1,215. For the season, those A's averaged a major league low of 3,787 fans per game, a grand total of 306,763. Those embarrassing numbers were the straw that snapped the Oakland Coliseum governing board's patience. They sued A's owner Charles O. Finley for $11.5 million in damages for not promoting the team in the Bay Area.

The Coliseum Authority then hired sports business consultant Matt Levine as an expert, someone who would testify as to what the proper marketing standards were for Major League Baseball teams, and then contrast them to what the A's were or weren't doing.

After extensive research, Levine concluded, "The A's under Charlie Finley were the worst marketed franchise in all of baseball."

Colorado-based oil and real estate tycoon Marvin Davis, one of America's richest men, expressed a strong desire to become the owner of an MLB team, and then move it to his home base in Denver. Finley was eager to sell after dismantling one of baseball's greatest teams, highlighted by their dominance earlier in that same decade, with three consecutive World Series titles in 1972, 1973, and 1974. Finley had been negotiating quietly with Davis to sell him the team. On December 14, 1977, Davis announced his purchase of the A's for $12.5 million, including a $5 million deposit. Finley had bought the Kansas City A's for $4 million in 1960.

One day later, the Oakland Coliseum Authority, the City of Oakland, and Alameda County filed a $35 million lawsuit against Finley and Davis, based on the A's trying to break their 20-year stadium lease, which Finley signed in 1967. Dancing with Marvin Davis didn't end there, all because of who was leading whom. Even with lawsuits tossed about like a baseball in a pepper game, in January 1980, the two men felt they had a new deal. The A's would be gone to Denver that very season. The Coliseum Authority quickly used a temporary restraining order to suspend the sale, thereby prohibiting American League owners from voting on the move.

Based on the dueling lawsuits, Oakland officials said "no" again, staking their claim on that 20-year lease agreement Finley had signed. Finley, Davis, and the American League had agreed to a $4 million buyout. When Oakland killed the deal, it meant the A's would play at the Coliseum in 1980. More importantly, they were back on the market, with this one caveat: the team would be staying in Oakland through 1987. Finley's dancing with Davis resulted in their toes being stepped on, for they weren't Fred Astaire and Gene Kelly.

Walter A. Haas, chairman of the largest apparel company in the world, was the great grandnephew of the original Levi Strauss, who sold denim pants to prospectors during the California gold rush. Haas inherited a major family fortune along with a tradition of hard work and dedicated community service, always with a sense of modesty. His low-key personality was 180 degrees different from the bombastic, egotistical, look-at-me Finley. Haas' decision to negotiate the A's purchase was put in the capable hands of his son Wally and son-in-law Roy Eisenhardt. The elder Haas believed that an imaginatively operated, community-focused sports franchise would be the most efficient way to become a major force in improving Oakland's sub-Bay level of self-esteem. The family's deeply rooted philanthropy was dedicated mostly to the University of California at Berkeley and environmental causes. Walter and his wife, Evelyn, or Evie, loved fly fishing as a hobby.

Wally, who went by Walter A. Haas Jr., worked for the Levi Strauss Foundation after a career in the music business, managing the Sons of Champlin, a rock group that later reconstituted a number of its musicians into the even more popular rock group Chicago.

Eisenhardt attended Dartmouth, served his country as a Marine officer, and then received his law degree from Boalt Hall at Cal. Roy married Walter's daughter, Betsy, in 1978. Roy fit the "Renaissance Man" image perfectly. He had an amazing thirst for knowledge, thus he mastered numerous skills—playing the piano, woodworking, languages, teaching, coaching crew at Cal, photography, science, and marine biology. He even found time to sleep.

Walter Haas' decision to enter the baseball business was influenced by his friend Cornell Maier, CEO of Oakland-based Kaiser Aluminum and Chemical Corporation. Maier's persistence brought Finley and Haas together. Maier was at Kaiser's helm when that company was the number one civic leader in Oakland.

Maier approached Haas knowing that his family had interest in getting involved with a Bay Area sports team. Maier's original plan was to head a group of local business leaders who would team up for the purchase. Kaiser would make a major investment stake in the acquisition of the A's and Haas would be a partner. However, at this same juncture, the global aluminum market tanked, and Maier knew Kaiser would have to bow out. Maier quickly sent a letter of intent from the Haas family to Finley in Chicago. Haas tasked his son Wally and son-in-law, Roy, to deal—successfully—with Finley and his lawyer.

On Thursday, August 21, 1980, the A's called a press conference for that Saturday at the Kaiser Center in Oakland. The reason for the conference was kept secret. Some secret, it turned out, for word leaked out that the team had new ownership in the Haas family.

Walter's son, Wally, remembered it this way: "We wanted to use sound business principles in the operation of the team. We also wanted to make sure that we ran the business in a very socially responsible way. Buying a baseball team gave us the opportunity to use the family philosophy in a powerful way. Even though my father was the owner of one of the largest clothing manufacturers in the U.S., it wasn't until we bought the team that he became well known."

Eisenhardt was typically direct at the press conference. "It is the responsibility of a business to give back to the community some of what it takes out," he said. "Levi Strauss is a classic example of this kind of thinking, and the Oakland A's will be run with the same philosophy. We'll be reaching out to senior citizens, youth groups, students, and areas of the community that haven't participated with the A's before."

Finley's neglect of the marketing side was a boon to the Haas family's plans on upgrading the franchise. They got off to a positive start, inheriting a headline-grabbing, but successful, manager in Billy Martin and a young team that was getting better all the time. Finley had run the team as a dictatorship, but the self-made millionaire insurance man was an absentee owner, making most decisions from his Chicago office. His cousin, Carl Finley, was the A's office manager, juggling the jobs of many as just one person. Finley often listened to broadcasts of entire games over a long-distance phone line from a transistor radio that Carl held up to the telephone. That connection seemed the makings of urban legend.

I, Andy Dolich, had worked for a number of less-than-successful teams, including my first stop with "Hoops Hades," the 1972–73 Philadelphia 76ers, who went 9–73, a record for putridity that stands as an NBA record to this day. But I was drawn to Matt Levine's business and marketing strategies, especially after working for teams defined by chaos and disaster. When the Haas family announced their purchase of the A's in August 1980, I got a call from Matt. He had been hired by the Haas family to work with team president Roy Eisenhardt and executive vice president Wally Haas, assisting them in the ramping-up process for their first year of directing the team.

I had known Levine for several years as my career in the sports marketing business was escalating, with stops in the NBA, indoor professional lacrosse, the NHL, and pro soccer. Levine was a welcoming strategic voice alike to league commissioners and team executives. He convinced them it was going to take more than just winning to market their franchises. He helped create the whole concept of proactive business operations as key parts of successful professional sports organizations.

"Andy," Matt asked, "would you be interested in talking to Roy Eisenhardt about a marketing job?" At that time, my wife, Ellen, and our two-year-old son, Cory, were living in suburban Maryland. I had just ended my time as general manager of the Washington Diplomats of the North American Soccer League. And I do mean ended, for team owner Madison Square Garden decided there was no future in soccer and shuttered the franchise.

The call from Levine was beyond fortuitous. If I could have flown through the telephone to meet with Eisenhardt, I would have. The job couldn't have been more perfect. Working for the family that owns Levi Strauss to replace the marketing chaos and disaster of the Finley years? Sign me up.

I flew to San Francisco to be interviewed by Walter, Roy, and Wally. It was exhilarating to meet these down-to-earth, high-quality people. In one of the interchanges with Mr. Haas, he asked me, "With all the experience you've had in professional sports, what one piece of advice would you give me as the owner?"

I figured it was time to show them my sense of humor, which is always a gamble when you really don't know someone that well. "Mr. Haas," I said, "the quickest way to become a millionaire as the owner of a pro franchise is to start out as a multimillionaire." Oops—no reaction. I saw my chance flying out the window until he cracked a smile and said, "I'll remember that and make sure it doesn't happen."

Whew! So let me tell you about my first day with the A's. I started work in early December 1980, my first visit ever to the Oakland-Alameda County Coliseum. Once I found my way to the A's offices, it looked like a ghost town. After entering through a glass door with the A's logo, I didn't see anyone inside. There was a black dial telephone on a desk that had a broken leg and was leaning to one side. A stained Oaktag sign on the desk read PLEASE DIAL O FOR OPERATOR. I finally got someone on the phone who buzzed me into the office. No one was there to greet me. Nice start.

When, finally, I entered the office that Roy Eisenhardt and Wally Haas shared, my eyes were drawn to what looked like a World Series trophy sitting on a corner desk. Upon further inspection, it was, indeed, the holy grail of baseball franchises. The metal flags attached to the trophy's base represented, honestly, each of the teams being used as file folder separators for incoming mail. I'm pretty certain this was the first and last clerical filing use for any World Series trophy.

Then I got better acquainted with Carl Finley. Together, we were able to hire more than 30 young, engaged, sports-career men and women to go forth and tell our story. Charles O. Finley viewed the A's market with a microscope, which stopped in the East Bay. With new ownership, we used a telescope, looking north through Sacramento, south to Monterey, and east to the Nevada border. The San Francisco Giants across the Bay were dealing with their own problems, and they didn't see us coming. We made business headway while their heads were down.

By sending out a new A's army of ticket sellers, we increased season tickets from 326 to more than 3,200 before our first game. And we didn't get started until mid-December, not exactly the best time to sell the game of baseball, yet we sold very well. Under Finley's ownership, A's customer service was nonexistent, which accounted for those lowest attendance figures in the majors.

My crystal-clear direction from Walter, Wally, and Roy: put the fans first. Wally told me to follow the guidelines of how Disney focused on customer service. Since I was already a Disney service devotee, it was easy making that directive an integral part of the A's Coliseum experience.

Early on, some media referred to the A's as the Nordstrom of baseball, which was high praise in being compared to one of the most respected service providers in the United States.

Roy and Wally told me that they wanted our growing business operations group to "create an enjoyable and economical entertainment package, so that when the fortunes of the team declined, that dual package might hold up at the ticket windows."

To gauge how we were doing with new fans, in our first two years, we worked with Matt Levine and his colleagues, holding focus groups and conducting regular surveys called "audience audits." Fan input helped us create programs that would pay immediate dividends in enhancing their experience. We termed it the "driveway to driveway experience." Every aspect of the fans' trip to and from the Oakland Coliseum was part of our focus.

Any improvements we wanted to implement were done cooperatively with the outside management of the Coliseum Authority. We hired a group of young men to work on developing a stadium operations department under Jorge Costa. Two seniors from Oakland's Bishop O'Dowd High School would, in time, become well-respected baseball stadium managers. David Rinetti still works for the A's as vice president of stadium operations with 38 years' experience. Kevin Kahn holds a similar position with the Colorado Rockies at Coors Field. I asked Kahn about those early days. "I think the Coliseum people were a bit shocked," he said, "when we started focusing our attention and money on improving customer service." The Finley years, obviously, had dulled people's perspectives.

The A's and Coliseum management made several key enhancements to the fan experience. One of the most significant moves: two new scoreboards. The A's installed a Diamond Vision video board for instant replays and close-ups of players and fans—"crowd-pumpers" to get the Coliseum rocking, plus the advertising to help pay for it. The team added a manually operated scoreboard, similar to Fenway Park's, to keep track of the daily action around Major League Baseball. During the last few years of Finley's ownership, the electronic scoreboard stopped working in the middle of games.

Rinetti recalled "adding television sets near all the concession stands so fans could track the action while waiting in line for the improved food selections we were offering. We piped in our radio broadcasts on KSFO to the restrooms."

Our marketing group came up with the concept of baby changing tables in both the men's and ladies' restrooms, while supplying free Pampers in a sponsorship deal with Safeway Supermarkets and Procter and Gamble. To introduce that idea, we held a press conference in one of the ladies' rooms (on an off day) and even served lunch. Safeway and Procter and Gamble warmed to the idea after seeing the positive stories it created.

We converted several Mezzanine Loge seating areas between the Coliseum's second and third decks into luxury "skyboxes." Constructing these upgraded boxes involved taking 40 seats and turning them into two boxes, one with 12 seats, the other with 18. In 1981 we spent about $120,000 on the project, charging $39,000 for the 12-seater and $48,000 for the 18-seater. We served high-end food in the skyboxes. We kept on adding, and in 1989 we had 35 skyboxes with 556 total seats, which became a significant profit center for the franchise.

Our sponsorship group was aggressive in reaching out to companies both large and small that the previous ownership had ignored for years. We wanted all our fans to be immersed in activities in and around the Coliseum. Right next to our broadcast booths, we created "A's Fantasy Play-by-Play." For a fee, two fans per inning could sit in the Budweiser announcers' booth we created to call the action while the game was going on. The fans left with a video tape of their performance. We had sponsors insert their ads in the facsimile broadcasts. This winning concept then went national in a number of ballparks, also sponsored by Budweiser.

The A's converted the space in the Exhibit Hall—which connected the Coliseum to the Arena where the Warriors played—by turning it into a family-friendly interactive "Foster Farms Family Place." The A's sponsorship team went to the CEO of Foster Farms Chicken, George Foster, a big baseball fan, convincing him that this would be a positive way for his company to engage families. A few years later, Foster purchased the A's Triple A franchise in Tacoma.

The major attractions in Family Place were Speed Pitch, Photo Booth, and Legoland. The team set up a speed pitch machine so fans could test how fast they could throw. There were some embarrassed dads who had told their kids they could throw 80 mph. When the screen showed a 67-mph pitch, the dads complained aloud that the machine was broken. I'll admit that sometimes we gave the operator the opportunity to throw up a bogus number for a young hurler hitting 90, thereby making this one of the most popular attractions, pregame or during the game. We created life-sized stand-up cutouts of our star players and let fans take photos with them. When lines formed for fans to pose between the Bash Brothers or next to Rickey Henderson and Dave Stewart, we knew we had another winner.

Tom Cordova of the A's corporate sales department remembers taking "an aggressive sales approach to local regional and national corporations who had shown interest in sports and entertainment. A sponsor could purchase a wide range of custom designed promotional packages. We had a group of companies that helped us create 'value added' premium giveaway days to attract fans to big games so that we could approach sellouts. These 'power promotions' gave the sponsors much more bang for the buck."

I recall our sales and marketing groups always pushing each other for creative and innovative concepts that could directly benefit the fans. We partnered with Safeway to present six "Saturday Barbeques." The first 10,000 fans were treated to a full BBQ lunch before the game, courtesy of Safeway and other major food companies that were able to fill up those fans' plates. We were concerned that these free BBQs would hurt our concessions during the six selected games. In reality, our receipts remained strong from food and beverage during games. We could, it seemed, do no wrong.

The Haas family also created the A's Community Fund and hired a former teacher, Dave Perron, to run it. Perron reached out to local companies who shared the Haases' philanthropic DNA in becoming funding members. Each A's staff member honored Walter Haas' commitment to Oakland by donating eight hours of community service time. By the third year of the Haas ownership, the A's Community Fund sponsored more than 30 programs, with Lucky Supermarkets and the A's combining to provide the money to rehabilitate, or build, community baseball fields, one field per year.

Also, a special service squad dressed in A's colors aided fans with special needs by helping them navigate the Coliseum during games. Fans were given access to pregame baseball clinics and free tickets to games. If an A's player homered, those kids received free tickets to another game.

Additionally, $1,000 donations were presented to a minority student pursuing a graduate degree in sports administration, sports journalism, or sports medicine. Free tickets were given to students who had read an agreed-upon number of books by the end of summer vacation. Fifth and sixth graders with outstanding academic records were invited to attend a pregame picnic and A's game as guests of IBM and the A's. These innovative ideas kept on coming.

The Haas family was all about a ballpark-friendly experience for the fans and proved it in ways that surpassed what other MLB organizations were doing or even thinking of doing. We even had a special program for the blind, inviting them to games and then escorting them from the parking lot to a special box, where the game's radio play-by-play broadcast was piped in and food and drink would be served. Then, after the game, they would be escorted back to the parking lot, where their rides would be waiting.

No baseball franchise was as imaginative, or fan-friendly, as ours.

When the Haases took over the team in 1981, they aspired for overall success. During their 14 years of guiding the franchise, they collected five division titles, three American League championships, and three World Series appearances, highlighted by the 1989

"October Classic" sweep of the cross-bay San Francisco Giants. The Haas-inspired increased attendance numbers painted an even clearer picture as to what a community-based baseball organization can mean to a city's pride.

Remember the A's paltry 306,763 attendance figure for the 1979 season under Finley's ownership? Under the Haas family flag, the A's set a franchise record of 2.9 million attendees in 1990.

Fast-forward to 2022 for further evidence of paltry home attendance figures in Oakland. A month into that season, after the A's had traded off their biggest stars once again, they ranked 30th, or dead last, in MLB attendance, at 7,965 per game.

During the previous season, 2021, the A's drew 701,430, their lowest Colisem attendance since the ill-fated 1979 campaign, though COVID protocols played a factor this time around. Also between 1979 and today, the A's have played at the Oakland Alameda County Coliseum, Network Associates, McAfee, and RingCentral—all at the same address—while looking at new ballpark sites in Oakland, Fremont, Santa Clara, and Las Vegas. Ah, nothing like stability.

John Fisher has owned the franchise for 17 years through 2022 and has rarely been quoted on the A's or hardly ever, it seems, seen in public. Three things can't stay hidden for long: the sun, the moon, and the truth. Fisher is doing a fantastic job of hiding his end game, other than his "parallel path" concept of either building a "rooted in Oakland" ballpark at Howard Terminal, or accepting an "uprooted in Oakland" outcome and moving the A's to Las Vegas.

Just remember—the current, hardly proven "rooted in Oakland" A's ownership has been searching for a ballpark location for years, though mostly outside of Oakland. Hence a portfolio of artists' renderings for proposed diamonds at Cisco Field in Fremont, Diridon Stadium in San Jose, the Victory Court and Peralta College sites in Oakland, a preliminary sketch in Las Vegas, plus Howard Terminal.

While A's management has been busy looking here and there, they've let All-Star quality players get away in Matt Olson, Matt Chapman, Marcus Semien, Chris Bassitt, and Sean Manaea, in addition to the winningest manager in Oakland franchise history, Bob Melvin, while expecting the terribly abused A's fan base to support the team as if none of the above departures ever occurred.

Well, the fans have more common sense than that, and so home attendance figures have sunk like a ballpark rain tarp in Oakland's Lake Merritt. In 2021, the A's finished 29th in MLB attendance, their lowest ranking since 1979, the tail end of Finley's fading franchise. In 2022, the A's averaged 9,973 fans, the lowest mark in MLB, and finished the season at 787,902, MLB's lowest attendance for the second straight year.

Meanwhile, the proposed Howard Terminal site was the target of multiple lawsuits by Union Pacific Railroad, Capitol Corridor Joint Powers Authority, Schnitzer Steel, and a coalition of Oakland port workers, truckers, and cargo terminal folks. Ah, friendly neighbors.

However, no matter where the A's decide to play ball—and this is vitally important information to remember—it will take a minimum of four years to build a new ballpark. Four years, Mr. Fisher.

As far back as May 2021, MLB Commissioner Rob Manfred gave A's management the green light to explore relocation options. A year later, the A's no longer were exploring because they had set their sights specifically on Las Vegas. Manfred's view is that the Oakland Coliseum "is not a viable option for the future vision of baseball"—even though Oakland is the 13th largest market in America, while Las Vegas is the 29th largest. Go figure.

Possibly awaiting the A's in Las Vegas is the same ballpark of their Triple-A affiliate, the Aviators, seating 10,000 maximum, slightly above the team's attendance average in Oakland through 2022. The Las Vegas ballpark is outdoors, and summer heat in southern Nevada can reach 115 degrees. Baseball weather? The Aviators also are owned by the Howard Hughes Corporation, which makes perfect sense as Fisher is identical to Hughes in public visibility.

Until a final stadium site is agreed upon—somewhere—the A's will continue to function on the cheap. The team's 2022 payroll sagged to last in MLB, $48 million, a sharp drop from $83 million, their skimpy payroll in 2021. And $48 million is their lowest player payout since 2008.

John Fisher is the ownership re-creation of Charles O. Finley.

The Haas family was, indeed, heavenly.

Chapter 6

Franklin Mieuli: The Ageless Hipster

Franklin was like a character in a novel. He truly was a fictional character.

—Tom Meschery,
Warriors player, poet, author

The Bay Area, combining San Francisco, Oakland, San Jose, and parts in between, produced Franklin Mieuli, who was this nation's most unusual sports franchise owner. During the 1960s, a decade of considerable social change—hippies, communes, folk music, incense, freaking out on LSD—Mieuli emerged as a senior-citizen flower child on his own (ego) trip.

Scott McKenzie sang the anthem of that culturally changing age, which actually related to Mr. Mieuli's neighborhood: "If you're going to San Francisco, be sure to wear some flowers in your hair…" Mieuli didn't wear poppies in his curls, but he covered them with, of all things, a deerstalker's cap, mostly associated with fictional detective Sherlock Holmes.

You couldn't miss the bearded Mieuli in that noticeable cap, cutting in and out of San Francisco traffic on his motorcycle. Then, when his basketball Warriors relocated to Oakland in the 1970s, Mieuli moved to nearby Berkeley, living near the University of California campus, the very home of idealistic conversion: fiery student protests, cultural upheaval, and sidewalk bead sales—a perfect setting for the hirsute Mieuli.

Mieuli was also nautical by nature, even sailing around the world. He fit in wherever the scene was shifting, land or sea. He went through motorcycles like Red Auerbach went through cigars, leaving bikes scattered everywhere and forgetting where he left them. He was an absent-minded, ultra-successful businessman, owning pieces of San Francisco's two other sports franchises, the 49ers and Giants. While a leather-jacketed aging biker doing wheelies and escaping from a three-piece-suit world may have looked odd, he somehow conquered the NBA.

"Franklin was so complex, and incredibly smart," said former San Francisco Warriors forward and current author Tom Meschery, "but he came off as a caricature in a way. I liked that about him because he never was ostentatious. He was a businessman, a romantic. He loved boating, and he was crazy about the Warriors. He kept them afloat with money out of his own pocket, because they weren't very successful back then."

Meschery added that Mieuli (pronounced MULE-EE) was "a hand-shake guy" who existed in a corporate world that was sometimes unkind, when others he engaged weren't true to their word.

"Franklin was a regular guy who liked to have beers with us after games," Meschery continued about those 1960s Warriors. "One time he said to me, 'Tom, I'm the owner of the team, and you never seem frightened of me.' And I said, 'Franklin, no one's frightened of you. You love the team, you love basketball, who's going to be afraid of you?' We were kind of pals in a way, and he wanted to be a pal of the players."

Mieuli desired that same pal-like relationship with the media, but he wasn't always successful.

"Franklin was a colorful guy," remembered beat writer John Simmonds. "But somewhere along the line, he went from being well-groomed, clean-shaven, and wearing a sports coat to this bearded guy with the deerstalker cap on a motorcycle. That's when he became a character. I remember the night in Oakland when he rode a motor scooter all over the court at halftime."

Simmonds covered the Warriors, both in San Francisco and Oakland, for the *Oakland Tribune*, finishing up with the 1974–75 NBA championship season. At the same time, Art Spander was the Warriors beat writer for the *San Francisco Chronicle* before becoming its lead sports columnist.

"Franklin was peculiar, but not strange," said Spander. "He was a Bay Area fanatic. With his ownerships in all three pro teams here, he had this decal made up, 'We Love Thee All Three', to stick on your car. He portrayed himself as the ultimate underdog, a mom-and-pop operation competing with the big cats in New York and Los Angeles."

Yes, but groceries?

"Franklin wanted positive news. He would come by the Chronicle with a big bag of vegetables, to try and get you on his side, a bribe in effect," Spander said. "But the Warriors in the late 1960s were an afterthought. The 49ers were the No. 1 team in the Bay Area, while the Warriors were the outsiders, with bad management, bad seasons, and bad draft picks. Franklin was a good guy, a nice guy, and he treated people that way. He drafted Al Attles in 1960, and he's still with the team today. Franklin was loyal, staying with the same people all the time."

When the San Francisco Warriors came to be in 1962, 33 investors with slam-dunk ambitions paid $850,000 to buy the team. And 32 of those investors blew their own dunks by buying their way out, leaving only Mieuli.

"When they brought the club out here from Philadelphia," Simmonds reflected on the 1962–63 season, "Wilt Chamberlain had scored 100 points in a game a few months before, and the Warriors thought they would be a great success. But it just didn't work that way as the crowds were 2,000, 3,000." (The Warriors' initial attendance average in San Francisco was a likely fudged 3,067, lowest in the NBA regardless.)

"Franklin also became very frustrated," Simmonds added, "because the local newspapers weren't traveling with the team; maybe to Los Angeles, but that was pretty much it. Finally, he started paying for writers to make some trips, but he still wasn't getting the coverage he wanted. The team played at the cavernous Cow Palace. The '5,000 attendance' announced one night…there must have been 1,500 there. It was pathetic."

That's when the initial large ownership group, including fashion store tycoon Cyril Magnin, bailed. Desperate, Mieuli shifted games to the smaller San Francisco Civic Auditorium, and then to the even-smaller University of San Francisco gymnasium, before playing "home games" in Oakland, San Jose, Richmond, Fresno, and even far off San Diego. The Warriors were received warmly, though not wildly, wherever they went.

"When they played at the Oakland Auditorium," Simmonds said, "there were ruts on the floor. So when you bounced the ball, you didn't know where it was going to go. It was awful."

Mieuli tried everything to boost attendance, even traveling to Italy to buy chandeliers to enhance the Cow Palace's bovine ambience. Then he had sportswriters wear tuxedoes the same night those glitzy lights were unveiled at a home game.

"Franklin wanted to be different, but not strange," said Spander. "He was unusual and erudite, but he tried to make people feel good."

Sadly for Mieuli, while he was shopping for those chandeliers abroad, star player Rick Barry went shopping too. He crossed the Bay Bridge to sign with the American Basketball Association's Oakland Oaks for $75,000 a year, more than doubling his Warriors salary. That was a great professional and personal loss for Mieuli, who considered Barry an adopted son. Ironically, Mieuli would "readopt" Barry in the future.

"Franklin was an emotional guy," said Simmonds. "He was kind and very easy to talk to, but then he would lash out, become angry. One night after a game in Oakland, after the Warriors had moved there, I asked Franklin if there were any chance he would change the team's name from 'Golden State' to 'Oakland'. He said, 'Absolutely not. I'll never do that.'"

Oakland saved Mieuli financially, yet he couldn't deign to honor Oakland by name, conceiving of the "Golden State" moniker. How ridiculous that was, when there isn't a governor or mayor or counties or zip codes in "Golden State."

"Franklin identified with San Francisco, where his businesses were," said Simmons. "That's why he had 'The City' on the team's uniforms, because San Francisco was referred to that way. He wouldn't lower himself to say he was 'Oakland.' He was hoping one day to put the team back in San Francisco."

That day would happen, though not on Mieuli's watch. He passed away at 89 in 2010, and the franchise didn't cross back over the bridge until 2019. Simmonds, when interviewed in April 2020, predicted the team will be renamed the San Francisco Warriors by 2023 at the latest.

"In those early years," he remembered, "the Warriors were just trying to get a following. With their games in places like San Diego, nobody here covered them. You'd get a four-, five-inch wire story of the game. That's hard to believe now."

Mieuli couldn't ever hide a gracious personality. When the Warriors played the 76ers for the 1967 NBA title, Simmonds recalled, "Franklin bought London Fog overcoats for the entire team and for writers covering the team. 'The City' was [stitched] on the outside of the coat, but Dick Friendlich of the San Francisco Chronicle asked that it be put inside for the writers, to look more appropriate. I still have that coat."

Back then, Bay Area sports teams presented "gifts"—either clothing store certificates or outright cash—to meagerly paid beat writers at Christmastime. Such generosity, which rarely influenced coverage, was done quietly until newspaper management found out, killing that Christmas golden goose.

Mieuli employed Shirley Figgins for 43 years, beginning in 1968 as an accountant, before she became his controller, and, later, his financial advisor. Figgins remained with Mieuli, even beyond the Warriors years, until his passing.

"Franklin made me a 25 percent partner in his companies," she said. "He was a big promoter of women's rights. I was the first woman controller in the NBA. And he was the first to see the future of women's basketball, starting the women's basketball league in San Francisco in 1969.

"I loved the Warriors, and I loved working for Franklin. We were like family, so close. He trusted me with everything. Of course, I admired

Franklin, such a generous person and so financially smart. I would never have left Franklin. Al Davis of the Raiders tried to hire me as his controller. I was shocked he would do that to his good friend Franklin, and I said no."

Figgins witnessed the transformation of Mieuli from a beardless coat-and-tie person to that 1960s hipster look.

"Franklin didn't like clothes," she said. "He just didn't care. He would take whatever was first in the closet, and if people didn't like what he wore, too bad. That was Franklin, who would say, 'Take me the way I am.' He was real; there was nothing phony about Franklin. He knew so much about all kinds of things. He listened to National Public Radio all day long. He loved the theater, jazz, and gardening."

Gardening? Mieuli grew up in San Jose, the son of a nursery owner. Selling flowers wasn't for him, so after graduating from the University of Oregon in 1944, he did marketing for a Bay Area brewery. He then sponsored radio broadcasts for 49ers games in 1954, and later produced the team's first telecast. Next up, he was in charge of radio broadcasts at the 1960 Winter Olympics in Squaw Valley before acquiring the rights to 49ers and Giants games. He even had his own FM radio station, KPUP, which he sold a few years later. By then, Franklin Mieuli and Associates were in full broadcasting swing.

Owning the Warriors for 24 years, Mieuli broke down racial barriers in making his team more inclusive than other NBA teams of that era. Ten of the twelve players on the Warriors' 1974–75 NBA championship roster were Black, as well as head coach Al Attles and assistant Joe Roberts.

"Franklin never had a quota, and he never intimated anything about race," Roberts recalled. "Otherwise, he wouldn't have hired Al to coach the team. I doubt there hardly were any people in the league at that time like Franklin. I always liked Boston, even though it was a racist city. Red Auerbach always took care of his players; regardless of what color they were, they all got a chance to coach. Franklin also should be saluted as a trailblazer, always putting the best team on the court. He told me in one discussion, 'You guys don't have to win every game, just have them play hard.' He was a fair-minded man."

Meschery viewed Mieuli as "intensely loyal to his players. When he sold the team, Franklin had the new owners put into Al Attles' contract that he would always be with the team in some capacity."

Dick D'Oliva was the Warriors' team trainer for 22 years, mostly with Mieuli before spending his last two seasons with succeeding owners Jim Fitzgerald and Dan Finnane. Then D'Oliva and his wife, Vi, opened a flower shop.

"Franklin was a better person than an owner, really," said D'Oliva. "He was personable, considerate, compassionate—all those good words— though his personality was sometimes weird. But he was a nice man."

D'Oliva was more than just a trainer with the Warriors. He arranged travel, was the equipment man, charted team fouls and time-outs during games, and supervised summer clinics.

"Franklin did things differently from other people," he said. "His office had a barber chair, a refrigerator, and a basketball hoop outside. Could he shoot? Uh, let's just say he was OK."

Mieuli, the divorced father of two children, had a 33-year relationship with Blake Green, a talented journalist with the *San Francisco Chronicle*. Their dating continued bicoastal after Green worked for Newsday in New York City.

Green was divorced from *Chronicle* sports columnist and later *Sports Illustrated* writer Ron Fimrite when she met Mieuli at a party in San Francisco.

"Franklin asked me to dance," she said, "and I was impressed by how good a dancer he was. Ironically, I was doing a column for the *Chronicle* on the 10 most eligible bachelors in San Francisco, and Franklin was chosen. He was selected because he was never around, sailing the South Seas on his catamaran with his Australian skipper, Don Marmo. Some people objected strenuously to that column, but Franklin thought it was very funny. So, he asked me out to dinner, and that was the beginning of it."

Green speculated that dinner date was 1977 or 1978, by which time Mieuli "was fully eccentric. He rode a camel during a Warriors game and fell off, cutting himself. I heard he even wore a monocle at one point.

But his eccentricity made him very endearing. He certainly wasn't your average date. After three dates, he asked me to go sailing with him on the South Seas. Marmo, his best friend, was the captain of that trip, and we had a great time. After I moved to New York, Franklin would come back frequently, because he loved the theater.

"I don't know that we would have had as long a relationship as we had if we didn't live on separate coasts. That's because he was independent, and he had a good time. Then, in old age, he became cranky because of all the medicines he was taking for pain. He was sick for a long time and didn't feel well. But he still was Franklin, fun to be with. We had a lot of memories."

Was the topic of marriage ever broached?

"We had a conversation about that early in our relationship," Green said from her current home in Virginia. "Don Nelson was getting married when he was the Warriors coach, and Franklin suggested we do a double wedding—not that Nelson was in on it. And then we both said, 'No.' We had [each] been married before, and we decided it would be better if we didn't marry."

Ken Flower met Mieuli in the middle of his Warriors ownership, timed perfectly with the team's ascendancy in the mid–1970s. They became fast friends, on both coasts.

"Franklin was a unique person, unquestionably," said Flower. "When I was working in New York at NFL Films, he would come to town with the Warriors, and he'd stop by for a visit at the NFL office. I'd get a call from the receptionist, who would say, 'Mr. Flower, I think you better come out here in the lobby. There's a man here who wants to see you and the commissioner.' It would be Franklin, with a leather sport coat, a Hawaiian shirt, and with a beard and his deerstalker cap. Everyone in the office would be in suit and tie, and the receptionist then asked, 'What do I do?' I told her that he owned the Warriors and part of the 49ers and Giants, and, 'Please let him in, and I will take him back to Pete's office.'"

Pete, of course, was Pete Rozelle, NFL commissioner and a longtime friend of Mieuli's. "Franklin would get all these crazy looks from people because of his nonconformist way of dressing," Flower added. "We all met later for drinks and a bite to eat, and it started all over again: 'There's a guy at the door,' Rozelle was told, 'who wants to come in. He says he knows you.' So Pete would go out and get him. We all went through that with Franklin. The only thing missing was his motorbike.

"But he was so much fun, never embarrassed, never apologetic. Franklin was just Franklin, someone with a big heart, and people loved him. He was something, a special guy. Bad things, organizationally, were never said about him. He was a very bright individual and a good businessman. Those were competitive times in business, and he coped with all that, handling things exceedingly well by holding shares with the 49ers and Giants, and owning the Warriors. He thrived in that age, and he would have thrived in this age as well."

Late in life, Mieuli described his business approach. He made his formula for success sound hardly complex.

"If I saw something that needed doing, I did it," he said. "Some of them made money, some of them didn't. But I did it anyway, even though I don't remember all the things I did. I just don't."

Hank Greenwald, the Warriors and Giants baseball announcer, saw right through that understated ruse.

"Franklin is the one man in the world," said Greenwald, "who works hard at having people underestimate him."

An elderly Mieuli attended Warriors games in Oakland, sitting court-side, no longer an owner, but still involved as a fan.

"He would sit there gazing at his creation," Meschery said. "I know it hurt him terribly to lose the team. But financially, he just had to give it up."

Shortly before dying, Mieuli summed up his life as follows: "I've had too many motorcycles and too short a memory." With such irreverent comments, he kept everyone guessing until the end.

Shirley Figgins gets the final word on her favorite boss.

"I was there every day at his bedside," she said of Mieuli's final days. "I was married all those years, but Franklin was like family to me.

Whatever I could do to make his life better, I would do it. I think of him all the time. All the time."

Blake Green gets the final, final word.

"He was a dear, dear man who enriched my life greatly," she said. "I miss him every day."

But a final, final, final word:

Franklin Mieuli, albeit a good man with a generous nature, didn't treat Oakland as generously as Oakland treated him in making this San Francisco devotee a very wealthy man.

Golden State, my ass.

Chapter 7

Dave Stewart: Oakland Embodied

I was just waiting for the right door to open, and when that happened, I was going to walk right through it and never look back.

—Dave Stewart,
A's four-time 20-game winning pitcher

Dave Stewart is Oakland, and Oakland is Dave Stewart. It's rare that an athlete and a hometown are so intertwined, most notably when self-preservation matters for both the athlete and the town. In that regard, Stewart and Oakland are gamers.

Stewart and Oakland: unflinching, two-fisted, perennial underdogs, blue collar in spirit, and both capable of creating turnarounds against significant odds.

Thus it was only natural with their strong link that Stewart would come to Oakland's rescue at critical junctures, when the baseball A's, for whom he won 20 games in four consecutive seasons (1987–90), were contemplating moving out of Oakland if a new ballpark couldn't be built.

The odds of the A's remaining in Oakland increased slightly when Stewart, 63 in 2022, swung into action. He led a group of minority investors who submitted a $115 million bid to purchase the City of

Oakland's share of its Coliseum site. The purpose of Stewart's group was to construct a baseball-only facility as part of a diversified commercial entity—hotels, housing, offices, and youth and amateur sports facilities—intended to entice consumer interest year-round.

The Coliseum property is divided: the City of Oakland owns one half with the A's owning the other half after purchasing Alameda County's portion for $85 million. Stewart's group offered itself as a stopgap measure to buy up the city's 50 percent share to prevent the A's from leaving town.

"I've been involved with the city forever," Stewart said during these negotiations while recalling his childhood fantasy of owning the A's. "But the one place that has been forgotten is East Oakland, and I have my footprint in that community."

East Oakland is where the Coliseum property is situated, with the outdoors Coliseum next to the indoor Arena. Only one other person in Stewart's group was identified initially: Lonnie Murray, the first and only Black woman to be certified as a player agent by Major League Baseball. Stewart's group made its offer in November 2020, banking on his history with the A's, which is everlasting, and East Oakland, where he grew up.

"That part of the city is lacking grocery stores and boutique shopping," he said. "And there's nothing recreational there for the youth of the area. So my thought is to make East Oakland a city within a city, to make it desirable with a facelift. That became my vision, and my dream."

Stewart's group competed with another minority investment body—the African American Sports and Entertainment Group (AASEG)—to buy Oakland's share of the Coliseum site. Oakland was given six months to negotiate with the two groups before recommending one of them to the City Council for exclusive negotiations regarding the 155-acre Coliseum site. Whichever group was selected then would work in concert with the A's, the one-half property owner.

"The capital certainly is in place to purchase the land," Stewart said in fall 2021. "I haven't been given a time frame by the city, just to do it in the right way, so the city can make the right decision. The Coliseum is a perfect site, but people haven't wanted to put their money into East Oakland, which has a stigma, a phobia, that's been there a long time. The thinking is the money would be a waste."

So, what were the odds of Stewart's vision becoming a reality? He didn't back off from that question.

"It's 50-50," he said. "But it should be better than 50-50, because I'm from the Bay Area, I'm investing in the Bay Area, and my motives are genuine, from the heart. East Oakland has been wearing the same clothes for years, so why not give it new clothes?"

Fifty-fifty, regrettably, then turned 90-10 against him in November 2021. AASEG was chosen unanimously by the Oakland City Council over Stewart's group to either purchase or lease the city's share at the Coliseum site. Stewart hung onto that 10 percent because the council's vote only directed the city to negotiate financial terms and a development agreement with AASEG. A final development agreement needed to be presented to the council before it voted, yes or no.

Stewart was crushed, nonetheless, by the outcome. "Everything I've done for Oakland—from the [1989] earthquake to all my involvement with the city, and to all the money I've put into the city—Oakland turned its back on me," he said, harshly, several weeks after his group was rejected. "They can't ask me to do another thing for Oakland."

Stewart wasn't reacting as a sore loser; his group was, in fact, iron-clad solid and largely homegrown. Stewart and Murray fronted a most impressive band of investors, whose names Stewart revealed only after his group was rejected: baseball greats Rickey Henderson and CC Sabathia, basketball standouts Gary Payton, Damian Lillard, and Brian Shaw, and superagent Aaron Goodwin. Supporting their bid were former A's executive Wally Haas and Pro Football Hall of Famer Ronnie Lott. Stewart, Henderson, Payton, Lillard, Shaw, and Goodwin are Oaklanders. And they still lost out, somehow.

"It was disappointing," Stewart said in a slightly calmer tone. "I was hopeful we could get it accomplished. But in dealing with Rebecca Kaplan, I knew it would be difficult."

Kaplan, an Oakland City Council member, supported AASEG because of that group's plan to bring a women's professional basketball (WNBA) franchise to Oakland. Stewart's group opposed that idea, believing the Bay Area belonged to the Golden State Warriors, regardless of which side of the Bay Bridge they played basketball—Oakland or, most recently, San Francisco. But the City Council believed in Kaplan's concept.

"She made unethical appearances with the other group," said Stewart, riled up again. "The WNBA was her thing, and the City Council only listened to her. On the final vote, we were supposed to get 15 minutes to make our presentation; it was cut down to eight minutes. We presented more substance in our plans and in our renderings. We told the city we would pay them the asking price of $115 million. We dotted all the 'i's and crossed all the 't's, but it came down to 'What have you done for me lately?' The other group had done grassroots work for a year, whereas all of my involvement...."

His involvement? Here was a hometown hero attempting to buy into a hometown facility with hometown capital to prevent his hometown team, the A's, from possibly moving to Las Vegas. The City of Oakland blundered badly in regard to its dwindling sports landscape by casting Stewart so cruelly aside.

Stewart, holding true to his tough, resilient nature, brushed off that mistreatment by looking 2,291 miles east to Nashville, putting together, in the spring of 2022, a revised, unnamed ownership group attempting to bring an MLB franchise to Tennessee. If successful in his latest endeavor, Stewart would lead the first minority ownership group in MLB history.

However, the clueless City of Oakland disregarded Stewart's humane hometown "save"—the 1989 earthquake that devastated the Bay Area and Oakland. There was Stewart, in the middle of the A's–San Francisco Giants World Series, bringing food, drink, and provisions daily to the quake's rescue team on Oakland's side of the bridge—a one-man relief party.

With the Raiders and Warriors gone, Stewart then endeavored to prevent a triple relocation sweep by retaining the A's. Oakland blew this one badly, but Stewart, in time, put this disappointment in a large drawer with his other setbacks.

"The experiences you have growing up are to benefit you, not to keep you down," he reflected. "I never took the viewpoint that there was anything wrong with Oakland. Maybe there are imperfections, but we all have imperfections. People preferred to live in Danville, Pleasanton, or San Francisco. But if I grew up in those places, I wouldn't be the person I am today.

"Successful."

Exactly. Whatever values he learned from growing up in East Oakland, either from family or circumstance, steeled Stewart through a rough transitory baseball period until he became the pitcher he had envisioned he could be all along: a 20-game winner.

Becoming a hometown hero, too, made his life even better.

"My youth manifested itself in everything I did in baseball," he said. "What I'm proudest of was taking my life lessons and showing them on the baseball field."

Stewart was one of eight children who became fatherless when he was a high school sophomore. There were chores to do at home—cleaning his room, cutting the grass, raking leaves, etc. There also were outside jobs to perform, with Stewart delivering newspapers and pumping petrol and servicing cars at Everett Henry's gas station.

Though Stewart's hands were greasy, his nose was clean. He joined a boys' club and then became a star athlete in football, basketball, and baseball at St. Elizabeth's High School, though his star shone less then in baseball. That's because 30 colleges wanted him to play football. Oh, how he loved to hit—in football, not baseball. He could punish like Ronnie Lott.

Distractions might have steered him on an alternate course. The Black Panther Party was housed a few blocks away from his boyhood home, and drug dealers loomed even closer. Police sirens pierced the neighborhood air during the night.

"There were domestic issues with the police—drugs, crime, pandering," he recalled of his East Oakland surroundings. "I had friends that went in the other direction. I was fortunate that I had a good balance."

With that balance, he took the correct future path—baseball.

"I was just an OK baseball player," he said of his high school years as a catcher. "I was a good basketball player, and a very good football player. But I had a chip on my shoulder in any sport I played. My focus was to destroy the opponent. I wanted to be the best at what I did."

He had visited Oklahoma and Nebraska, plus he had West Coast offers from Cal, USC, and UCLA—all to play football. He was a ferocious tackler at linebacker, but at 6'0", 190 pounds, he was recruited as a safety. While mulling his top choice, USC, the Los Angeles Dodgers drafted him in the 16th round in 1975.

"That was the first time I knew I could play baseball, that I was good enough to play," he said. "But when I got to my first assignment, Bellingham, Washington, I was told that I wouldn't put on catcher's equipment ever again."

He was, suddenly, a pitcher. "I have to be honest, if I knew that was their intent, I wouldn't have signed," he reflected. "I would have taken that football scholarship."

He had pitched only twice in high school, otherwise focusing on throwing fastballs from behind home plate to cut down base stealers. But the Dodgers loved his strong arm regardless. After all, his boyhood nickname was "Smoke."

"I got a good crash course on how to become a thrower, not a pitcher," he said of his rough pro indoctrination. "My first two years, I didn't win any games, and I walked more batters than I had innings pitched. I was throwing fastballs and trying to learn a curve and other breaking balls, all at the same time."

He grew to 6'2", 210 pounds, but pitched like a linebacker.

"But I couldn't come back home as a failure," he told himself, "because it would have been embarrassing for me and my family. That's just not who I was: quit wasn't in me."

He needed that strong balance, plus a transformative moment that would resonate with a pitcher of any age: Sandy Koufax became his mentor. The iconic Koufax was part of a Dodgers instructional league and took Stewart under his wing.

"He revamped my mechanics," Stewart said. "He took everything away, and then we restarted. I learned from him about getting my balance. I learned from him about getting my chin, shoulder, and elbow as my sight, like the sight on a gun, when I got ready to throw to the catcher. It was some of the best lessons I ever learned, and the easiest for me to understand, everything there was to know about pitching."

Had Koufax materialized, magically, as a pitching guru?

"That's what he was like for me at that time," he said.

Years later, when Stewart was an established 20-game winner in Oakland, the opportunity arose to thank Koufax.

"In 1988, when we played the Dodgers in the World Series, I thanked Sandy personally on the field," Stewart said. "He said to me, 'You did all the work.' That's Sandy."

When first encountering Koufax, Stewart was a relief pitcher with an iffy future, moving from the Dodgers to the Texas Rangers to the Philadelphia Phillies, where his career crashed.

"I never doubted my ability as a pitcher if given the right opportunity, so I never wavered," he said. "It's tough when you're in the bullpen, then you're starting, then you're back in the bullpen, then you're starting again in three days. That way, you have no opportunity to plan or to get into a routine."

His unbridled confidence through difficult times came from his father, David, a longshoreman, and his mother, Nathalie, who worked in a cannery and a post office after her husband died. Their strong work ethic was instilled in him early.

Stewart came to the Oakland A's in 1986, still carrying that same undying belief in his ability. Oakland is where it all came together—besides the four 20-win seasons, there would be three postseason MVP awards, and, in 2022, having his number 34 retired by the A's. (Rollie Fingers' 34 was retired earlier by Oakland.)

Tony La Russa was named A's manager midway through the 1986 season. Needing pitching help, La Russa remembered how the idling Stewart, then with Texas, shut down his Chicago White Sox team. So

La Russa started him against Boston, and Stewart, stunningly, outpitched Roger Clemens.

Those Oakland teams grew as Stewart's reputation grew, although he encountered an early clubhouse doubter. Mouthy A's pitcher Joaquin Andujar chided Stewart, "I'm a 20-game winner, and you will never win 20 games." Stewart replied curtly, "Anything you can do, I can do better. You'll see."

What then changed for Stewart was the forkball, an unused pitch in his arsenal, which previous teams had nixed. A's pitching coach Dave Duncan felt otherwise, and that forkball made Stewart…worthy of Cooperstown consideration?

"The best way I can put it: I've done some Hall of Fame things," he pointed out. "Nobody is going to win 20 games four years in a row ever again. I may be the last guy to throw 270 innings a year, or the last guy with 15 or more complete games in a season. I've been an MVP in both the postseason [league series] and the World Series. I may be the only guy to win two games in the postseason and two games in the World Series. My bulk numbers—169 wins and 3.95 ERA—don't make me a Hall of Famer, but over a four-, five-year period, there wasn't a more dominant pitcher in baseball."

Stewart was also 10–6 with a 2.77 ERA in the postseason. There was also the matter of his utter domination of the great Clemens, beating him nine of 10 times, in what became a heated rivalry. Wouldn't ownership of a pitching legend, added to everything else, make Stewart a Hall of Fame candidate, even remotely?

"Reporters would ask me what it was like to go up against Clemens," he said. "The only way to change that question would be to pound on him, and beat him, until he's no longer a factor. Now the question to Roger was, 'How do you beat Dave Stewart? You haven't beaten him since he was with the Texas Rangers.' I intimidated him. If he threw at one of our hitters, I'd throw at two of his. When he looks back on his career, the one thing he won't want to talk about is pitching against me."

Stewart might have been a heavyweight boxer with his fighter's physique and his "Death Stare." He did deck Cleveland manager Pat

Corrales one day by the mound. "He called me a 'dirty ——' because I threw at Julio Franco," Stewart said. Corrales should have thrown in the towel before ever confronting such a fierce combatant.

Though Stewart pitched in three straight World Series, 1988 through 1990, the A's won only the middle "October Classic" against the Giants. Stewart analyzed why years later.

"In 1988, we got a reality check in that first game," he said, reliving Kirk Gibson's jaw-dropping, game-winning pinch hit home run off Dennis Eckersley, who had relieved Stewart. "We didn't recover for some reason. Against Cincinnati [in 1990], there was chaos in our clubhouse. José [Canseco] was a big factor, and one factor can destroy everything."

However, the Dodgers and Reds played terrifically, with multiple heroics. Still, the A's three straight World Series, win or lose, remain an achievement.

Since Stewart retired as a player, he has been a pitching coach (Toronto, Milwaukee), an assistant general manager (Oakland, Toronto), and a general manager (Arizona). He now runs a sports agency and does studio television work for NBC Sports Bay Area.

Stewart's nobility is second to none in baseball, as evidenced by his involvement during the 1989 World Series earthquake.

"This is something I don't talk about much, because it's pointing the finger at myself," he said. "But what took me there (to the quake's site) was tragedy. I brought whatever the people needed. I grew up in Oakland, a gift I could never pay back to Oakland. So the four days I was at that site, I was able to give back what Oakland has given me."

So, then, what has it been like for this proud hometown kid in seeing two of Oakland's three pro sports franchises leave?

"When you look at the Golden State Warriors, which they were called in Oakland, they originally came from San Francisco. So even though they went back to San Francisco, I still look at them as a Bay Area team," Stewart said.

"The Raiders are a totally different story. I've been a Raiders fan since they were at Frank Youell Field. When they first moved, to Los Angeles, I lost some love for them, but still embraced them. They returned to Oakland, and it was like, 'We don't love you, but we're glad to have you back.' Then they moved again, to Las Vegas. Now I can say that I don't support the Raiders in any way. I could never root for them again."

Does Stewart, deep in his heart, fear the A's leaving, too? "No," he said. "I don't think [A's owner] Mr. [John] Fisher will move the team. I just don't see him relocating. If he does sell, it will be to someone who'll keep the team in Oakland. It would be the worst thing ever to see the A's leave, too. Oakland is a championship city. I live in San Diego now most of the time, but when people ask me where I'm from, I always say Oakland."

Stewart starred in a league where a designated hitter took away pitchers' at-bats; both leagues now do likewise. But this pitcher stepped up to the plate in a princely way to try and prevent the A's from leaving his Oakland. To negative nabobs who feel Oakland isn't a big-league city, by citing its sports departures, beware in expressing that sentiment to Stewart.

He'll turn his Death Stare on you.

Chapter 8

Joe Lacob, Mark Davis: Stealing Off

*John [Madden] believed in the town of Oakland.
He believed in the [Oakland] Coliseum. Most of all,
he believed in the Raiders—the Oakland Raiders.*

—Virginia Madden,
speaking at her husband's memorial
on February 14, 2022, at the Oakland Coliseum

There are two proven stepping stones to owning a sports team: venture capitalists and Daddy. Oakland has experienced both diverse entries and paid dearly in either capacity.

Joe Lacob was a venture capitalist, which earned him an immense fortune, but not the exposure he craved. He sought fame, for no man lacks ego quite like a wealthy man. And so Lacob bought a professional sports franchise. Thus, he could be televised at courtside, next to the athletes he would be paying.

Mark Davis was just the opposite—an unsuccessful nobody, yet the son of an NFL owner. Only this Daddy wanted no part of his only child in the football business, for the son lacked sense in general, skidding through adulthood as a trust-funder. Then Daddy died and—poof!—Sonny wound up owning the team.

97

Lacob bought the Golden State Warriors, and Davis inherited the Oakland Raiders. These two disparate characters then took leave from Oakland, hurriedly. Lacob vanned his Warriors to San Francisco, while Davis hijacked the Raiders to Las Vegas.

Oakland had given the Raiders life, even a second life. Oakland rejuvenated the Warriors, yet the city's reward for its charity was twin abandonment—following 340 consecutive Warriors sellouts at the Oakland Arena. The Athletics remain as Oakland's last sports tenant, tenuously, a sad outcome as its three teams won 10 world championships.

The Warriors motored to Oakland from nearby San Francisco, only to reverse course and head back across the Bay Bridge to The City That Knows How (to lose franchises, that is, as the football 49ers also fled San Francisco to Santa Clara).

The Raiders are practitioners of fleeing—or fleecing. Las Vegas is their third home—Oakland to Los Angeles, back to Oakland, and then on to Las Vegas. A father's failed example of stability and loyalty was passed down to his son, who has emerged capable, just like Daddy, of screwing up matters too.

Oakland built and retrofitted a stadium for the Raiders and also constructed and retrofitted the arena that housed the Warriors. Though both of those tenants' attendance figures hovered at capacity in Oakland, the two misfits couldn't wait to skip town. Oakland's only problem, it turned out, was that it couldn't avoid being stigmatized as un-sexy Oakland.

The Warriors' relocation to San Francisco, however, came with a going-away gift from Oakland: a state appeals court ruling in August 2020 that stated the Warriors owed Oakland and Alameda County financially for construction at the very same arena where they played for nearly a half-century before thumbing a ride back to San Francisco. Though the court didn't list the debt, it apparently topped $30 million.

The deceitful Warriors initially intended to escape Oakland without owing the city and Alameda County a single penny, even though the 19,000-seat arena had been renovated, and enlarged, in 1996 at a cost of $150 million in bonds, to be paid off over 30 years. That '96 agreement contained a provision that allowed the Warriors to leave after 10 years by paying the renovation debt in full or to move after 20 years by making debt-service payments, less any offset, until 2027. But any departure, even one allowed by contract, would be considered a termination, thereby leaving the Warriors responsible for any remaining debt.

Thus, Oakland proved smarter than Lacob had envisioned before he bolted. A Warriors' official, while upset by the ruling, said, "We will fulfill our debt obligation." Hell yes, you will!

Lacob wasn't planning on staying in Oakland from the start. Three of his first four press conferences as the new Warriors owner were held outside Oakland. At the fourth, to announce the team's shifting to San Francisco, who just happened to show up but NBA Commissioner David Stern, 2,565 miles from his New York City office, sticking it to Oakland meanly.

Oakland has been violated so many times by its three teams, including the A's turbulent, yet triumphant, ownership of Charles O. Finley. Thus, the city's winning even one court case against its elusive tenants felt like a Supreme Court decision.

"There is a scrappiness and persistence about Oakland, and there is a heart in this city," Oakland Mayor Libby Schaaf said in spring 2022. "One of the reasons that Oakland always is in love with its sports teams is that sense of competiveness and grit in the field. We have that same sense about our city, even in the face of [negative] national opinion. Don't underestimate us, because we do have a heart, a soul, a resistance that nobody else has ever seen, and we will win."

Oakland's will to win certainly is there, but two-thirds of the city's sports teams still hightailed it elsewhere, leaving behind only the equally antsy A's. A mayor only can do so much in the face of ownership greed. But to avoid a third Oakland franchise from relocating on Schaaf's watch before she was termed out in November 2022, her unwise decision to cram an unnecessary ballpark at an unsuitable waterfront location wasn't the wisest political strategy for her future higher-seeking ambitions.

After Lacob transformed the Warriors from a woebegone franchise into a model NBA team, suddenly his hat no longer fit his swelled head.

During the Warriors' five-year championship series run, he boasted that his franchise was "light years ahead" of other franchises in future planning. Bad timing: Cleveland then upset his team in the NBA Finals.

Lacob, to his credit, countered brilliantly. A week after losing to the Cavaliers, Lacob, coach Steve Kerr, and a group of players flew back East and convinced Kevin Durant, playing out his option in Oklahoma City, to come join the party in Oakland. That collective brainstorm was the most brilliant NBA front office move of the century, leading to back-to-back league titles. But the Warriors couldn't hold on to Durant, who now sinks 25-footers across the country in Brooklyn.

So who is Joe Lacob? Born in 1956, he received a master's in business from Stanford University before becoming a partner at Kleiner Perkins, a venture capital firm since 1987 and an early backer of Google, Amazon, and Genentech. Big, *big* bucks!

Lacob, in 2006, became part owner of the Boston Celtics. Four years later, together with an investment firm, he bought the Warriors from Chris Cohan for $450 million. Lacob and Hollywood impresario Peter Guber are the principal owners, though Lacob oversees the team's day-to-day operations.

Lacob wasted no time establishing authority, firing Hall of Fame coach Don Nelson and replacing him with Warriors assistant coach Keith Smart—though only temporarily, for Lacob coveted NBA broadcaster and former player Mark Jackson as his first true coaching hire. Jackson, it turned out, was a motivator, not a coach. During Warriors time-outs, while his assistants diagrammed plays, he stood and watched.

Jackson projected himself as deeply religious, and he strove to drive the gospel into the Warriors. On one road trip, he asked the team to attend a certain church, although not all of them showed up. Jackson got under too many skins, including ownership's. Lacob fired him in 2014 with this explanation: "Part of it was he couldn't get along with anybody else in the organization. And, look, he did a great job—and I'll always compliment him in many respects—but you can't have 200 other people in the organization not like you." Of course, but *you* hired him, Joe! Jackson returned to television when no other NBA franchise coveted him as a head coach.

Lacob, in another coup with better results, reached into the television world once again to pick Jackson's successor, Steve Kerr, who instantly coached the Warriors to glory during a streak of six NBA finals in eight years. Kerr, a man of clear strategy and a deep soul, earned his fourth NBA title in 2022, with the very same Mark Jackson providing TV commentary.

The day after the Warriors eliminated Boston in six games, the *San Francisco Chronicle*'s Page 1 headline—"Fourever Champs"—honored the franchise's fourth Bay Area–related NBA crown this century, which, truthfully, would have occurred in Oakland, too. It's not the home facility, folks, it's the team.

But that exceptional ride would have been derailed if Lacob had traded Klay Thompson for Kevin Love. Jerry West, then a Warriors senior advisor, intimated he would quit first and blame Lacob for making such an ill-advised deal. Fortunately, the swap didn't occur, but West wound up leaving anyway.

Lacob wanted out of Oakland despite nightly sellouts and the NBA's best basketball atmosphere. Despite his snubbing of Oakland, the Warriors' championship parades in Oaktown remain the best on the planet, with an estimated 1 million in attendance, spreading from downtown to around Lake Merritt.

But the snobbish Lacob preferred hobnobbing with San Francisco's elite and the mega moneymen in Silicon Valley. Thus the 18,064-seat Chase Center was built in San Francisco for $1.4 billion; Lacob's and Guber's money for sure, though partially funded by taxpayers and season ticket holders.

Lacob then revealed a dastardly heart in concert with incredibly bad taste. In the Warriors' 47 years in Oakland, not once did the name "Oakland" appear on the players' jerseys, even though Oakland made the team's various owners into multimillionaires with consistent capacity crowds—who watched mostly inferior basketball. But as soon as the franchise left Oakland, "Oakland" appeared on the team's jerseys in San Francisco. How vicious was that? Thanks, Joe.

Lacob's "light years ahead" comment backfired on him right away as the Warriors descended from the league's penthouse suite into the NBA basement. Durant departed the franchise after a dust-up with teammate Draymond Green. Then injuries to key players and poor roster decisions led to the team's collapse. General manager Bob Myers, so instrumental in the team's rise, slumped once the franchise hit San Francisco. But, just as quickly, he rebuilt the team into a force again, winning an NBA championship in 2022. Even so, the Warriors dynasty, Oakland-built, is a thing of the past.

San Francisco still must prove that it's a quality NBA city after failing once earlier, forcing the Warriors to head over to Oakland. Will San Francisco now support a team with ultra-expensive ticket prices and cutback inducements for ticket purchasers? Fewer than 1,000 parking spaces exist at the Chase Center, and transportation to Warriors games in the inner city is challenging. Such handicaps weren't ever issues in Oakland, with its abundant parking and easy access. But, beware—if these Warriors start to lose, snobby, corporate San Franciscans will chase them right out of the Chase Center.

Thus, their future is hard to predict, unless Myers can find reasonably younger facsimiles of superstars Stephen Curry and Klay Thompson. But Myers is a most valuable resource, with an unerring eye for talent— even the discarded, such as Andrew Wiggins and the much-traveled Gary Payton II, who helped bring the franchise another NBA championship in 2022.

And although Lacob couldn't wait to ferry his Warriors from Oakland to San Francisco, he publicly stated in June 2022 that he tried to buy the A's and keep them in Oakland—and at the Coliseum site. He first tried to buy the team in 2005, but lost out to John Fisher and Lew Wolff, the latter then selling his share to the Fisher family in 2016. But Fisher appears intractable; his mind-set is Howard Terminal, and he doesn't wish to sell…to anyone.

But a more perfect example of just how underappreciated Oakland feels as a sport town involves those itinerate Raiders. The Warriors have left Oakland once, while the Raiders have bailed on Oakland twice. That is Oakland's reward for dealing with the renegade Davis desperados, padre and hijo.

Nevada put itself into hock in luring the Raiders to leave Oakland. In 2016, Nevada governor Brian Sandoval approved a hotel room rate tax increase to accommodate the $750 million in public funding for a new stadium to house the Raiders. At that price, the Raiders had better be winning, which happened, fortunately, for them in 2021. However, these same vagabonds know only too well how Las Vegas treats its losers.

Al Davis had gravitas when it came to pro football, whereas Mark Davis hasn't any gravitas. He just had Daddy, and a really bad haircut. Mark had some form of education at California State University at Chico. Beyond that, he hasn't shown much aptitude. He owned a T-shirt company together with the late, great Raiders wide receiver Cliff Branch. Mark also had a dubious hand-warmer business that Daddy funded, followed by a Raider Image store that Mark ran ineptly. Making it on his own has been Mark's major problem. Daddy grew so frustrated at one point that he kicked the son out of the house.

Al Davis passed away in 2011, and—voila!—Mark wound up owning the Raiders, with his mother, Carol, holding a 47 percent share. But, Mark, clearly, was running the show, even though his face hadn't ever appeared beforehand on the team's masthead. Daddy, you see, viewed him as a boob. And now here is Sonny, miraculously, as an NFL owner. There is nothing quite like a human success story, except that Mark has already created disarray throughout the organization.

Nonetheless, Mark is worth $500 million, although none of it was his own making. But if the father could run out on Oakland, the son could, too. Mark looked at San Antonio, he looked again at Los Angeles, and, secretly, he started talking to Las Vegas. Then in February 2015, he announced that the Raiders would purchase a shared stadium in Carson, California, with the then San Diego Chargers. Huh! Hah! Flailing leads to failing, i.e., Mark's business card.

Instead of San Antonio or Carson, Sonny finally rolled the dice with Las Vegas, the craps capital of the country. "We can turn the Silver State into the Silver and Black state," he announced, cornily. He first teamed with billionaire Sheldon Adelson, who discovered quickly that dealing with incompetent Sonny wasn't the most suitable partnership, and so he bailed. Sonny, nonplussed, increased his contribution from $500 million to $1.5 billion in order to build Allegiant Stadium in Las Vegas when $500 million easily could have financed a new stadium in Oakland.

NFL owners, who screwed Oakland earlier when the Raiders moved to Los Angeles, then screwed Oakland again, this time by a one-sided 33–1 vote, in allowing the team to head to Las Vegas. New England Patriots owner Robert Kraft said, soullessly, of that second move, "I think it would be good for the NFL." NFL owners turned into multi-millionaire rats being led by a pigskin Pied Piper, Mark Davis, into a sea of hypocrisy.

These same vicious NFL owners couldn't wait to stick it to Oakland again by awarding Super Bowl LVIII to Las Vegas to conclude the 2023 season. "It's a big day for the Raiders," Sonny projected." It's a big day for Las Vegas." But it was a bad, bad day for Oakland, which hasn't ever hosted a Super Bowl.

"I had a feeling you would ask me about the Raiders tearing the heart out of this Oakland girl," said Schaaf.

Schaaf's loyalty to the Raiders is understandable because the Raiders started in Oakland, unlike the A's and Warriors. But she wasn't chosen by voters to build playpens for sports owners. She needed to run a city that was struggling financially pre-pandemic. Those struggles increased with protests and lootings in downtown Oakland, with limited police presence.

Meanwhile, Mark Davis gathered Raiders players around him in their new stadium on August 21, 2020. "Welcome to the Death Star," he spoke, excitedly, into a microphone, "where our opponents' dreams come to die." Nobody understood what this desert dunce was talking about, but few ever do with Sonny.

His ensuing words were captured on three enormous video boards: "My father always said that the greatness of the Raiders is in its future. Well, today, that future really starts. This magnificent stadium was built on the backs of thousands of players, coaches, administrators, and fans, who for the past 60 years have proudly worn the Silver and Black. This is our field of dreams. This is our house."

His father spoke, identically, about the future greatness of the Raiders after moving the franchise to Los Angeles in 1982, winning then wilting. So what future is that again, Sonny?

"This stadium's personality will be defined by you," the younger Davis blathered on as Raiders players gathered for the first time on their Las Vegas turf. "You are the Raiders. There'll be many personal accomplishments out here on this field. Someone on the field today will make the first tackle. Somebody will score the first touchdown. And somebody will make the first interception. But, most importantly, it's what we do as a team."

He could have added that someone would be the first Raider to jump offside, or to be called for holding, for the Raiders are consistently one of the most penalized teams in the NFL year in and year out. But only positives were accentuated that day.

The Raiders players cheered when they initially stepped inside Allegiant Stadium in 2020, yet they would hear no home crowd cheers that same NFL season as the stadium was empty from September through December because of the pandemic.

"I haven't seen a stadium that looks like this ever," Jalen Richard said upon his first visit. "It's blacked out. It looks like a nice limousine or a blacked-out H2 Hummer. It just looks nice and big and aggressive. And then you get inside and it's just beautiful. I definitely won't take any of this for granted."

Sonny then grabbed the microphone again with an all-too-familiar closing message. "I'll leave you with three words: just win, baby," he said. "Welcome home." That's five words, though Sonny wasn't ever a mathematics whiz.

Welcome home? Which home—Oakland, Los Angeles, or Las Vegas? With a Davis in charge, options remain open. Always. But in the case of poor Libby Schaaf, there's a problem awaiting her in front of the home fires. "My son doesn't want me to come to his basketball games," the mayor admitted, "because I might embarrass him with his teammates."

So, what happens inside her house if the A's also leave?

For that move to happen, get ready, Las Vegas. Who will pay the approximately $1.4 billion dollars for a convertible, domed, air-conditioned ballpark needed to fend off the stifling desert heat, thus preventing sun stroke in the A's new home? Team owner John Fisher has been adamant in stating that any new ballpark will be 100 percent privately financed, guarding his own personal fortune. But what person or entity will step forward in southern Nevada, willing to pay the building and infrastructure costs for a new ballpark? Speak up, Silver State.

Nevada Governor Steve Sisolak opposes any special session called to approve hotel taxes for the ballpark project. "I don't know if they know what they're looking for," he said of the A's. "I explained to them that I didn't want to be a stalking horse." Or a talking Mr. Ed, neighing for A's ownership.

The A's are seeking the first ballpark built for them since Shibe Park in Philadelphia in 1909. But built where—in Oakland or Las Vegas? The A's and Los Angeles Angels play in Major League Baseball's oldest stadiums, both built in 1966, if you exclude Wrigley Field, Fenway Park, and Dodger Stadium. Of those five facilities, the Oakland Coliseum least resembles a traditional ballpark. The Oakland A's reflect the cinematic version of *Major League*, in which the franchise's owner purposely devalued the team to try and move it elsewhere. However, in reality, the Oakland A's could be the next Montreal Expos, having vacated a big-league city with no second MLB life guaranteed in either place.

But if the A's do settle on Las Vegas, John Fisher should prepare himself for a huge lawsuit from the City of Oakland.

That would be Oaktown's way of waving goodbye.

Chapter 9

Greatest Fans Anywhere...and the Most Abused

I actually thought [Warriors] fans were better in Oakland—that's one of the most fun places I ever played. These San Francisco fans are annoying, to be honest with you...

—Charles Barkley,
NBA great and commentator, in June 2022

Oakland has the most loyal sports fans in the universe and easily the most dumped upon. They sold out two athletic facilities despite having teams that failed to sniff the postseason in decades. These fans pushed loyalty to a new level, wearing costumes to create a unique game-time atmosphere and then chastising opponents in support of their hometown franchises—which then showed their gratitude by moving.

These loyalists also padded the wealth of Oakland sports owners, who chortled at such generosity before relocating with no sign of remorse. This morality play became the heart versus the heartless—the great divide between Oakland fans and Oakland sports owners, bringing unparalleled spectator torture.

Abused Oakland fans have lived through the unique experience of one franchise moving away twice and a second franchise departing after five consecutive sold-out championship series appearances. But the abandoned aren't silent martyrs. They share deep feelings of hurt and anger, including those deeply devoted Raiders Boosters who frequent Ricky's Sports Theatre & Grill, abutting Oakland in San Leandro.

Ricky's, once rated the No. 2 Sports Bar in America behind the "Cheers" pub in Boston, has fallen off its pedestal since the Raiders escaped a second time. Ricky's reliables spoke out in March 2020, prior to the Raiders debut in Las Vegas:

> **Rob Rivera:** Black Hole Rob is my handle because I founded the Black Hole back in 1995. You've got all these whipped dogs—that's what I call us, fans who just want Oakland's teams to stay. We love them; we just want them to love us back. Now we're whipped, underfed, and undernourished, a beaten-down old dog. Nobody cares about us; everything is slanted toward San Francisco, not Oakland. We feel like the stepchild, the ugly kid, the poor vagrant, with our soul ripped out.
>
> I've been in Hayward (just south of Oakland) my whole life. I became a Raider fan at 10, and that just got me locked and loaded. And their Super Bowls locked me in forever. When they left us the first time, I was crying because it was painful. Other people said they weren't going to be supported in Los Angeles. I said I'm going to support them; I just had this blind loyalty. And when I heard they were coming back, some buddies of mine in Hayward, we came up with this idea of the Black Hole, kind of like Cleveland's Dawg Pound. We had these meetings, we camped out at the Oakland Coliseum the night before games, we had these giant tailgates—it just consumed us. The love and the passion, it didn't matter even if the Raiders were losing, we weren't going to leave *our* team.
>
> We just kept multiplying in numbers. You're 10 years into their coming back to Oakland, and then it's 15, 20 years, and you start hearing the rumors, the rumblings. You start to see the dysfunction in the City of Oakland and Alameda County, making decisions having to do with the land that is the Coliseum Complex. You see the writing on the wall all

over again, but you still don't want to believe it. Then you see that the Raiders don't give a heck about us. They're looking here and there, dangling ideas, so are they truly authentic when they say they want to sit down and work things out in Oakland? Or is it all a smoke screen? Then you start to realize: "Our time is limited here."

Then everything gets super emotional. The volume on your emotions gets super turned up. You have all these relationships from going to games, and you start seeing the tears. You hug a little longer, and you talk about memories. Then Ronnie Lott and Fortress Investments come up with a viable option for the Raiders staying. They've got the finances and the vision, giving us some hope. Then you see it isn't going to happen, and that it's going to be Las Vegas. Then you see fans mobilizing with Save Oakland Sports, and you finally realize that you've been taken advantage of—again. The team, itself, doesn't give a rat's ass about you. Some of these [NFL] owners have to see this by now, but then the vote came down and only Tampa Bay supported Oakland. All the other owners cared about was the Raiders getting their fancy palace in Las Vegas. Just a ton of hypocrisy among the owners, ripping the soul out of Oakland—again.

And then there's the media. You turn on the TV or the radio, and it's always the same thing in terms of coverage: 49ers before Raiders, Giants before A's. Once in a while, they'll toss us a bone, but then they'll talk about the class of San Francisco fans. After awhile, it just beats you down. Oakland fans are loyal to a fault. We love our teams, we love our sports, and we had the ability to keep three teams, and now we've lost two of them. I have zero love for Oakland's owners. When the new owners bought the Warriors, I knew from the beginning they were going back to San Francisco. As soon as they were halfway across [the Bay Bridge], I threw away all my Warrior stuff. I also knew that they would put 'San Francisco' on their jerseys, when they never had 'Oakland' on when they played here. We got 'The Town' instead. Were they that embarrassed to be in Oakland? What a slap in the face.

We've been smiled at so many times in Oakland, and then here come the knives. There's [team president Dave] Kaval with the A's. Yes, he's doing some nice things to make the experience better at the Coliseum, dressing it up a little bit. But is that a true effort to stay here, or a showcase for someplace else? Are the politicians going to drop the ball again, and the A's move to Las Vegas, too? You may laugh, but if they left, we don't have anything else. And what happens to that Coliseum Complex site—does it grow weeds and become dilapidated? Maybe that's what Oakland mayor Libby Schaaf wants, to get all of that out of there, and then let's go high tech. What is the true agenda, and why are Oakland's fans lied to so much? Nobody is telling the truth, and it gets frustrating. Even so, I will go to games in Las Vegas, just like I did in Los Angeles, though the Raiders' home-field advantage won't be the same as it was in Oakland.

But it's all because of six guys in Hayward who came up with something special—the Black Hole, which grew and grew until we had chapters all over the world—Australia, Germany, Mexico, etc. Black Hole fans have fun, we really enjoy it, and we're not ready to let that go, to take our ball and go home. We still want this ride to continue, and so we will watch the Raiders in Las Vegas. Are we happy about it? No. Can we afford the season tickets? For the most part, no we can't. I work for myself at 54, running the Black Hole 24–7. I was in sales for almost 30 years before committing myself to growing this fan organization. I get by financially, but with a wife and two teenage daughters, I may have to get another sales job.

"How is the Black Hole handling the Raiders leaving a second time? Those last two games in Oakland, you should have seen the tears. Everybody was crying and hugging; it was a river of tears. I couldn't even hold back my tears. It really hurt, because I may never see those people again. Even talking about it now, I feel like I want to cry. There definitely are mis-characterizations about the Black Hole, like we're just located in the end zone. We've taken over the whole stadium; one big giant Black Hole. Everybody is in black—standing, cheering, sucking the other team in; that was the Black Hole's goal. We even have members in club seats and luxury boxes. We all wear black, but we don't all dress up in costumes like your Gorilla Rilla, your Violator, your Senor. It's a fanatical crowd, almost like a soccer vibe.

But you see these big fans with goatees, and you see trouble. We have baseball player Alex Rodriguez's attorney, plus district attorneys with painted faces, sitting in end zones. We also have a finance manager from an NBA team, Chevron executives, and people high up in the Air Force. The Black Hole is a Who's Who of people who mirror society. We look harsher than we really are, and we may not be for everyone, but we're a family, a true family.

Jim Zelinski: I'm the co-founder of Save Oakland Sports with four other people: Chris Dobbins, Joe Audelo, Jorge Leon, and Garth Kimball. We started in 2012, meeting at Ricky's with the idea of retaining all three of our teams. So when Mark Davis decided to move the Raiders to Las Vegas, I called him up directly. He had just told a radio audience that he wanted to help Oakland fans get through this change. So I said, "You know, Mark, if you really want to help us, why don't you help us get another team? It's a great market that deserves an NFL franchise." He just listened, then he said, "It's not about the fans. We have the best fans in the world. But we can't get a new stadium built here."

Of course, I disagreed, knowing that in this area, one of the richest regions in the world, we couldn't get investors? Amy Trask, the former Raiders chief executive, told me that the Coliseum site is the best in the country from a transportation standpoint. I told Mark, "You'll have excitement in Las

Vegas the first couple of years, but you're going to learn what your father learned, that the fan base in Oakland and the East Bay is irreplaceable. You'll never have the same mystique and atmosphere, no matter how hard you try. You'll be playing in a hermetically sealed dome. You won't be able to smell the grass or the hot dogs." He just listened.

Right now, the NFL needs atmosphere at its games, not less of it like in Las Vegas. Football needs to be played in the cold, not under a dome. And where else but Oakland can you go into a parking lot for tailgating, and every socioeconomic level is represented? You can hear a famous rock band, Metallica, playing. I never wore face paint or got a tattoo, but I'm as diehard a Raider fan as anybody. My connection to sports goes back to the 1960s. I went to California Golden Seals hockey games in Oakland with my father, a big hockey fan from Lynn, Massachusetts. I saw the last American Football League championship game ever played, Kansas City winning the AFL title in Oakland in 1969. So I've been a loyal fan.

But I believe loyalty goes both ways. Here was a team, the Raiders, who moved to Los Angeles even though Oakland fans showed unbelievable loyalty. When they moved back, I was so excited that I bought two season tickets. Eight years later, they moved again. Oakland and its fans are like Rodney Dangerfield; they just don't get any respect. What other community would welcome back a team that had abandoned them, and then renovate the stadium? And then to be abandoned again is a miscarriage of justice. For me, it goes beyond football.

I saw the A's first game in Oakland in 1968. I'm just as big an A's fan as a Warrior fan. The weather, the fans, the location, the demographics—Oakland is right there with the best location in baseball. And A's fans can be as passionate as Raider fans. As for the Warriors, I knew from the beginning they were leaving Oakland. Sometimes, leagues underestimate the moving of franchises. Some of those moves are unsuccessful. But what bothered me about the Warriors is that they didn't put

'Oakland' on their jerseys one time when they played here. And then they put 'San Francisco' on both their arena floor and team jerseys right away, plus 'Oakland' on their home jerseys occasionally. All of this is a slap in Oakland's face.

Oakland's fans are the most disrespected, unappreciated fans in the history of professional sports, anywhere in the world. Our Save Oakland Sports group is committed to keeping the A's here, no matter where they play—even on a barge floating down the estuary. The A's are just as much a civic treasure for the East Bay as the other two teams. Sometimes, that gets lost. I send out information constantly to keep people informed about Oakland sports, but I don't feel I'm the lonely voice in the wilderness. I just keep people abreast of situations. With two teams leaving Oakland, a lot of people lost jobs at the stadium and arena. That's important, too.

I'm a former newspaper reporter and longtime public relations consultant, so to me information is essential. I'm 61 now, and it's tougher to keep that information flowing because I have medical issues. I was diagnosed with high-grade bladder cancer in February 2012, a week after we started Save Oakland Sports. I had the bladder removed in 2017, but then I had a lesion and they discovered three more [cancerous] spots. Some of the things I've gone through are horrible, but I feel Save Oakland Sports is an important cause that goes beyond me. I'm pretty resilient, and I'm doing better than a year ago. I'm glad to be alive. I have a developmentally and physically disabled daughter with special needs. I read her stories at night. I also have a son and a wife, and I want to be around the three of them. So I'm trying to survive.

I just hope one day that I'll be sitting in a new A's stadium, wherever that is. Oakland has invested heavily in its teams economically, and I don't think it was right for the Warriors and Raiders to move. People have said to me, "You know, Jim, if you were owner of the Raiders, and someone dangled $750 million in front of you in free money, you'd do the same thing." I can say this without reservation: I absolutely would not. These teams in Oakland became rich and famous. If Mark Davis had stayed instead of doing what his father did in leaving, I would have erected a statue to him.

Wayne Deboe: I joined the Oakland Raiders Boosters Club in 1997 and became the club's president in 1998. I've seen a lot of good days and a lot of bad days, but it's going to be a challenge again to keep the club going now that the Raiders moved to Las Vegas. I put that to the club members at Ricky's, and they do want to keep going. Even though the Raiders also left Los Angeles, their booster club still is going, calling themselves the Original Los Angeles Raiders Boosters Club. We should be called the Original Oakland Raiders Boosters Club because we've been around since 1967. The Raiders used to send players to our meetings, which meant standing room only, 50 to 60 people. Now we might get 20 to 25 people to a meeting, but it's still a loyal fan base. Raiders fans are different than other [NFL] fans. You saw it at their tailgating parties, and Ricky's Sports Lounge the night before games. People came from all over the country, even from England, to party at Ricky's. When the Raiders played their last game for good at the Oakland Coliseum [in 2019], people came to our tailgates even without tickets. They just wanted to be there—a big, loyal fan base.

People in our club dressed up in costumes at games, just like people in the Black Hole. Wearing costumes is part of the Raider tradition. I remember this guy who used to walk though the Oakland Coliseum on stilts. True Raider fans, regardless of where the team plays, are still loyal to the team. They may not root as hard with the team in Las Vegas, and may not feel as bad if they lose, but you're still a Raider fan. A Raider fan would never be a 49er fan or Charger fan. Your loyalty always will be to the Raiders, just like my loyalty to the Original Oakland Raiders Boosters Club. I can give the club more time now because I'm 73 and retired twice—from AT&T after 34 years, and from a nonprofit after 11 years.

I'm disappointed, not angry, that the Raiders moved again. Like everything else, there's a lot of politics involved. But the efforts to stay in Oakland by the Raiders were never there. Mark [Davis] wanted to be himself. Even though his father ran the team for years, when the son's time came around, he had another agenda. Oakland couldn't offer the same money that Las Vegas offered anyway. If the Raiders went to the taxpayers and asked for $750 million, somebody would have hung. I didn't go to any games in Los Angeles, but I was told those fans became unruly, and visiting fans there felt unsafe. I don't remember that happening in Oakland.

Las Vegas will be different, too. There will be as many visiting team fans as Raider fans because of people wanting to go to Las Vegas. I'm sure there will be Raider fans from Los Angeles and Oakland who will be going. I know 10 people from my club bought season tickets. I plan to be our booster club's president, even if the Raiders don't move back again. They won't if it costs money. Fans shouldn't pay to build a facility; put that on the owners. But I can't say I see any difference between Al Davis and Mark Davis. Al loved Las Vegas, too.

Kenny Mellor: I was born and raised in Oakland. I remember the Raiders coming to Frank Youell Field, and Charlie Finley bringing the A's to Oakland, with Rick Monday as their big star. So I was very impressed with both teams, and my football coach at Skyline High School in Oakland was Clem Daniels, the Raiders running back. I also remember when the Oakland Alameda County Coliseum complex was built. I also liked the Warriors, who moved from San Francisco to Oakland.

After I got married, I bought season tickets to Raider games, where everyone went under the Coliseum bleachers at halftime and smoked dope. It was a little crazy back then, a blue-collar atmosphere that people loved, so it was great. Gene Tenace, who played for the A's, became a neighbor. I worked in high voltage electric construction, so I did some wiring at Gene's house. I played golf with him, and he helped me coach Little League. But when Finley didn't pay pitcher Catfish Hunter what he was worth, and he went to the New York Yankees, the A's dynasty fell apart. That's when I really got involved with the Raiders. Quarterback Kenny Stabler married Miss Alabama, and they moved within four blocks of my home in San Ramon. So I got to meet Stabler and Raider defensive lineman Art Thoms, who also lived nearby. Then Al Davis decided to move the team to Los Angeles. That's when I got season tickets to the A's, a package for half their games.

The Coliseum once was a nice venue to watch games. You could see the Oakland hills. When John Madden's wife bought a bar in Dublin, you'd go in and there was John Matuszak and other Raiders. When Mount Davis was built after the Raiders returned, I didn't want to go back. Eventually, I bought four seats in the middle of the Black Hole, which had a mystique about it that was electric. Everybody stood up the whole game, cussing out opponents and the officials—me, too; I was a diehard fan.

Then in 2012, Joe Audelo approached me about joining this new group called Save Oakland Sports. If somebody didn't do something, Oakland could lose all its teams. Well, I'm still a board member of Save Oakland Sports and also its treasurer. We'd have 80 to 100 people at every meeting at Ricky's, plus we did fundraisers and passed out literature. When Al Davis died, his son, Mark Davis, took over the Raiders, and he didn't want anything to do with us. I met Roger Goodell, the NFL commissioner, at an event, and I invited him to join us in the Black Hole. And here he came with these bodyguards, and he stayed 15, 20 minutes. People couldn't believe it really was the commissioner. I had bad knees, so I've moved to the west side of the Coliseum, and I kept those four seats until the team moved to Las Vegas.

The Warriors, with the panache of San Francisco, were leaving Oakland no matter what. We supported them for 14 years without a winning team, and then when they got a winning team, they moved. It's a nightmare now trying to get to one of their games, I'm told, but with either the Warriors or Raiders, there was a fan base in Oakland they can't replicate elsewhere.

It's all about money, I realize, but I'm bitter about the Raiders leaving. Ronnie Lott had a group that wanted to buy the Raiders, but [NFL] owners wouldn't even listen to him. Their mind already was made up to go to Las Vegas. And here's what they're going to get: half the fans there will be rooting for the Raiders, and the other half will be coming from out of town. The Raiders will never have in Las Vegas what they had in Oakland. Will I watch them in Las Vegas? Well, I'm a gambler, and I already go there six times a year. I didn't see them play in Los Angeles, but I might go to a game or two in Las Vegas.

You've got to admire the A's for wanting to stay here, but that new waterfront location they're looking at, Howard Terminal, there's no parking, no BART, and no freeway. I'm 73, and I'm not going to walk 10 blocks after a night game to the 12th Street BART station. But they don't want guys in my demographic. Here's my prediction: the A's already have a farm team in Las Vegas. I could see the A's, in four or five years, packing their bags and, like the Raiders, moving to Las Vegas. Losing the Raiders, Warriors, and A's, you lose your mystique. And if you take away a world-class team, you also lose your identity, your pride, and respect in the community.

Joe Audelo: I have friends who think I'm crazy, just because I had season tickets for all three Oakland teams simultaneously: the A's, Raiders, and Warriors. These friends wanted to know how I got to be that way. Well, I grew up in California in the Central Valley, in Fresno, and also on the Central Coast in

Lompoc, areas that had no pro sports. I had followed those A's dynasty teams, 1972 to 1974, so after I moved to Oakland, I started going to some of their games.

I really enjoyed them, but I was buying individual tickets in the third deck, sitting in the top rows, wondering, *How do I get seats down there in front?* I decided being a season ticket holder was the way to go. I'd get a better seat and enjoy a closer view. It all started with the A's in the early 1990s, and I've had those season tickets for about 30 years. I had four at one time, but I'm down to two. But I did have eight tickets for their spring training games.

I became interested in the Raiders in the 1980s, when I was attending a company management school in Berkeley. I bought tickets when I could afford them. Then when the Raiders came back from Los Angeles, I saw my opportunity and bought two season tickets. But eventually, I bought eight season club seats and eight season Black Hole seats.

I went to Warriors games occasionally, but my grandson really developed an interest in basketball, so I bought two season tickets to their games. I'm not a Google guy; I didn't hit it rich that way. I'm in construction management, and let me put it this way—I spend more on sports and entertainment than the average guy in my income bracket. There have been years where I've spent in excess of a hundred thousand dollars on three sports. And when the Raiders went to that Super Bowl against Tampa Bay in San Diego, I bought a suite for that game. I'm 62 and pretty much an avid sports fan.

To this day, I have those A's season tickets. The Raiders and Warriors have left Oakland, and I did not keep those tickets. With the Warriors, I only had season tickets for four, five years. With the Raiders, I had them from the time they came back to Oakland from Los Angeles to the time they left for Las Vegas. Different people have hobbies they spend extraordinary amounts of money on, like hunting. Attending sports events was my hobby. I'm trying to get the most out of life where I live, and I've lived in Oakland quite a while. And I've backed the home team there at Ricky's, too, but I've never worn costumes or had my face painted. I did have a friend, a banker, who came into town in a business suit to go to a Raider game with me. He asked if I had a room where he could change. When he came out, he had face paint and the craziest costume you ever saw.

I've supported those three teams even in years where they didn't win. Now two of the teams have left Oakland, and I feel a little bit abandoned. It's like I've been left behind, but I have no regrets about my investments. I was lucky to be in a city that had three major league sports. How many cities can say that? The one thing I'm going to miss with the departures of the Raiders and Warriors are the tailgates, which won't be the case with their new facilities. There aren't adjacent parking lots like in Oakland, where tailgates were as Americana as apple pie.

Tina Ricardo: [Authors' Note: Rickey Ricardo, 75, owner of the popular sports bar in his name in San Leandro, California, that has been frequented for decades by Raiders fans, died in November 2020 from a stroke and complications of Alzheimer's disease. Patrons brought bouquets of flowers to the bar to honor a truly good man and an East Bay institution.]

Ricky's Sports Theatre & Grill is the bar I run with my husband, Ricky. We're closed right now because of the coronavirus pandemic. With no sports being played anywhere at the moment, it makes no sense to stay open. We may open again, or we may not.

But as far as the Raiders and Warriors both leaving us, Oakland has lost its reputation as a major sports city. Its local government is at fault, just like the first time the Raiders left. We got over that, but this time around, we got the rug pulled out from underneath us. That's sad, because when the Raiders play, it's like Disneyland at our sports bar. Ninety-nine percent of the people who come here are from out of state or even out of the country—Australia, England, Japan, everywhere.

The whole thing is really sad. Because of the people who come to Ricky's, including locals, we've watched their families grow up, and now we'll never see them again with the Raiders gone. We got to know the players, the coaches, and even guys trying out for the team. We've stayed in touch with them for a long time. They send us Christmas cards.

Ricky's now is a sports bar without sports, and that pretty much shut us down. With the Raiders leaving again, it's like a girlfriend leaving. And when she comes back, it's like fool me once, but not twice. We thought the Raiders might get a stadium extension, but that's over. Former Raiders would come back to Ricky's, like Rod Martin, Jeff Barnes, Kenny Stabler, Derrick Ramsey, and Phil Villapiano. Our patrons would go out of their minds. The players would stay all weekend, and they were just as happy to see the fans as the fans were to see the players. Fans got to wear the players' Super Bowl rings and have a drink with them. A fan in the parking lot started screaming, "I met Jim Brown! I met Jim Brown!" We have a lot of good memories.

I've met seven or eight fans who are moving to Las Vegas. The cheapest seat there is $650, and the cheapest club seat is $3,500—for one game! Who can pay that? It's crazy. Jon Gruden has been the Raiders' coach twice. When he came back, he threw a party here and picked up the whole bill. It was an insane atmosphere, and he stayed day and night. He was great.

I don't think teams leaving Oakland had to be done. I don't mean to be political, but I think Mark Davis is trying to keep up with Al Davis, his dad. Without the Raiders here, though, Ricky's will be like a ghost town. People don't want to get hurt again, and they can get games now on their iPhones. They don't need to come to a bar. Ricky used to be on top of our roof, setting up the game on satellite. Those days are gone. Mama said there would be days like this, and I'm now taking care of Ricky, who has dementia. Taking care of this place and my husband, too, it's brutal.

Ricky and I met in 1989, and we got married in 1993. It's been a lot of fun, like watching the Raiders play in London. One thing about Raider fans, they're loyal from their toes to the top of their heads. It's inbred; I've never seen anything like it. The Raiders beat them up by leaving, and the fans stay loyal. The Raiders come back and the fans love them all over again.

Ricky and I don't live together anymore, but we're still together in a way. I'm over here at the sports bar, eight to 10 hours a day. I take care of Ricky, and we take the cat for a walk every day. I'm out there in the bar with the people instead of being buried in the back with the books, though I'm still taking care of the books. If I knew it was going to be like this, I would have jumped off the bridge. I'm kidding, but like I said, it's brutal. You give your heart and soul, and everything in your purse, to keep it going. I could work every day for the next six months and not get caught up. I can't keep up; there are no more hours in the day. Nobody in his or her right mind would do this. The French Foreign Legion would be like a vacation.

It's definitely been quite an experience, but do I open the restaurant again in a panic? People, after this pandemic, may not go out to restaurants like they did before. People going back to the way they were? I don't think it's going to happen.

Chris Dobbins: It's idealistic, but I'll throw it out there: John Adams is my favorite president. He represented King George III and the British at the Boston Massacre, a horrible time in our history with the British firing on these poor defenseless colonists. John Adams defended the British in court, and he won, so he was super vilified. But he had this idealism.

I've been a lawyer for 25 years, and I ask myself, *What would have happened if John Adams had defended Al Davis in court?* Davis is doing what the British did, using his power and influence to get what he wanted. If Davis were president, he'd be King George III, who made a lot of smart decisions, but became irrational as he aged. Davis would have made a lousy president, though he was difficult to defeat in court, which every Ricky's loyalist knows all too well.

I was 10 when the Raiders left for Los Angeles. I didn't watch football for 15 years, but when they came back in 1995, I bought season tickets, which I kept until they left for Las Vegas. I also make it to 50, 60 games a year with the A's. I don't doubt that Las Vegas will go after the A's, too. I'm the type of person who can't sit still, so I'm involved with Save Oakland Sports, a group that also tried to keep the Warriors in Oakland. But when Joe Lacob bought the Warriors, he had his first press conference in San Francisco, so you could see the writing on the wall right then.

Lacob used his own money to build an arena there, but it's still heartbreaking. He screwed over the City of Oakland, so I'm not a fan of his. I've had Warriors season tickets for 10 years. I've been to a few games in San Francisco, which is more corporate, lacking the same exciting, passionate vibe the team had in Oakland. You watch, they'll be the San Francisco Warriors in a couple of years.

I do both criminal and civil law, split 50-50. But in law school, we did study the Raiders moving the first time, to Los Angeles, and how Oakland used eminent domain as part of its defense. That didn't seem like a good argument, and the Raiders left. And now they've moved again, to Las Vegas. I was mad at both departures, but I think they'll be better at controlling the situation in Las Vegas than in Los Angeles.

Mark Davis, Al's son, now runs the team. He fired Amy Trask, who was phenomenal as the Raiders' chief executive, the highest-ranking woman in sports. The Raiders are super paranoid about everything, regardless of which Davis is running the team. But I loved going to games with family and friends. I'd pass out business cards, I got to know the vendors, and so it was a great time. It's been rewarding to see the passion of people in trying to keep these teams. It was a process, but I think we put up a good fight. I'll just say that other factors did us in. Our focus now is the Oakland Athletic League, trying to raise money to help our high school teams. We're viable, and more tangible, and we think we can help those schools. With the A's, we started the Green Stampede after-school tutoring program. Kids who aren't getting their homework done, they come to the Coliseum from 4 to 7 PM, we help them with their homework, and then they get free tickets to watch the A's.

The sports situation in Oakland is disconcerting, especially with the Raiders and Mark Davis kicking us in the gut a second time. He told us that he was working real hard to get things done in Oakland, and then a month later he's going to Las Vegas. You see what a jerk this guy is, disingenuous.

Not that I've always been a fan of other Oakland owner-ships. When Lew Wolff owned the A's, he invited three of us to sit in his box on the same day, in 2010, that Dallas Braden pitched his perfect game. But in the seventh inning, Wolff got up and left. It was one of the greatest days in Oakland A's his-tory, and the team's owner left the ballpark. I didn't see him anywhere in the postgame celebration. That's when Wolff was trying to move the team to Fremont, just before he attempted to move the A's to San Jose. He failed both times. Perfect.

John Fisher, owner of the Gap stores, now owns the A's. I've read that he's the 15th-richest owner in baseball, but he doesn't want to spend money on the team. I believe an owner should try everything to help his team, short of moving vans.

Mark Acasio: I started dressing up in costume after the Raiders returned to Oakland from Los Angeles in 1995. It was in my DNA, because I was born on Halloween. So I dress up for everything, from Santa Claus to the Easter Bunny. With the Raiders, I started out with face paint, but it would get into my eyes or on my blouse. I needed to make a change.

We were playing the Kansas City Chiefs, and I went to a yard sale in Oakley, where I saw the complete set of a gorilla costume. I said, "That's what I want to be." I would be covered in the rain, and I could hang out with the kids. I would fit right in, ape before man. It was like an instant likable character. I was like the king of the jungle, only with beads. I'm a gorilla from my feet to the top of my head. I'm 5'7", and the costume fits me perfectly. I can see through it good, I can breathe through it good, and I can drink through it good.

The only problem is the weather. When John Madden entered the Pro Football Hall of Fame, I went back to Canton, Ohio, for his induction. It was so hot, and I got sick, heaving…it was the worst weather ever for a gorilla, in or out of costume. But I've been Gorilla Rilla in the snow, the rain, and the wind. Chicago was the worst ever. However, I sweat in that costume no matter what the weather is like. I've been to 30 NFL stadiums. When I go to Miami, that heat can be rough, man. But by working in the fields, and in construction over the years, I can adapt to it.

People get to know me because they get to see me. When the Raiders are at home, I start on Friday in full costume with all these functions to go to for the full weekend. Plus I sit in Row 1 in the Black Hole, which is a melting pot of races and religions, and we come together on that day, man. I'm family oriented. I spread the love, and I watch over the Raider Nation.

Gorilla Rilla never talks; he shows action. He's lovable, friendly, and funny. And he's very mobile…he's alive. He'll jump up and down, shake your hand, and take a picture with you. He's not King Kong; he's a furry friend. But he's one busy ape. I go through two gorilla suits a year. I have 10 home games a year, including preseason, and three or four away games, where there are events I get invited to, including a free room and free flight. So it's a bonus being an ape.

Body replacements aren't hard to find, but I have a special designer who makes the gorilla's head. I pack them in carry-on luggage, so I can bring them with me on a plane. When I show up on the road, people say, 'Aren't you the gorilla we see on TV?' I have 40,000 followers on my fan page, and 18,000 more on my Twitter. I've become quite connected to the Raider players.

When my wife and I married, we had a church wedding and then a Raider wedding. Two former Raiders, Jeff Barnes and Rod Martin, attended the latter ceremony along with the Raiderettes. Violator was my best man, and Senor and the Pirate were there. We're very close as costumed guys. I speak to Violator twice a week. I live in Brentwood, and he lives in Los Angeles. I've got pictures of me with Tiger Woods and Bo Jackson. Al Davis has walked by me, but he was kind of quiet, though he wanted the best teams, and the best fan base.

Do fans buy me beer? All the time, and I try not to get inebriated, although it's happened. But I haven't ever been hurt physically. I got two season tickets and a personal seat license for Las Vegas—it ain't cheap—but that's down from the five season tickets I bought in Oakland. It will be a different experience in Las Vegas, like starting over again. I look at it like this: it's a bad divorce for the fans. Some are going to Las Vegas with Dad, and some are staying in Oakland with Mom.

Being Gorilla Rilla doesn't take away from my work. I'm a contractor who does resort-style landscaping. I design it, I install it, and I manage it. So I set my own schedule. In 25 years, I've been to golf tournaments, funerals, and I've also married three people as Gorilla Rilla, for I'm also a minister. Three months ago, I flew up to Washington to marry a couple. Another time, in costume, I walked a woman down the aisle to get married. I got paid both times, including travel.

I've had an awesome life. But let me say this about Raider fans: they are one of a kind. It's like a melting pot, and when you stir it, there's nothing like it, man. If you haven't lived it, you wouldn't understand it. It's all about love.

And if Oakland fan rejection isn't depressing enough, the late Joe Raposo, with unsolicited help from this book's co-author, Andy Dolich, jointly composed a sing-along arrangement titled "There Used to Be a Ballpark". Musical backdrop is optional.

There used to be an Oakland Coliseum, where the field was warm and green,
And Oakland's teams thrived in that complex with a joy we've never seen.
The air was always fragrant from the bratwurst and the beer,
Yes, there were year-round sports with three teams right here.
And there once were world champions, Hall of Famers, and sellout crowds,
Fireworks exploding across the Oakland hills and framed by billowing clouds.
Fans watched in wonder, how they'd laugh, and how they'd cheer,
Yes, there used to be a Coliseum, with a Black Hole right here.
Oaktown's loyal fans used to get so rowdy,
Thus opposing teams never expected a "Howdy."
Spring, summer, fall, and winter brought seasons of cheer,
But now Oakland fans can only shed a collective tear.
Yes, there used to be an Oakland Coliseum right here.

A dedicated dirge, a lamenting of franchises lost.
Stephen Sondheim, eat your heart out.

Chapter 10

Mike Jacob:
Port in a Storm (of Conflict)

*A ballpark on our inner-harbor basin wouldn't leave
room to turn shipping vessels around.*

—Mike Jacob,
Port of Oakland maritime executive

There is one powerful—and integral—presence in the City of
Oakland, and it has absolutely no connection to sports, regardless
of what disloyal, ego-inflated team owners at the Coliseum Complex,
past and present, think of themselves.

The big economic cheese in Oaktown is the Port of Oakland.

Oakland has the sixth-largest container port in the United States, and
its valued port is the economic engine that drives northern California.
Now there is a home-run hitter! The port's world-class facility provides
union jobs, 84,000 in its logistic chain, stretching to China. Now that
is a slam dunk!

Two sports franchises have left Oakland, and a third has loaded a
moving van in preparation. But a disabused Port of Oakland would have
an even greater negative impact on the city. Thus, the port's importance
to Oakland was jeopardized by the A's proposed ballpark jutting into
the Oakland Estuary.

127

The port is Oakland's No. 1 financial resource. But Oakland Mayor Libby Schaaf believes, nonsensically, that a new ballpark at Howard Terminal is more vital to Oakland's economy.

"Simply put, a dormant Howard Terminal is not the future of shipping," she said in May 2022. "But it can be the future of baseball, public parks, desperately needed housing, and recreation—and give Oakland's waterfront back to the public."

Give the waterfront back? Was it ever taken away? And Howard Terminal isn't the future of shipping—seriously, Mayor? At the Port of Oakland, ships are loaded and discharged by workers 24/7, even during a challenging pandemic. The Port faced a shortfall in cargo space, but in fitting a ballpark there—the big squeeze—a supply chain crisis would worsen.

"The Bay Conservation And Development Commission released a preliminary recommendation," Schaaf continued, "that Howard Terminal be removed from port priority use…because it's a parking lot."

A parking lot? Good gracious, Mayor, really? Where is the logic in disfiguring the prominent Port of Oakland, and in making Oakland appear more foolish in its failing, or failed, relationships with its sports tenants? For among the 50 major U.S. ports, Madam Mayor, not one has a sports stadium or arena in the middle of, or abutting, a shipping zone.

Oakland's past mayors have shown good sense in leaving the successful port alone. Schaaf opined that a new ballpark would create good union jobs. That's true, while a ballpark is being built; then it reverts to lower-paying jobs, such as ticket takers and beer vendors, thus having minimal impact.

Jacob is vice president and general counsel at the Pacific Merchants Shipping Association, which represents Port of Oakland clients. The PMSA is headquartered at Jack London Square, where the proposed ballpark would be situated.

"There are a couple of issues we have problems with," Jacob said of the ballpark plan. "We only have so much waterfront acreage to be used for maritime operations, and we guard that acreage to preserve it for the future. We're having a hard time understanding what the A's

Part champion builder, part con man, Al Davis believed, "I can charm anybody. But in order to run an efficient organization, there has to be a dictator. And I'm going to dominate."

When Charles O. Finley moved the A's franchise from Kansas City to Oakland in 1968, Missouri Senator Stuart Symington called Oakland "the luckiest city since Hiroshima." Ouch!

Longtime Oakland Councilman Dick Spees said, "I don't think the people of Oakland truly understood or appreciated their sports teams in terms of what an asset they were to the city."

"We are the most progressive, most liberal city in America," pronounced former Oakland politician Ignacio De La Fuente. "But we are mismanaged…Oakland is its own worst enemy."

"Franklin never had a quota and he never intimated anything about race," onetime Warriors assistant coach Joe Roberts recalled of team owner Mieuli. "He was a fair-minded man."

Dave Stewart was the pitching ace of the A's World Series presence in the late 1980s, with four straight 20-win seasons. "I never took the viewpoint that there was anything wrong with Oakland," said this Oakland native. "Maybe there are imperfections, but we all have imperfections."

Ricky Ricardo owned Ricky's Sports Theatre & Grill, an Oakland Raiders fans watering hole voted the No. 2 sports bar in America behind the "Cheers" saloon in Boston. "I don't think teams leaving Oakland had to be done," said Ricardo's widow, Tina, who closed the bar during the pandemic.

Jim Otto was the iron man's all-time team captain, never missing a Raiders game at center despite repeated medical warnings. "I always played," he reflected proudly. "I didn't want to let anyone down, including myself." His dedication led to a physical overhaul, including an amputated leg.

Rick Barry is among basketball's greatest players, though often overlooked. "People pick players ahead of me whom I thought I was better than," he said, disappointedly. "I won't mention names, but people don't understand the game as well as they think they do."

Bill Patterson was an Oakland playground director who groomed superstars—Bill Russell, Willie Stargell, Frank Robinson, Joe Morgan, Curt Flood and Vada Pinson. "If they rose above where they were when I met them," Patterson said, modestly, "I didn't need anything more."

Paul Cobb was an Oakland kid who became an Oakland newspaper publisher. "Oakland sits at the heart and vortex of information," he noted. "We're the engine of creativity, culturally and athletically."

Tony La Russa has amassed the second-most wins by a big-league manager, trailing only Connie Mack. And La Russa is the first Hall of Famer to return to managing, with the Chicago White Sox, all because he missed "being down on the field where the action happened." He retired again for medical reasons after two seasons.

Dr. Aleksandar Obradovic left Yugoslavia to manage Oakland's first national professional sports champion, soccer's Oakland Clippers in 1967. "In two, three years, we will be good enough to play anywhere in the world," Dr. O. predicted. Alas, in three years, they were no more.

Scout Jethro Mcintyre was a valuable asset to Oakland youth with his free baseball clinics. "I want to see a kid who's a late bloomer," he said. "But you got to beat the bushes to find that kind of kid."

Co-author Andy Dolich's three A's rings from the AL Championships in 1988 and '90 and the 1989 World Series (center). *(Courtesy of the authors)*

A claymation figure of the A's mascot, Stomper, used in the team's advertising campaign in the mid-1980s. *(Courtesy of the authors)*

The Oakland Coliseum and its adjoining Arena became, jointly, the House of Champions, with the A's, Raiders and Warriors all achieving royalty. Now this sports Complex feels like a stripped kingdom.

Co-author Andy Dolich's World Series trophy from the A's 1989 victory over the San Francisco Giants. *(Courtesy of the authors)*

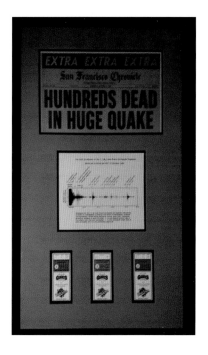

The 1989 baseball season concluded with the earthquake-interrupted World Series between the San Francisco Giants and Oakland A's, the only October Classic meeting between the two Bay Area franchises, ending in an A's sweep. *(Courtesy of the authors)*

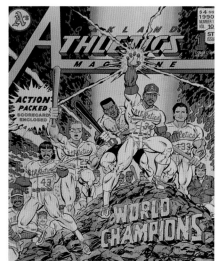

The A's Bash Brothers of the 1980s became so popular that they graced the cover of a game magazine sold at the Coliseum in the 1990 season. *(Courtesy of the authors)*

John Madden enjoyed a singular iconic sports career as Raiders coach, famed broadcaster, and mega-successful video game entrepreneur. Here he receives a gift in the 1970s from Oakland Raiders Booster Club president Al Kieselbach.

and the City of Oakland are arguing, that [the waterfront] is a vacant parking lot. That's just fundamentally untrue.

"Before the pandemic, if you looked at what the waterfront was used for, it was a staging area for shipping cargo, and for loading and unloading trucks. The last 15 years, there has been pressure on us to reduce our impact on our neighbors in West Oakland, because of environmental issues. So we've been consolidating trucking operations at the Port, and one of the places we've been able to do that is at the Howard Terminal.

"Pre-pandemic, we were seeing 325,000 truckloads a year, 1,200 for a working day, and those aren't insignificant numbers. Post-pandemic, that activity has increased, and it is a very busy yard right now."

The pandemic wasn't over when Jacob made that comment, but it's good that the port is, financially, above water. However, he's right that a new baseball facility would cut into the Port of Oakland's functioning capability—drastically.

"It's unfortunate," he commented. "One of the things we wanted to see which hasn't happened yet, even though it has been on the A's radar screen for four years, was how to address the impact a ballpark would have on maritime operations. The A's don't believe that impact exists, that our concerns are remote and speculative. That's why we have such opposition to the ballpark project, because there would be no positives for our operations, and a whole lot of risks that haven't been mitigated. But the A's and the City have paid us lip service."

Jacob stressed that this conflict goes beyond the A's and the Port of Oakland, to where it impacts what the City of Oakland "wants its economic base to be. Oakland is an industrial, blue-collar town, not San Francisco lite. That's not what Oakland was built on (strategically), and how it has evolved, with the port you see today."

The port, he noted, isn't a tax burden on Oakland residents because it's a priority public agency, meaning it operates off port revenue. Its infrastructure also has been developed without state and federal support, backed instead by revenue bonds emanating from terminal operators and customers.

"The model we've created," Jacob said, "has been very successful, making our investments profitable, and then re-investing those profits into further expansion, technology, and efficiency improvements. That's a cycle we need to continue, which means we have to re-invest capital to show that our operation is profitable. For that to happen, we must grow. And we cannot grow if we are constrained from our efficiency."

Thus, removing, or invading, Port of Oakland property would be "a real step backward for us," he emphasized. "It's an open question: Where do those misplaced trucks go? What type of congestion does [a new ballpark] cause? Do we lose business, and where do we grow?

"We don't want to analyze these costs, because the A's are coming into *our* neighborhood. We've asked the A's and the city to make us whole, and they've refused to do it."

Then comes the tightness question, for the A's and the City haven't figured out how to turn ships around, creating a serious snag in cargo transportation. These aren't toy ships in a bathtub, Mayor, so why "sink" an industry?

Jacob also mentioned that traffic, noise, and air quality, all of which a new ballpark creates, haven't been thought through. "And if it hasn't been analyzed, then you don't know what the impact is," he emphasized. "And they've refused to analyze it."

This follows a zany pattern, he added, since the A's and the mayor have discounted contrary opinion in their haste to construct, or jam, a ballpark into a crowded space that lacks parking, rapid transit access, a railway system, or an adjacent freeway—four plusses available at the Coliseum Complex.

What the A's and the City of Oakland have provided as answers to the Howard Terminal negatives are "in no way satisfactory," Jacob noted. "Our shipping vessels won't be able to transit, plus there will be a problem for recreational boaters. The project the A's envision is a re-creation of McCovey Cove [the waterfront ballpark site of the San Francisco Giants]. But the difference is that McCovey Cove is a cove, while the Port of Oakland is an active navigational channel. The A's and the City said they plan to have Oakland police monitor that area.

We don't think that's an adequate solution to the problem, for that area has to be monitored 24/7."

Howard Terminal is "just a tough location if you're trying to beat what the Coliseum already has to offer," Jacob added. "People seem to have their heads in the sand, because they don't want to answer the tough questions."

Did Oakland's termed-out mayor, like an ostrich, have her head in Oakland Estuary sand, unable to see reality? A's president Dave Kaval analyzed in May 2022: "We put so much into Oakland; we haven't given up. But we have to run the table. We can't afford any losses." Run the table? He's talking like a Las Vegan, perhaps already counting on becoming a Nevadan.

The A's may be using Howard Terminal as a smokescreen, albeit a costly one for the city, in enabling their sneaky move out of state. The rub: A's billionaire owner John Fisher could pick up that Oakland ballpark bill easily, even leaving a generous tip behind.

Jacob was asked in the spring of 2022 if he believed Howard Terminal would materialize as a ballpark site—or just end up as an architect's blueprint in some office wastebasket.

"The ballpark is not going to look like the way it's proposed," he noted. "The biggest issues are the new residences, hotels, parks, and office space that are being proposed, which is going to take re-zoning of the area. The long-term effect we're looking at regarding the project isn't the stadium. It's what happens when you move people into an industrial complex area. Over time, those areas become constrained, which then brings quality-of-life issues. That's why there is re-zoning. The stadium you can live with, but putting 3,500 residents on your doorstep, and millions of visitors coming to see you every year, that's something the A's and the City haven't addressed."

Jacob assessed not only ballpark fans, but those partaking in the entire Howard Terminal business concept. Nonetheless, he hammered against the sagacity of that waterfront concept.

"The odds are against the new ballpark being built, honestly," he said. "It's an audacious project, because it's hard to get waterfront projects approved and through the system, even when they are conventional. There are environmental issues, plus maritime projects take years to get approval. Also, it will be difficult to build housing on that site because of regulatory changes and legal approval."

Then he hammered harder: "There are other physical constraints at that site, a PG&E sub-station and 3,000 trucks going in there every year. If you are going to pick a site for a new ballpark, Howard Terminal is a tough little corner of the world."

A tough little corner in which to build a massive project doesn't make much sense, not when you're trying to reroute shipping traffic or to make the Port of Oakland, Oakland's greatest financial asset, genuflect to a baseball franchise that has moved across the country, willy-nilly, in its existence—Philadelphia to Kansas City to Oakland…to Las Vegas?

"I can't put a percentage on whether the new ballpark will be built," Jacob concluded, "but it will have to look a lot different. And if it does look different, then why have they been messing around all this time? Maybe it's because this really isn't about the best place for a ballpark, which the Coliseum is, but instead maximizing property for profit."

Meanwhile, ships could be stuck in Oakland waters until this navigational matter is solved. Turnabout isn't always fair play.

Chapter 11

John Beam:
Harbinger of Hope

> *Coaching is around the clock, it is around the year,*
> *it is...hope.*
>
> —John Beam,
> revered Oakland youth football coach

In the wide, wide spectrum of sports, there is one area that's nearly invisible: the junior colleges, that netherworld hidden between high schools and four-year universities.

A prime example of a junior college's unseeable existence is Laney College of Oakland. In the fall of 2018, Laney won the state JC football championship. One Bay Area newspaper mentioned that achievement in a single paragraph the next day, while another Bay Area daily failed to mention it at all.

That slight wouldn't have occurred if a local high school were playing in a state title game. Or, on a larger scale, if a local four-year school was participating in a bowl game.

And that's a shame because junior colleges often are the last bastion of hope in keeping athletic careers alive, sometimes against overbearing odds. Junior colleges, in truth, rescue as much as they recruit, while educating those who endure.

John Beam is living proof of this ongoing, unnoticed drama.

133

Beam is the football coach and athletic director at Laney College, having been employed at its downtown Oakland campus for 18 years through 2022. Nobody understands that environment, and its inherent problems, better than Beam, who previously coached for 22 years at Skyline High School in Oakland's hills, a combined 40-year commitment in influencing the mind and the heart.

"In suburbia," Beam compared, "there is much more parental involvement, whether it's good or bad. In Oakland, parental involvement isn't always the case, but that's good in one sense, because I have more of an involvement in shaping a kid, and in giving values to those I work with.

"Another thing that I find remarkable in Oakland is the competition. Take De La Salle High School [in Concord]. Nobody wants to be in a football league with De La Salle. But at Skyline High School, I can't remember one time when a fellow Oakland Athletic League coach didn't want to play us. Even if we beat someone 50–0, they couldn't wait to play us the next time, because of the scrappiness you find in Oakland kids. They just have this toughness, to where they won't back down from anyone at any time."

Beam's Laney teams demonstrate that same toughness. His job is "to show them the values of teamwork. Once they believe you're in it with them, then you have loyalty, and it's nonstop."

He is consistently successful in taking rosters with diverse personalities and a myriad of off-field obstacles and getting them all on the same page. This takes around-the-clock coaching and around-the-calendar monitoring, which can be burdensome on some coaches, often leading to burnout.

"That's what I wanted to do anyway," said a somehow unburned Beam. "Coaching is a total commitment, but it is your family, right? That's OK. You want to become part of the fabric of their lives, and they become part of the fabric of your life."

Thus, it works both ways, yet obstacles are more challenging at the junior college level. Beam coaches players who are parents. He coaches players who must work to make ends meet. He coaches players who live outside the area and who have travel difficulties. He coaches players abused by parents. Adding to their hardships, these same young people must stay eligible to play for the Laney College Eagles. By encouraging his players to succeed on the football field and in the classroom, Beam's players regard him as a paternal figure.

"But I'm not trying to replace anyone's dad," he insisted. "I talk to my players about people who are in gangs. What does anybody want, to be involved as a family, right? That's what a gang is, so why not make that gang your baseball team or football team? Kids anywhere, not just in Oakland, want to belong to something that has meaning. I give my kids that [meaningful] role on the team, and they love it."

Beam, in the big picture, lived a largely unknown, unpublicized life for four decades until 2020. Then a Netflix series on junior colleges focused on Laney and Beam, spotlighting his challenged players and the amount of behind-the-scenes involvement required to develop a state champion. Suddenly, Beam became nationally known in preaching his most vital message—structure—to a broader audience.

"Kids want structure whether they're from suburbia, the ghetto, or in between," he pointed out. "They need it, and we have to give it to them. With structure, there is no confusion in their lives. They know what is good for them, and for the team."

Beam's teams personify Oakland: young people from various backgrounds pulling together successfully. Beam is different, genetically, from most coaches; he is half American, half Korean. He also coaches a team that often is entirely African American.

"I would be at a coaching clinic, and I'd get questions like, 'What is it like to coach an all-black team?' " Beam said. "I would tell those coaches, 'Kids don't see color. They want to know if you'll answer the phone at three in the morning. That's all that matters to them.' "

That brings up the possible burnout factor, which 3 a.m. phone calls could lead to if sleep continually is interrupted.

"There could be burnout," Beam acknowledged, "but I get so much energy and purpose back from the kids. I'm not a savior, but to see a face light up when they get a scholarship, or get their degree, or get their first job, or when they get married, or when they have their first son or daughter—to be a part of their accomplishments, I get super energy from that."

Having enjoyed success at both the high school and junior college levels, does Beam see any similarities between the two?

"There's no comparison," he replied. "At Laney, we get kids from everywhere, which makes it hard to build community. And the culture we're trying to build changes rapidly, because half the team leaves every year. So it's definitely tougher than at a high school in getting, and maintaining, a continuity."

With inner city issues confronting him at either level, did Beam exit Skyline for Laney chiefly for financial benefits?

"Not at all," he replied. "I had won 10 OAL football championships at Skyline, so what is the next challenge? I would make more money coaching at a four-year school, yet it was a no-brainer in terms of where I would impact more lives.

"People don't realize the value of junior colleges. Kids still want to play football, and we pump them up, give them the drive to continue their education. In high school, I'd have a kid for an hour and a half [of practice] At the JC level, I'd have them for a four-hour block daily, giving me a real chance of making more of a difference in their lives."

Perhaps Netflix's national exposure of Beam altered, in magnitude, his player relationships. He laughed at the thought.

"I'm grounded because I have a fabulous wife, Cindi, who won't let my head get too big," he said. "I have two daughters, so it's the same thing. But Oakland reminds you of who you are; you're part of the town, right? The Warriors and Raiders got too big for the city, and they moved. The messages I get from people are that I'm still the same guy, kind of quirky. I still ride a skateboard at practice, I still play the quarter game, and I'm still a big kid at heart."

The quarter game?

"A kid puts a quarter in his hand, palm out," Beam explained, "and I put my hand on top of his, palm up. So I have to turn my hand all the way around to take the quarter out of the kid's hand. And I never lose, but I always give the quarter back."

However, he is no sleight-of-hand trickster. Since Beam, 62, came to Laney, it has improved its athletic facilities to the envy of other JCs. But whether it's high school or junior college football, straight talk is the best coaching approach.

"The impact, though, is bigger in high school, because you're getting them at such a young age. You're building the foundation for a 14-year-old," Beam said. "At a JC, you're helping them get to the next level. At a four-year college, you're part of a business, because it's wins and losses, and not whether you make Johnny into a better human being."

Are there more heart-warming Johnny tales at the JC level?

"Oh, it's tremendous," Beam concurred. "Kids after leaving high school are more often left on their own. Survival then becomes a part of their lives. They have to put food on the table. I've had Laney kids bring their own kids to practice. We're fine with that. But coaching is harder at our level just because of the economics."

Those economics mostly affect JC athletes, who aren't on scholarship and often struggle to make things work financially and educationally. Therefore, a special togetherness evolves.

"After we won the state title," Beam reflected on 2018, "and had celebrated on the field, our kids made a beeline for the end zone to be with one of our players, Ramon Sanders, who had broken a leg in a previous game and developed cancer. He would die from the cancer within a year, but that scene still stays on my mind."

Netflix changed Beam's image, yes, but not his coaching life.

"I don't see myself stepping down until I find that it's no longer fun to go to work," he said. "I don't even call it work. I get to wear shorts and tennis shoes, and I get paid good money to have fun with young people all day."

He only wishes that he could more easily resolve players' issues and, on a bigger scale, alleviate society's ills as well.

"We're always looking at our differences as people," he said, philosophically. "But if we looked at all the things we have in common, we'd be a much better society. We focus too much on the negatives, and not on the positives."

Beam's commitment to young men, on and off the gridiron, is more essential at the generally more needy junior college stage. While bettering lives there, he's likely also saving lives.

In the diverse City of Oakland, it takes that kind of open arms embracing, which isn't that essential in well-off suburbia.

"Oakland's story is like my story," said Beam. "I grew up with two parents, neither having graduated from high school, but who provided me with great support throughout my time growing up. But I had to have a tough skin, like Oakland."

He has received offers to coach at four-year colleges. While interested at first, he then was put off by the continual delays in arranging interviews.

"I realized that I couldn't control my life," he said. "I couldn't have as much private time with my wife and daughters."

Cindi is an independent psychological therapist, working with family members. Their two daughters played sports and are interested in athletic administration. The Beams, parents and children, are all about helping others.

So how would John Beam best describe the complexity of Oakland to someone who hasn't ever visited there?

"Think about the most beautiful quilt you've ever seen, and look at all the individual pieces," he responded. "They don't look so beautiful by themselves, but when you put them together, the tapestry they make is vibrant. That's Oakland, which has as much diversity as any place in the world. Put all of that diversity together, and you have a beautiful quilt."

Spoken by the master quilt maker himself.

Chapter 12

Jim Otto:
Mr. Raider

If someone came from another planet and wanted to know what a football player looked like, you'd show him a poster of Jim Otto.

—John Madden,
Oakland Raiders coach and football legend

Jim Otto was stunned to learn how appreciative America was about his perfected ability to snap a football. The National Football League reached its 100th anniversary in 2020, when a fans' poll was taken to determine its greatest players. Otto was chosen as the pro sport's definitive center.

"This is the first I've heard of it," he said in May 2020. "It surely is an honor. I can't believe it, but I'm happy. It's making me feel great. I don't know what else to say or how to handle it, except to say that it's a once-in-a-lifetime honor."

Well, Otto is that once-in-a-lifetime football player, whether it's a selected list of the NFL's all-time greatest competitors or an all-inclusive list of alumni who competed at the pro level.

But nobody who ever played center or, for that matter, any other football position gave more of himself physically, either in attaining legendary distinction or merely journeyman status.

Jim Otto also is the NFL's poster child.

Otto's hardship of grinding through 15 seasons, all with the Oakland Raiders, is unparalleled in NFL annals. His singular physical commitment, though, is even more evident today with the frequent pain and suffering he endures in his eighties.

An amputated leg is his ultimate sacrifice.

What Otto endured bodily during his celebrated career, and well beyond, would be more understandable if we were discussing an entire football team, and not just one player.

Otto has so many artificial parts that he has lost count. He has gone through, at least, a dozen artificial knees. He has endured 50-plus major surgeries scattered all over his savaged anatomy. And he has had just shy of 20 near-death experiences. Only a strong faith, a loving wife, and a battery of surgeons have combined to keep him alive, but just barely.

His struggles never cease. Three more ordeals occurred after he turned 80, each one life-endangering. First came an aortic valve rupture, secondly an aneurysm, and thirdly a hernia. How much abuse can one human being withstand and still survive?

Otto, it seems, has lived a hundred lives.

"I kept playing," he said of his life in general. "I was like that as a player. I'd tell the coaches, 'If I can't play, I'll let you know.' And I always played. I didn't want to let anyone down, including myself. I'm still the same way."

A football center is less noticeable than the football itself once the quarterback takes it from the center's haunches and either hands it to a running back or drops back to pass. So, then, what made Otto so visible?

"What they saw in Jim Otto was a kid who wouldn't give up, no matter what was going on out there on the football field," he replied. "He was going to be known as one of the best line blockers in the league. And that's what I tried to do on every play, to take on an opponent like I was the best that ever was."

Ah, the Roy Hobbs of football centers, a natural. But Otto stood out in ways beyond his excellent blocking. Wearing a double "00" throughout most of his pro career also made him more visable than other centers. He was the American Football League's only all-league center in the AFL's 10-year existence. He and George Blanda (Houston, Oakland) and Gino Cappelletti (Boston) are the only three to play a full schedule in each of the AFL's 10 seasons. Otto started in 210 consecutive league games, a Raider record, though that number increased with preseason games.

Otto was the ironman's ironman. And he is Mr. Raider, a testimony earned through productivity, longevity, and loyalty.

"You wrote about that a long time ago," Otto reminded me, referring to *Jim Otto: The Pain Of Glory*, a book I, Dave Newhouse, co-authored in 2000. "I still feel the same way, encouraging guys to go forward. To be included with those guys on the all-time team is wonderful. I'll get to see them before it's over with, and we'll spend time as buddies, having a few beers together."

Those all-time teams, 11 players per side, were chosen by a vote of fans (offense) and a selection panel (defense), albeit with some obvious slights, notably with the fans' picks.

On offense: quarterback Joe Montana; running backs Walter Payton and Barry Sanders; wide receivers Jerry Rice and Randy Moss; tight end Tony Gonzalez; offensive tackles Anthony Muñoz and Jonathan Ogden; guards Larry Allen and Bruce Matthews, and center Jim Otto.

What, these myopic fans don't know of Jim Brown, Jim Parker, and Don Hutson, three iconic figures? That's blasphemy. Brown should be listed as a fullback, dropping Gonzalez at tight end, because there weren't tight ends when Brown was a rookie in 1957. Parker replaces Ogden, and Hutson supplants Moss. Those who disagree obviously failed NFL History 101.

On defense: ends Bruce Smith and Reggie White; tackles Joe Greene and Alan Page, linebackers Dick Butkus, Ray Lewis, and Lawrence Taylor, cornerbacks Deion Sanders and Rod Woodson, and safeties Ronnie Lott and Ed Reed.

This is a more solid grouping, historically, except that Gino Marchetti replaces Smith at end, and Willie Brown or Jimmy Johnson bumps Woodson at corner. Marchetti was a monster. Brown was better than

Woodson at man coverage, and Johnson still played cornerback at 38, remarkably getting beat on just one touchdown bomb the entire season.

But there's no doubting which man belongs at center. Otto beat out a terrific trio of Mel Hein, Dwight Stephenson, and Mike Webster, all of whom were included on the larger all-time comprehensive team. Hein, a phenomenal two-way player in the 1930s and 1940s, would be a close second to Otto.

Nonetheless, Otto is a most deserving choice, embodying the image of a superstar who left everything on the playing field. Pro football greats applauded this man's greatness and grit.

"Jim is the most skilled center to play the game," said San Francisco 49ers coaching legend Bill Walsh, an Oakland assistant in 1966. "He had techniques others tried to emulate but couldn't. I used to marvel at his skills. He played every down with intensity. He is an amazing man. He has given his life to football."

"Jim was an ironman. He never missed a game, danced every dance," said former Kansas City Chiefs coach Hank Stram. "He had a passion for the game. He took charge of the Raiders up front. He was very special."

"Jim and I grew to have some legendary battles," said Mean Joe Greene of the Pittsburgh Steelers, "but I learned a lot about how to play my position from him. Not only was he strong, he was smart. Jim had that big ol' bucket head. He'd use it as a weapon, and a lot of his power generated from his head."

Otto's complete life is a testimony to sacrifice. He grew up in Wausau, Wisconsin, in impoverished means, living with his family in a chicken coop for a time until his father, a delivery man for a meat company, could afford better living conditions.

Otto remembered his mother saying, "Jimmy always wanted to be a football player, but there were so many things keeping him from getting there. But he kept on doing it, and that's what made him a great player."

What, in the legendary man's own words, contributed the most to his Pro Football Hall of Fame induction in 1980?

"The love of football," Otto said. "I wanted to show my parents and my brothers and sisters that Jimmy Otto could be a Hall of Famer.

Everyone at home called me Jimmy Otto, and I wanted people to know I was tougher than 'Jimmy.' My grandfather really respected me, and he would say, 'Butchie, you can do it.' Football was my game. Every time I looked around, it was football for me. But it was a long road."

The longest road imaginable, health-wise, if you lumped together Otto's countless hospital stays and unending surgeries with his fierce football commitment. Once again, that sense of pride traveled back to his cheesehead childhood in Wisconsin.

"As I boy, I wouldn't say no," he said, "and so I wouldn't give up. And as I got into football and grew up, I told myself that I would be better than the other guy. I wanted them to know Jim Otto was a tough football player, and so that's what I did."

That unrelenting determination served him well in achieving peerless fame, but it produced a medical malaise.

"Of course, I didn't know this would happen," he said of his physical deterioration. "I just thought that I could keep on going, thick or thin, and they would have to put up with me."

A typical example of Otto's battle-it-out toughness is exemplified by a severe knee injury suffered during a 1972 preseason game, five ligaments torn in the right knee. His ironman streak was at risk, for the team doctor prescribed major surgery. But Otto sneaked out of the hospital in Los Angeles, flew to Oakland, squeezed his damaged knee into a tiny Volkswagen, and drove to the team's summer training camp in Santa Rosa, 90 agonizing minutes away.

After his knee was taped by a nervous, though obliging, trainer, Otto dressed in uniform and limped onto the practice field. Coach John Madden threw a fit, throwing him off the field after berating him for sneaking out of the hospital. Otto patiently waited until practice ended, then he cornered Madden with this offer: if he practiced without hindrance the next few days, possibly surgery could be delayed. Madden agreed reluctantly, but how does one say no to Jim Otto? He survived subsequent practices, played the full season, kept his consecutive streak alive, and made the Pro Bowl. Piece of cake.

"If you think of what a pro football player should be—tough, dedicated, an ironman—that would be Jim Otto," Madden wrote in his foreword to Otto's biography.

Following that 1972 season, Otto finally underwent surgery on the damaged right knee—the same leg, unfortunately, that would be amputated after Otto became a senior citizen.

"Jim played through pain I can't understand," recalled Raiders fullback Marv Hubbard. "One day, he took off his pants, and one leg was a deep red. He had torn a leg muscle, but he pulled on his sweats and went out and practiced. Jim covers up so much. He doesn't want to show any sign of weakness. Guys like Jim never let you down."

Teammates would review Otto's unending injuries and shake their heads at his unequaled commitment. But nobody could coax him to leave the field, not even for a single play.

"My right leg is black right now," he said of the thigh area, or what's left of the leg. "I'm still worried about it a bit because they might have to take more of the leg off. But I'll seriously worry about it when the time comes."

Seriously? How much more serious can it get?

Otto conditioned himself mentally, and mightily, to give maximum effort, regardless of the medical unknowns waiting up ahead. Suit up now, he told himself, deal with it later.

"I should have kept score of all those surgeries," he reflected. "But I wanted to be an ironman, there's no doubt about that, and I wanted the respect of everybody. In order to do that, I was going to have to play every week."

Even if that ironman commitment would affect him physically—and mentally, as he has grown forgetful with age.

"I'm sorry, but sometimes I can't think straight," he said, acknowledging his memory lapses. "But I've never said, 'Poor me.' I don't believe in that crap."

His multiple concussions aside, Otto encourages today's Raiders to, if possible, stay on the field instead of living in the training room. "Let's play it out, without a doubt, and let's win the game," said this ultimate trooper. "I still see some teammates who are right there with me [in commitment]."

Those old Raiders aren't today's Raiders, who no longer win nearly as often. But, to Otto, they are Raiders, whether they play in Oakland, Los Angeles, or Las Vegas. He doesn't question their location, only their dedication. Just win, baby.

Back in high school, Otto was a menace on the football field, offensively and defensively. He was menacing, too, on the ice as a hockey goalie, often leaving the crease to punish opponents.

"I can't remember Jim missing a practice. He was self-motivated," said Tom Yelich, Otto's football line coach at Wausau High. "He came from a hardworking family. He was above-average in ability but had great desire. I have a quotation from Teddy Roosevelt: 'I'm only an average person, but I work harder than the average person.' That was Jim."

Otto received All-State honors in football, but he required considerable work academically, taking mainly shop classes in high school. He earned a football scholarship to the University of Miami (Florida), where his first two knee injuries occurred as a freshman. Miami's coaches considered giving up on him, but, determinedly, he fought his way back as a two-way player. He became a standout center and linebacker, as well as a late bloomer academically, earning a college degree. He proved an ironman in the classroom, too.

"The thing I remember about Jim from college was that he was one of the few interior linemen who played with a real flair," said *Miami Herald* sports editor/columnist Edwin Pope. "You always noticed him. 'There's Otto again.' He was a real hero…maybe the best offensive lineman the school ever had. And this has nothing to do with what he did in pro football."

Otto failed to receive All-America recognition, and the NFL didn't draft him, which made him feel worse, though his size, 210 pounds, was suitable for a linebacker, not center. But the AFL projected him as a prospect, assigning his rights to a franchise in Minneapolis. That's when the NFL jumped in and claimed Minneapolis as an expansion site. So that AFL franchise, slotted in the Twin Cities, shifted to Oakland,

with Otto tagging along. And then, like college, he had to battle his
way onto the Raiders roster.

"I told myself, 'I can kick their butts. I can kick their butts,'" he
remembered. "I felt I could do it, and I did it every week."

Though light in weight, he demonstrated to Oakland's coaches his
toughness, flattening larger players during blocking drills. Through vita-
mins and supplements, his weight shot up to 247 pounds, enabling him
to hold his own against linemen up to 50 pounds heavier. Over time, he
increased his weight to 260, growing into Mr. Raider in evolving stages.

It wasn't only Jim Otto seeking to improve, but the fledging Raiders
themselves. "We had a long way to go," Otto said. The Raiders lacked
an Oakland stadium during their first two seasons, playing "home"
contests in San Francisco while losing 19 consecutive games. A long
way to go, indeed.

"I had no idea that I would be a Raider forever," Otto remembered.
"There were plenty of opportunities to leave. For some strange reason, I
stayed even though Oakland barely knew it had a football team. When
it built us a stadium, it was more like a high school field."

Youell Field, with 22,000 seating capacity, opened during the
Raiders' third season, 1962. Youell Field wasn't a football garden, but
Otto bloomed like a sunflower nonetheless.

"I remember Jim's competitiveness," said Chuck Allen, a San Diego
Chargers linebacker. "On offense, he'd come out and drill me a few
times. On special teams, I'd try to get even, hitting him on the snap.
Then he'd chase me all over the field. He was an original, the mold,
the one everyone tried to emulate."

Otto and quarterback Tom Flores became Original Raiders, launching the franchise in 1960. Flores, who later coached the Raiders to two
Super Bowl wins, still can picture young Jim Otto.

"Jim loved life. He loved practice. He loved the game. He loved
being one of the guys," said Flores. "Jim set the standard on the Raiders.
We had to prop him up when he played, but he always bounced back.
He's still bouncing back. Here he comes, just like when he played."

Oakland, as a franchise, bounced back from utter failure after Al Davis was named its general manager and coach in 1963. The Raiders' time as a punching bag was over—they had become the puncher. Otto's loyalty to Davis is eternal, the former unable to say anything disrespectful of the latter to this very day.

Otto and the Raiders grew in stature together. He played in the first three AFC–NFC Pro Bowls, always striving to win, still bitter over the NFL's disrespect of the AFL. He would claim seven division championships and an AFL title in 1967. He was the third AFL player inducted in the Pro Football Hall of Fame, elected in his first year of eligibility. And his Double 0 is the only uniform number retired by the Raiders.

This same poor kid who lived in a chicken shack and took shop classes in high school then built himself into a millionaire businessman after football. He was a walnut farmer, bank owner, burger franchise king, and property owner whose wise investments also included a llama farm. Then, in 1995, he rejoined the Raiders as a special projects director, reporting to work with two shoulder replacements.

There's not much left, physically, of the young Jimmy Otto. No retired NFL player, in fact, has a body as mangled. Television's Six Million Dollar Man is a few million—dings—behind Otto. A lost leg is the ultimate sacrifice—but ask Otto if he would do it the same way again, of course he would. His mind-set: Pro Football Hall of Fame, greatest center, Mr. Raider.

"At the Canton Hall of Fame parade," said Kansas City Chiefs linebacker Willie Lanier, "I rode in the same car as Jim. I asked him about his mind-set. I could understand the first surgery, but not the third, fourth, fifth, and sixth. I had a different mind-set. Jim spoke about where he grew up, and how football raised him up to accept the downside that comes with it. I can't think of anyone who has had as many surgeries as Jim, and as many artificial replacements. I still struggle with that because my own views are different. I never had a major surgery."

Otto's health worsened in 1998. Over an eight-day period, his body temperature reached 105. A reading of 106 meant funeral arrangements were pending, but he won that battle.

Eight years prior, Otto's back surgery lasted 11 hours. Then a bacterial infection developed in his kidneys and bladder from a catheter placed inside him for urinary purposes. That infection lasted six months, but he survived that ordeal, too.

But Otto's worst scare might have been a second ordeal in 1998, lapsing into septic shock as his kidney, lungs, and liver shut down. He was in California, his medical specialist was in Utah, and time was of the essence. Wife Sally drove him to an airport in time to catch a plane to Salt Lake City, where he was rushed into surgery at the University of Utah Medical Center. Filled with antibiotics to bring down the fever, artificial knee No. 5—the culprit—then was removed. Six months later, he received artificial knee No. 6. Finally, in a new century, that same leg was amputated.

And he's still managing to live—and to win—somehow.

"I always thought Pops was the ideal gladiator," said Raiders linebacker Phil Villapiano. "To watch him play—the beating he took, the bleeding—the guy was incredibly tough. Nobody was going to take his job. I loved that attitude. Once he showed me his legs. They were all fat except for two muscles that were working. He was so proud of those two muscles. We always said Pops loved pain, but I don't think he wanted this much."

Otto, additionately, would have foregone breaking his nose 20-plus times—busted so often that the nose has no cartilage left. Sally straightens his nose for him; she is wife and trainer.

Otto visualizes himself as a Roman gladiator, triumphing over enemies, regardless of wounds and against all the odds.

"Having a gladiator's mentality has given me the resolve to survive," he said. "I'm from an era when NFL gladiators weren't well-paid, but there wasn't any question about our commitment to duty. You don't see that same gladiator attitude anymore. These Raiders don't dominate the way the old Raiders dominated.

"Generations change. The lion's as tough as ever, but the Christians don't put up the same unconditional fight as the gladiators of my era.

And although my battle wounds greatly outnumber everyone else's, you can count on me to be the one gladiator standing at the end of the fight."

A gladiator on one leg, yet with his sword still held high. Look in any arena you want, NFL fans, but you won't find a gladiator even on two legs who can match Oakland's finest.

Chapter 13

Rick Barry:
Misunderstood Superstar

*Rick is one of the most unappreciated players in basket-
ball because of his personality, which I saw as angry.*
—Jerry West, NBA legend

Rick Barry is the Bekins of basketball. He is the sport's most traveled
superstar, largely through his own itinerary. His bouncing ball was
more than a metaphor. He started in San Francisco, then it was on to
Oakland, Washington, D.C., Virginia, New York, Oakland again, and
finally Houston. Barry was his own moving van, hauling his successful
career, and his personal baggage, around the country from the National
Basketball Association to the American Basketball Association, and then
returning to the NBA, a singular and iconic journey.

The San Francisco Warriors drafted him in 1965, but he jumped to
the ABA's Oakland Oaks two years later. The Oaks relationship lasted
one year, winning an ABA championship before the franchise moved
to Virginia, then leaving just as quickly to the nation's capital, where
Barry played one season before the team shifted to New York City. He
stayed two years in the Big Apple before rejoining the Warriors, now
based in Oakland. However, his one NBA title, in 1975, occurred in
San Francisco because of an ice show conflict in Oakland, where he

starred for six seasons. He spent his final two seasons in Houston before drifting, or dribbling, into the basketball ether.

Barry's hoops career was akin to a cross-country excursion, with extensive exit ramps. "On the Road Again," sung by Willie Nelson, captured Barry's nomadic life. But the decision that launched his travelogue was switching leagues in 1967, which forced him, legally, to sit out one season before filling up baskets once again. The man truly was a scoring machine.

Barry simply couldn't stay still. He grew up in New York City, attended the University of Miami in Florida, and now splits his time between Florida and Colorado. But his first pro stop—with the Warriors franchise he abandoned—still bothers him to this day.

"I gave the Warriors every chance to keep me. I didn't do it for the money," he maintains, though Oakland guaranteed him twice what the Warriors paid. "[Owner] Franklin [Mieuli] called me a 'mixed-up boy' when I left. I became his 'prodigal son' when I came back. But we ended up getting along great."

Travel luggage—and personal baggage—delayed that process. Barry led the ABA in scoring, just as he had done in the NBA, and the NCAA before that, the only player to lead all three in scoring. The Warriors and Oaks battled over him in court, so he missed that one season. Then a knee injury altered the way he played basketball—still brilliantly, just differently. Regardless, he ranks among the best who ever played, wherever he played.

Now more rooted as a senior, Barry berates himself over his younger, gazetteer-like motivations.

"If I had to do it all over again, I would not have joined the ABA," he said. "We had just played in the NBA Finals, I had led the league in scoring, and I was the MVP in the NBA All-Star Game. So what would my reputation have been like if I had come back to the Warriors instead of going to Oakland?"

Dominant, yet he still ranks among the pro game's 20 greatest players and is clearly its best all-around small forward. Besides his scoring prowess, he led the NBA in steals and free throw percentage and was among its leaders in assists. He scored from the outside or inside, hooked accurately with either hand, and though his build was on the lean side, he was physically resilient. Other great forwards—Bob Pettit, Elgin Baylor, Larry Bird, Julius Erving, LeBron James, Kevin Durant—lack Barry's overall package.

But because of his transient lifestyle, and perhaps his volatility, his exploits on the basketball court are disregarded or downplayed, an undeserved curse he lives with today.

"I think a lot of people have short memories," he said in his own defense. "They don't know that the greatest center was Wilt Chamberlain, because they're younger, and they don't know how great Wilt was. People are caught up in the moment, and that usually means current players. That's OK, but don't say that someone is the greatest player because you can only pick by a certain era. So whether the center is Shaq [O'Neal] or Kareem [Abdul-Jabbar], that's fine. But I recently watched some video, and Wilt blocked three of Kareem's skyhooks at the end of Wilt's career. That's how great Wilt was."

As for Rick Barry, how great was he, Rick Barry?

"I don't mean to blow my own horn, but people say that players from my era couldn't play today," he responded. "I say to them, 'You're out of your mind.' I would be better today, because these guys have so much training that goes on. Plus, with the game's technology, I'd be stronger, faster, and jump higher. It would be a joke. And I'd wear shorter shorts; I hated those long shorts."

So where does Richard Francis Dennis Barry III place himself among basketball's greatest players?

"People pick players ahead of me whom I thought I was better than," he answered quickly. "I won't mention names, but people don't understand the game as well as they think. I do know that I have great respect among Blacks over my ability."

That last sentence seems bold, and in need of substantiation, which former NBA guard Butch Beard, who is Black and a Warriors teammate of Barry's, provided.

"Rick was a miniature Black guy," Beard said. "People forget that when he first came into the league, he ran like a deer and he could jump. So he was looked upon as a 'brother.' He was a great scorer and rebounder, but what people don't talk about was his ability to pass the ball. That was important for us when we won the championship, because we ran our offense through him. He was one of my favorite teammates because of his I.Q. on the floor, which explained his ability to steal the ball.

"He has to go down as one of the all-time greats. I played with a lot of great players, and I tell them that Rick was misunderstood. He had that demeanor on the floor where he'd be whining or bitching if he didn't get the call. But you really have to look past that and give him credit for what he did on the court. Look, the great ones like Rick would be great even in this era."

Typically, as Beard stated, Barry whined when he spotted a "foul," which included the 1974–75 Warriors' omission in basketball annals, which he deems a gross injustice.

"I had a chance to be part of a team that had the greatest upset in the history of NBA finals," he said in 2020. "But we never get any kind of recognition, not even a documentary."

Those underdog Warriors were supposed to be swept by Washington, but they, instead, swept the Bullets in the NBA Finals. The greatest upset, indeed.

"With all the b.s. that is put out there today," Barry persisted, angrily, about sports documentaries in general, "nobody has ever done what we did."

Ironically, while Barry was interviewed for this book, his Warriors teammate, Charles Dudley, had begun the process of interviewing other Warriors about their special championship run for a documentary that Dudley is producing. He just hadn't gotten to Barry yet.

"No one has recognized our achievement—the greatest upset in NBA history," Dudley said for this book. "We were the third team up to that point to win the NBA title in a four-game sweep, after Boston [1959] and Milwaukee [1971]."

The third team, yes, although the first underdog. Dudley, interviewed in May 2022, planned to have his documentary ready for public consumption sometime in 2023.

But, using that same historic perspective, does Barry see any NBA legend comparable to himself?

"Bird played the same way I played, but I was faster and quicker than Bird," he said. "He was taller [6'9" to 6'7"], but I was a very good rebounder until I hurt my knee. I averaged 25 [points] and 10 [rebounds] my rookie year and made All-Pro, which doesn't happen very often. And did you know that in college, my rebounding numbers were better than Kareem's?"

Even so, Barry's career is denigrated, though he averaged 23.2 points in the NBA and 30.5 in the ABA. Perhaps that denigration is tied into his hobo-like existence, his quick-trigger temper, his eternal outspokenness—or all three.

"It has to do with my going to the ABA," he thinks otherwise. "No question about it. I had just averaged 35.6 points with the Warriors in my second NBA season before changing leagues. Then I had my knee scoped out in the ABA."

Prior to the ABA, he was a fierce driver to the basket. Then because of the knee, he no longer crashed to the hoop with his early NBA ferocity. His game, subsequently, moved outside.

"My game was righty-lefty crossover dribble," he said. "I was a very good ball handler and passer. I could see, really see."

Seeing in basketball is creating, and Barry had that knack, offensively and defensively. Even at age 32, he ranked fifth in the NBA in assists (6.1) and fourth in steals (2.49), strengthening his image as the most diversified small forward, but finishing fourth in the NBA's Most Valuable Player balloting, perhaps because of his personality. Perhaps?

"I played hard every game," he said. "I only remember one quarter of one game in which I wasn't mentally ready to play. I just took great pride in playing hard. When you're getting paid to do something, how can you live with yourself if you're not playing as hard as you can? Basketball wasn't work. I loved it."

Jeff Mullins, a Warriors teammate and deadeye backcourt marksman during a twelve-year NBA career, places Barry in elevated company in the game's pantheon.

"I've always been of the opinion that Rick's stardom has been held back by those four years he missed in the NBA," Mullins said. "He rates with the best all-time small forwards. I put him right up there with Larry Bird and Dr. J. [Julius Erving]. And, overall, he deserves to be right up there with Jerry West, Oscar Robertson, and all those guys."

Mullins believes Barry's competitiveness, by itself, qualifies him for greatness. "He just strove every night," Mullins said, "and he was very underrated as an athlete. Once in practice, Rick lined up with the Warriors guards for a race, and he beat us easily down the court. And he had a standing start, while we took off from a sprinter's kneeling start."

Another example of Barry's athleticism: a charity decathlon involving Bay Area athletes, including footballers John Brodie, Gene Washington, Fred Biletnikoff, Daryle Lamonica, and tennis star Barry MacKay. Everybody was tested for their skills in swimming, running, tennis, shot put, longest golf drive, etc. Barry was so far ahead in overall points that he skipped the final event, a mile run, and still won comfortably.

"He was a great athlete," Mullins said. "He had that characteristic of what I call the old-time player, not being afraid of taking a beating. Going to the basket, being fouled, and getting to the free-throw line, Rick was the best at that.

"And just like Michael Jordan would do, if you weren't having a good game, you'd hear from Rick at halftime. He was very competitive and wanted to win. In 1975, Rick put the team on his shoulders, and we got that NBA championship."

Jerry West, one of basketball's greatest players, places Barry on that same lofty level, while also thinking of him—get this, Barry-bashers—as a friend, not a menace.

"Rick wanted to win at all costs," said West, the Los Angeles Lakers' perennial all-pro guard. "His energy level was amazing, it really was. The great players are like that; their effort is there every night. Rick wanted to compete."

Barry's temper was amazing, too.

"He wasn't the most fun person to be around," West acknowledged. "The way he reacted to things hurt him. He played angry, which some people resented. But he was an elite player. He could shoot the ball, finish with both hands, and he could put it on the court. And he wasn't a self-promoter."

West perceives Barry differently from his critics.

"We still speak after all these years; I'm happy to hear from Rick," he said. "I also interact with his kids a bit, because I've known them a long time too. Rick is willing to participate in things that some players don't do, like the league's players association, which shows me that he does care. He's come to my basketball camp. I've always gotten along with him."

West admires Barry in another capacity, "Rick was a pioneer in a sense. He went to the ABA when some people just wouldn't have done that, and the first [NBA player] to do it," West said.

Barry topped the ABA in scoring (34.0) in 1968–69, when the Oakland Oaks were league champions, although a leg injury sidelined him throughout the postseason.

"It was a pretty good team, but not outstanding," Barry said of the Oaks. "Henry Logan was a special player, kind of ahead of his time in the way he handled a basketball. Unfortunately, he tore up his knee and couldn't play. Warren Armstrong [Jabali] was an outstanding player. Doug Moe and Larry Brown were outstanding. Ira Harge and Jim Eakins were nice centers, and Russ Critchfield was a backup guard. We had some nice talent."

How well would those Oakland Oaks have done in the NBA?

"We would have been competitive, no question," Barry replied. "The only difference: we wouldn't have been up to the quality of some NBA teams and their great centers. On the Warriors, we had a two-headed monster at center in George Johnson and Clifford Ray. But the Oaks wouldn't have embarrassed themselves in the NBA."

Perhaps had he played strictly in the NBA, Barry wouldn't have encountered his ABA-generated knee difficulties. Who can really say, but, in the final analysis, which Rick Barry was a better basketball player, pre- or post-knee surgery?

"The one after," he said, quickly. "I learned to do other things, becoming a better facilitator, making my teammates better. Though I was a big-time scorer my first two ABA seasons, I was never selfish. But I was a better passer afterward."

Barry then made a startling career statement.

"If I had to do it all over again, I would be a point guard," he said. "I was quick enough and fast enough to do that. I would have worked on my ball-handling skills, but at point guard, you control the destiny of your team with the basketball in your hands. Late in my career, I gained more satisfaction in getting the ball to a teammate than in scoring myself. I loved doing that. I may still have the NBA record for the most single-game assists by a forward—19 on the road in Chicago.

"Playing today wouldn't benefit just me, but any player from my time, because we played the game the right way. So many guys now get by on sheer athleticism, way too much one-on-one. That's why I love the way the Warriors are playing during their championship run this century, because they pass and run. Remember, players from my time never lifted a weight, and we didn't have strength-and-agility coaches or dieticians. Also, our travel was brutal. In my second NBA season, we played on the road Thursday and Friday, had the All-Star Game banquet in San Francisco on Saturday, played the All-Star Game Sunday, and then had a road game Monday."

However, it wasn't uncommon then for an NBA team to play six games on the road in eight nights. Late-night flights, sleeping on planes, eating on the run, catching a mid-afternoon nap before yet another evening game—all that cramming was a handicap in trying to perform at their best nightly. Today's NBA is a waltz, Barry noted, compared to that marathon dance.

And—don't forget—young Rick Barry was a punching bag in sneakers. Though on the thin side, he'd drive defiantly to the basket between two hefty defenders, who'd pummel him.

"I wanted to get fouled," he explained. "I knew I would make a bunch of free throws, so I would get three points [by scoring a field goal first] instead of two points. By playing today, like I played back then, I'd get 15 free throws a game. That's because you can hardly touch a guy these days. LeBron [James] should benefit this way, but he's not a great free throw shooter. And so he doesn't like to be fouled going to the basket."

Barry had fewer critics among sportswriters, for he was the NBA's most accommodating interviewee, sharing that role, historically, with Charles Barkley. Those two weren't ever short of quotes, filling up reporters' notebooks after games.

Barry's unique legacy includes his family tree. Two of his three marriages produced five sons, all of whom played professional basketball, including on foreign soil. Brent, Jon and Drew played in the NBA, while oldest son Rick IV, or Scooter, played in Europe. These four are from his first wife, Pam, along with an adopted daughter. The fifth son, Canyon, from third wife, Lynn, has played minor league basketball. No other father has such a hoops pedigree, with Division I scholarships for all five sons, another Rick Barry feat.

Canyon is the only son, though, to utilize the underhanded free throw popularized by his father. "It's the best possible way to shoot a free throw, a much softer shot, with less moving parts," papa Rick pointed out. "What bothers me is that Canyon has NBA ability, but he just hasn't gotten that opportunity."

Canyon, who stands 6'6", has a master's degree in nuclear energy after finishing his college career at Florida, where he was the second leading scorer on the team and the Southeastern Conference's Sixth Man of the Year.

Rick Barry has been married since 1991 to the former Lynn Norenberg, a dynamo herself—athletically, culturally, and academically. A prom queen in high school, she was a basketball record-setter at William & Mary College, where she was homecoming queen with a 3.97 grade point average. After earning a master's degree in athletic administration at Kentucky, she met Barry in Moscow at the 1986 Goodwill Games. What ensued was a long, long, long courtship.

"I was working for USA basketball with the women's basketball team, and Rick was doing the broadcasting," Lynn recalled. "He would say that he made an instant connection, but I would say not right away on my part. Our first date was at the opening ceremonies of those Goodwill Games on July 4, 1986. Then he said it was five years of relentless pursuit until we got married. He had a lot of baggage, so I had to be sure."

Baggage? Envision a platform of suitcases waiting to be loaded at a train station, i.e., Rick Barry's baggage.

"I do think he is a tad misunderstood," Lynn pointed out. "That's because people judge him on the fiery, competitive personality he had when he played. I never saw him play, and I didn't know anything about him then. But there's always so much more to a person than his on-court demeanor. I loved him because he is competitive, but he's always been kind and loyal. He would give you the shirt off his back, and he does so many wonderful things that people don't know about. He's been a wonderful husband and father. We've had an amazing life, a great ride, and we're truly blessed to have a son together. As for Rick's other sons, I love them and their children."

A harmonious relationship with Barry's other children obviously took some doing because of damaged feelings and a prolonged bitterness resulting from his first marriage.

"There have been hardships," Lynn conceded, "but in the end, all you really have is your relationship with your family—your children, grandchildren, and your spouses. As Rick has gotten older, he sees the importance of it, and has the time now to invest in it. Things are very good now in the Barry family."

Barry's oldest son, and namesake, is Scooter Barry, who won an NCAA basketball championship at Kansas, and was the last cut of the Boston Celtics before playing 17 years professionally overseas. He openly addressed his father's first marriage and the ensuing family fallout.

"I was born in 1966, my dad's rookie year, so I always say that we both had the same rookie year," he said. "I remember when I was five, he'd take me to practice. Later on, I'd come home from school, do my homework, and my dad and I both took our power naps. We'd have a pregame meal together and go to the game. In the locker room, we'd both get dressed—I had my own little Warriors uniform—and I'd go out and shoot baskets. During the game, I'd sit under the basket and sweep the key with a mop. Then I became a Warrior ball boy."

Scooter recalled family trips—father, mother, four children. "My parents had things they kept from us, but I don't remember it being a volatile marriage," he said. "Then he announced, and my mom announced, that he was leaving. I was 13 and about to start high school. My dad saw me play one basketball game in four years. Our relationship was rebuilt during my college years when we had a heart-to-heart talk.

"Then when I was overseas, he would come over and see me play once a year, staying for a week. His best advice to me was, 'Shoot the ball, Scooter. I didn't fly all the way over here to see you pass the ball.' My first game afterward, I scored 33 points and still had a lot of assists. My dad said the same thing about all five of his sons: We have a court vision you can't teach."

Like father, like sons.

Reflecting on his father's first marriage, Scooter said, "There were some unresolved things with my brothers that led to animosity. But I was the oldest, and so I took on the role as the man of the house. After I left for college, my mom married Bill Connolly, and he took on that role. But any divorce involving children is difficult. I'm experiencing it myself with two teenage children. My father then had Canyon, who's half my age, and now my girlfriend wants to have children. So I'm going through the same [child age difference] thing."

The four sons from Rick Barry's first marriage each have two children, adding up to eight grandchildren. The adopted daughter is married but childless. The families are spread out across the nation, which limits family get-togethers. However, as Scooter made public, the Barry siblings do get along.

Scooter was 53 when he was interviewed for this book in 2021. He works in sales in the Bay Area. "I don't want people to think that we have this dysfunctional family," he noted. "Any time you have a divorce, where it's not mutual, then it's not nice. But all the [Barry] children are upstanding citizens: God-fearing, kind, all-around good kids, who came out of this [divorce] unscathed. Our family would be a good candidate for a TV reality show."

Pamela Hale Barry Connolly was widowed several years ago, "and is having a hard time," Scooter said of his mother, a caring individual who is, by nature, friendly and likable.

Canyon Barry, like his mother, is a two-time Academic All-American. Thus, the influence from his parents extends beyond the basketball court. He earned a bachelor's degree in physics before receiving that master's in nuclear science.

"I felt Canyon would be pressured to go into basketball, so I tried to introduce him to all sports and to music," said his mother, who played the French horn and sang in the choir during her adolescence. "But he wound up playing basketball, just like all the other [Barry] boys. He plans to play as long as he can, but he definitely has a fallback position."

As for the parents' own athletic genes, there is intensity in Pickle Ball doubles at the Barry home. 'We play with Canyon," said Lynn, "but I always feel sorry about the fourth member, because the competitive juices still flow from all three Barrys."

Including Mom, who is quick to defend her husband.

"There is so much more to Rick than going to the ABA, and contract issues, and being a demanding teammate," she said. "I'm very fortunate to have gotten to know the real him."

Barry's hoops-playing sons haven't had Snickers bars thrown at them. Rick Barry promoted that same candy as a young Warrior. During a contentious playoff series with the St. Louis Hawks, he was pelted with Snickers. Something he did or said, possibly a display of temper? Rick Barry, temperamental?

"That temper never bothered my game," he stressed. "It wasn't a temper; I just got upset when the officials wouldn't do their job. If they wouldn't do that, and they're making mistakes, I'd get pissed off. Some of those officials were horrible, and I'd get upset at their lack of ability. I know it's a difficult job, but to this day, they don't know the difference between a block and a charge. So when guys grabbed me on a charge, I'd get mad.

"But when you say temper, I was the hardest on myself. I was demanding of my teammates, but just as demanding or even more so of myself. Michael Jordan got mad, too. He'd get upset if his teammates were giving a half-assed performance."

Barry married the daughter of Bruce Hale, his coach at the University of Miami. The father-in-law then was working in the Oakland Oaks' front office when Barry joined that franchise. With all the varied twists and turns of Barry's interesting life, why doesn't he write a book? It could be a best seller.

"I've been asked to do another book," he said, having co-authored *Confessions of a Basketball Gypsy: The Rick Barry Story* with Bill Libby in 1972 (Prentice-Hall). "But why would I want people pissed off at me, when they're pissed off already? I've always told the truth. Lynn said, 'Honey, you're the most truthful person I've known in my entire life.' I am brutally honest, but sometimes people can't handle the truth. So I don't know if I want to [do a book]."

Barry was 76 when he was interviewed for this book in 2020. Analyzing his journey, does he have any serious regrets or misgivings?

"Everything I've done in my life, I've never tried to hurt someone intentionally or to take advantage of anyone," he replied. "I have hurt people by some of the things I did, but it never was intentional. That's not the way I was brought up.

"People who really know me will say, 'Rick Barry was someone who gave the best that he could throughout his life. And, deep inside, he is a good person.' But you read some of the quotes my teammates said about me, and you can see they were taken out of context, and all because they didn't put the whole quote in there.

"Mike Dunleavy Sr. said, 'If Rick went to the United Nations, he would start World War III.' He also said I was a nice guy, but that didn't appear in the quote. Billy Paultz said of me, 'Half of the guys in the league don't like him. The other half hate him.' And it was made to sound as if he was half-serious."

Half-serious? Sounds completely serious, although truth is in the ear of the listener.

"[Sports analyst] Bill Simmons called me a 'dick' in his book," Barry continued. "I've never met Bill Simmons, so how does he know me?"

Regardless, Rick Barry will be vocal—always. That's who he is—he doesn't hold back, and he is brutally honest. Find another athlete who is more honest, more real. Good luck in that quest.

Or, for that matter, find someone who is a more athletic senior citizen. Barry spends up to three hours playing pickleball. He fractured his pelvis, was laid up several months, and then resumed his pickleball wars. Nothing slows down this perpetually driven man. His next goal: fly-fishing in Alaska.

After playing for the Warriors both in San Francisco and Oakland, what are Barry's thoughts about that franchise leaving Oakland in 2019 to return to San Francisco?

"It's unfortunate because the fans in Oakland were very support-ive—that is, other than the baseball A's, who haven't gotten the same support as the Warriors and Raiders," he said. "During that one period in the mid-1970s, all three teams won national titles. So there was that special time.

"But in terms of the fans, it's way more convenient for them to come to Oakland than San Francisco. The only people who find San Francisco more convenient are San Franciscans. Oakland is more con-ducive to the greater number of fans.

"The roots of the team are in San Francisco," he said, overlooking Philadelphia. "They were the San Francisco Warriors, but they never were the Oakland Warriors in name. And they had a nice arena in Oakland, unlike the Cow Palace, though we had good crowds in that building my second year. It's unfortunate that Oakland has lost two of its three teams, but the holy dollar rules.

"I do feel sorry for Oakland as the Warriors were there a lot longer than they were in San Francisco. But from an international standpoint, people know about San Francisco, they don't know about Oakland. That gives the Warriors a little more panache."

Showing class even in the face of rejection, nobody from Oakland hurled Snickers bars at the Warriors as they left town.

The NBA player who knows Rick Barry the best is Clifford Ray, his Warriors teammate and close friend. Barry is white, Ray is Black, but their close bond crosses racial lines.

"Rick is one of the best players to come down the pike, someone we should appreciate like Bill Russell, Jerry West, Oscar Robertson, and all the great players of that era," said Ray. "Everyone in the Black community knows Rick Barry, and they think of him as the best white player ever. He did everything all the great basketball players do, adding players like Magic Johnson, Kareem Abdul-Jabbar, Michael Jordan, Kobe Bryant, and LeBron James to that list.

"When I came along, there weren't many great white players, though people don't like to talk about that. You can devise all the defenses you can to stop Michael Jordan, and you can't stop him. It was the same thing with Rick. I believe the NBA has used him as a whipping stick, because he played in the ABA. But Rick is a basketball icon superstar."

Ray knows a totally different individual than the Barry who is normally portrayed as whiny and self-centered. Ray hasn't forgotten that the first player to greet him when the Chicago Bulls traded him to the Warriors in 1974 was Barry.

"I liked him because he was honest," Ray said. "He would put his foot in his mouth and say stupid stuff, but he spoke his mind and his heart. He has a good heart, and he is generous. He found me a place to live when I came to the Bay Area."

Ray believes the reason critics misread Barry "is because he's introverted and, I think, actually shy. He's not the most socially graceful person in the world. I told him when he shakes someone's hand, he has to look at the person or he'll look like a jerk. He's just not graceful when it comes to that."

Ray doesn't understand why the Warriors haven't erected a statue of Barry, either in Oakland or San Francisco.

"Just like Larry Bird [in Boston] or Magic [Johnson in Los Angeles] or Michael [Jordan in Chicago]," said Ray, statue-campaigning for his friend. "And why haven't the Warriors given Rick a chance to make his mark as a head coach? He's a smart guy who really knows the game."

The Barry–Ray relationship grew after their playing careers ended. "We talk every day or just about," Ray said, "or I can drive to his house in two hours when he's in Florida." Ray lives full-time in Florida, whereas Barry splits his time between Florida and Colorado.

When interviews for this chapter occurred in May 2020, Ray, Barry, and two others were about to leave on an Alaskan fishing trip. "Rick and I fish together all the time," Ray said.

Ray wished to make this final point about his close friend and true superstar: "Teams hated to see that boy coming. All those cats, they hated to see him coming. Rick could beat you off the dribble, he could beat you with the jump shot, and he could beat you by posting you up. His game was complete."

But don't ever think of challenging Barry, even now in his late seventies. Basketball or pickleball—he's waiting for you to show up. Just beware, he's still prepared for battle, his competitiveness is endless, and he plays only to win.

And if he doesn't win, you will hear about it.

Chapter 14

Bill Patterson, Paul Cobb:
A Racial Perspective

Oakland is the can San Francisco loves to kick down the road, even though San Francisco could learn a lot from Oakland when it comes to racial diversity.

—Paul Cobb,
Oakland newspaperman and vocal activist

Bill Patterson fought back tears as he named the sports legends he groomed long ago at an Oakland recreational facility. Sadly, some of those legends have predeceased him.

"I taught Bill Russell, Curt Flood, Willie Stargell, Joe Morgan, Frank Robinson, Vada Pinson, and Paul Silas," Patterson, now in his nineties, wept while reliving his playground directorship at DeFremery Park in West Oakland in the 1940s and 1950s.

Of the above athletes, Russell, Stargell, Morgan, and Robinson achieved Hall of Fame status, and all but Silas has died, which affects Patterson deeply. Merely mentioning their names is enough to make him emotional.

Patterson brought purpose and direction to the lives of countless youngsters, the majority of whom lacked big-league ability but who thanked him regardless. Did guiding those who reached the top give his life a certain fulfillment?

"It really has," he said, pausing to collect his feelings. "And it came from mentoring. I saw the dark side and light side of athletes, but you have to guide them through. If they rose above where they were when I met them, then that was my accomplishment. I didn't need anything more."

Patterson was interviewed for this book in the summer of 2021, during a time of further loss. His loving wife of nearly 60 years, Euradell, had just died, and his heart was broken further. He had outlived those he had a profound effect upon and who also graced his life. Such reflection evoked deep emotion.

The kindly, sensitive Patterson, who is African American, was an Arkansas transport who migrated to Oakland and steered the lives of mostly African American youngsters. Therefore, he has a clear perspective of the city's impact, positive and negative, on its Black neighborhoods.

He has observed signs of civic improvement in this regard.

"I guess the configuration of Oakland is part of it," he said. "The other part is history as it relates to how Oakland has provided for ethnicities. Oakland was segregated all the way up to the [Byron] Rumford Fair Housing Act."

The Rumford Act, passed by the California Legislature in 1963, ended discrimination by property owners and landlords who refused to sell or rent to "colored" people.

"Oakland was occupied by the white community, which made all the decisions [prior to the Rumford Act]," Patterson recalled. "There was available land where you were not welcome, and not just African Americans, but Hispanics."

Patterson pinpointed westward Black migration during World War II. With Americans heading off to war, there were job openings in Oakland. And so Black people journeyed there from other states, settling in West Oakland and East Oakland.

Shipyards and steel mills were the first main draws for Black transients in Oakland. Kaiser Hospital, a future institution in Oakland, was built to accommodate the increasing work force. Housing was constructed for Black residents, but racial inclusion at that time was analogous to a marathon, not a sprint.

"Some [Black transplants] stayed in Oakland, and some didn't," Patterson remembered. "Land is key to everything; it makes communities. We didn't know what gentrification was back then. Some moved two, three times before finding housing they preferred in Oakland. Others just moved away.

"But we do know now what gentrification feels like, for Oakland has a makeup of all the cultures, all the ethnicities. And we have other components coming forward. All people, regardless of their gender or [sexual] persuasion, they all have equal rights. Groups were formed for the betterment of the community in Oakland.

"I later conducted a recreational program in East Oakland, where we taught our kids what to look out for, and how to get along better, which built social mores on how to work together. West Oakland then followed my direction, and we had success together, like in track and field. Those are the things that unite us, though it wasn't just about sports. We taught young girls how to be ladies, with a strong moral side."

But, Patterson emphasized, it's a continuing struggle.

"Oakland is a changing community," he said. "We've had some things that have turned us back, like redevelopment. People have moved here from San Francisco and from all over the world, bringing good things and also bad things. Whole communities were changing, and that's how the Black Panther Party got started, with kids that grew up under me. The Panthers did some good, which doesn't get recognized, but you can't rule with the gun."

So, then, in assessing this advancement, what are Oakland's biggest assets and its biggest remaining drawbacks?

"Its positive asset is what has always been here: location," Patterson answered. "Some of the people coming into Oakland now are the techies, with the big bucks. What you're seeing today is an economic boom. Housing is at a very high market price. The ethnicity of Oakland is changing. You can walk the streets at night or walk in the park and see babies in strollers. Oakland is no longer seen as just a Black city.

"But the worst thing we have now—not just in Oakland, but in all the major cities in California—is the housing problem. Housing is not affordable. It's not about people getting along. People are forced to sell, they move, and then they can't afford to buy their way back into Oakland. To work this out, this is our future."

That future comes down to, in Patterson's frank opinion, "the bitter and the sweet. Gentrification is a good thing, but every time there is a protest, people want to come down on Oakland. Windows are shattered, buildings are gutted, car dealerships are broken into—these are the negatives that happen. People want to dramatize things, but the bad is always the bad. And when they talk about Oakland's population, a lot of that population is living today under the freeway or in vans.

"Oakland has problems."

Suddenly, Bill Patterson—civic thinker/youth developer/Oakland conscience—felt his eyes moisten.

"All my guys are dying out," he said. "I always go back to Curt Flood, who knocked down walls so baseball players could have free agency. He was one of my charges, following me from Poplar Park to DeFremery. I met Joe Morgan when he was 12, Willie Stargell at 14. At one time, Cincinnati had an entire outfield of kids I had worked with out of McClymonds High School: Curt Flood, Vada Pinson, and Frank Robinson."

And Cincinnati later added another Patterson product, second baseman Joe Morgan, twice the National League's Most Valuable Player.

"We taught our kids leadership and responsibility, caring about each other," said Patterson, "and they were able to bring these factors into focus. Joe Morgan gave back to this community through his foundation, giving more than all the athletes coming out of Oakland combined. That's what I mean by leadership, and Joe did it quietly; he didn't need the publicity."

Combining Morgan, Robinson, Flood, Russell, Silas, and Pinson with Don Budge, Jim Pollard, Jackie Jensen, John Brodie, Rickey Henderson, Gary Payton, Jason Kidd, Damian Lillard—was it the water in Oakland, or the mentoring and coaching, that brought out such athletic greatness?

"If you want to know the future of a nation, you have to look through the eyes of the children," Patterson said, prophetically. "I could see Bill

Russell's greatness long before anyone saw it. I used to recommend things for him to read and study. We enjoyed each other's company."

Patterson instructed Black youngsters on football, basketball, and baseball techniques, but he also educated them on how to use a knife and fork and proper table etiquette.

"We made sure they were sensitized," he said. "We wanted them to perform at the highest level, both as athletes and as people. We had a purpose, and our young people carried it out. That's my story, and I'm sticking with it."

Paul Cobb turned 79 in 2021, when he was interviewed for this book, though he was nowhere near retirement. He publishes the *Oakland Post* newspaper, specifically directed at a Black readership. Cobb, an impresario of sorts, owns 10 other minority newspapers, stretching from Oakland throughout the Bay Area. By enlarging his syndicate, remarkably, as a razor-sharp senior citizen, he is living proof that old age is no deterrent to continued growth.

Cobb believes deeply in Oakland, the city of his birth, even though he hasn't always felt Oakland was racially inclusive.

"There was so much going on," he recalled. "My mother had a master's degree, but she couldn't get a job teaching school. My father was a longshoreman, so we weren't in any extreme poverty. We lived in West Oakland in the same neighborhood where I live today. I had a newspaper route with the *Oakland Tribune*, and I shined shoes on Seventh Street in front of Slim Jenkins' nightclub.

"I went to the same school as Huey Newton and David Hilliard of the Black Panther Party. There were plenty of sports activities and recreational outlets in those days. We had great park directors like Bill Patterson and Willie Steele. I remember Bill Russell walking by my house to go play pickup basketball games at DeFremery Park, where Black kids played sports."

Life was comparatively calm in those Black neighborhoods until Emmett Till was lynched in Mississippi after whistling at a white woman.

"We didn't get into social consciousness and racial advocacy until that happened," Cobb reflected. "That was a wake-up call. People started paying attention, listening to Martin Luther King's speeches, and opening up social discussions about racial disparity and how Blacks should be given a chance."

A chance to succeed, he meant, which didn't come to pass with great emphasis until the turbulent 1960s, when student demonstrations at the University of California at Berkeley spread nationally to other campuses. At the same time, a national struggle for civil rights turned ugly in the Deep South, where police dogs bit and police batons cut peaceful Black marchers. And right here in Oakland, the Black Panthers and local police engaged in their own mini wars. All these conflicts still are logged in Cobb's memory bank.

Comparing the 1960s to today, "In some ways, it's gotten better, and in other ways it's probably gotten worse," he said. "That's because people are still fighting for what they wanted to achieve back then."

It's gotten better, he believes, because Oakland's diversity allows its residents to coexist more harmoniously in terms of race relations than what has transpired in other major cities.

"Because of its size, and the fact that we didn't have an issue of strict turf rites over living in certain neighborhoods, Oakland didn't always have a history of telling its residents that you…must…live…here," he said. "I lived in West Oakland, but I could ride my bike around Lake Merritt. And sports are a great integrator of how to get along. Even though there was tension, sports have a way of bringing people together. Republicans or Democrats, inner-city people or suburbanites, gay people or straight, they all come to sporting events."

Cobb mentioned that Oakland produced the first Black mayor of a large city in Lionel Wilson, the country's first Black symphony conductor in Calvin Simmons, the first Black NBA coach in Bill Russell, the first black MLB manager in Frank Robinson, and the harbinger of sports free agency in Curt Flood.

Oakland has produced an amazing list of athletes, dwarfing other cities, but Oakland, itself, tends to get lost in the conversation—any conversation about its worth, its stature.

"There's a bias about Oakland that I call the reverse San Francisco bias," said Cobb. "Most of the negative descriptions of Oakland have come from the biased San Francisco media, which looks at Oakland as the home of the Black Panther Party, or the home of the Hell's Angels, or the city that will challenge authority, or the city that's an interesting oddity, a sideshow."

Those same looks ignited Cobb's support of Oakland.

"Oakland is the main show in the Bay Area because of its creativity, whether it's sports or musicians," he stressed. "Don't forget that Jack London, as a child, was breastfed by Jennie Prentiss, a Black woman. I'm always quick to defend Oakland, because I love Oakland."

Cobb picked up more speed.

"Now let me tell you why Oakland is booming economically," he said. "It's because of Silicon Valley. The digital industry has created all these $150,000-a-year jobs. It costs a billion dollars to live in San Francisco. So people are moving to cheaper places like West Oakland, where you can renovate a house much cheaper than in San Francisco.

"So the digital tech people are buying up buildings in Oakland at the same time that building codes are being relaxed. That started under mayor Jerry Brown—the gentrification wave of Oakland. That wave was the major driver of pushing real estate prices up in the tech industry."

Cobb then addressed the same old Oakland image problem.

"Oakland suffers misfortune because we aren't San Francisco," he said, angrily.

Oakland also suffers from lost sports teams. But once Cobb gets started on this topic, it's difficult for him to stop.

"Al Davis' personality drove the future of the Raiders more than any owner of any other team," he said. "He went from a minority stockholder to managing general partner to league commissioner, which made him think, because of his ego, that he wanted to be the greatest sports owner in the world. He was driven by a huge anger toward the city administrators of Oakland. So he took the Raiders to Los Angeles, found that wasn't working, came back to Oakland with egg on his face, and then hustled Las Vegas.

"Then you have the Warriors, who had the greatest fan base in the history of sports in Oakland. But [owner Joe] Lacob wanted more—he wanted to be in San Francisco so he could hob-nob with other billionaires. It wasn't anything that Oakland or its administrators did wrong, and it wasn't economics; it was the ego, status-climbing aspect of the owner. Lacob's personality is different from Al Davis', but the outcome is still the same."

Cobb shifted topics to the A's, and their moveable desires.

"It's always been an upscale real estate play," he said. "[A's owner John] Fisher wanted to build a new ballpark in Oakland around some high rises that would attract million-dollar tenants. That's what it's all about, not about downsizing a stadium to 35,000 people. It's all about upscale revenue, but who wants to be there with all that noise of hearing train whistles every five minutes? It's not about finding a nice place to play ball; it's stupid."

Toot, toot, everybody.

Cobb then aimed a bean ball at deserving targets: money-grubbing sports owners who don't give a hoot about Oakland.

"It's not the people of Oakland, or Oakland's crime rate, that is forcing teams to leave. It's the greed and the corporate-seeking image of those sports owners," he charged. "And, besides, now you have Al Davis' son, Mark, running the Raiders. Mark is a spoiled brat who wants to hang out with superstars and to mingle with the beautiful women. Those are two of the main reasons why he moved to Las Vegas."

So, finally, the earthquake-sized question: What happens to Oakland if all three teams leave? How can it fill *that* hole?

"Oakland's going to continue to be great," Cobb countered. "I have a prediction that you might not be ready to hear. If the A's move, to Las Vegas or wherever, I predict that in two or three years a new baseball team will come to Oakland."

Really? How?

"Racial diversity," Cobb offered. "There's a movement in this country that Oakland could benefit by, because of its diversity. Oakland sits at the heart and vortex of innovation in this country. There's always going to be dynamism and activity in the Bay Area. Oakland is located on the sunny side of the Bay, and people always want to come here. Oakland is the engine of creativity, culturally and athletically."

Contrarily, if Oakland is wiped out as a major sports market, has that engine lost its firepower? Paul Cobb doesn't believe so, and neither does Bill Patterson, who predicted, "Oakland will rise again. I wouldn't be surprised if Oakland gets another franchise—football might be the easiest one."

However, whenever an Oakland sports fanchise has departed, replacing it with an expansion team hasn't happened. Oh, well; optimism soothes the mind better than pessimism.

Oakland is, unfairly, the city that is flogged continually—by San Francisco, by sports franchises, and by sports leagues in general. But Oakland, defiantly, sticks its nose out at the floggers. As Patterson and Cobb pointed out, Oakland doesn't need to feel embarrassed, or to feel a need to apologize about anything, which isn't necessary in either instance.

It's not Oakland's fault; it's just Oakland's predicament.

Chapter 15

Andre Ward:
The Perfect Fighter

Was I a great fighter? I'll say this: Yes, I was a great fighter. Just look at my accomplishments and leave it at that.

—Andre Ward,
Oaklander and undefeated boxing champion

Andre Ward is that rare boxer who achieved perfection. In the centuries-long pantheon of pugilism, few champions end their careers undefeated. From the modern era, there is Rocky Marciano, Floyd Mayweather, Andre Ward, and…that's it.

Ward, the super middleweight and light heavyweight champion from Oakland, California, had a record of 32–0, including 16 knockouts, 15 decisions, and one disqualification before his early, by boxing standards, retirement at 33.

His distinguished ring career, which ended in 2017, also included a gold medal at the 2004 Olympics in Athens, Greece. Ward is the last American boxer to win gold at an Olympic Games.

"It wasn't my ultimate goal," he said of an unblemished professional career, "but it was high on the list, along with establishing a legacy and having all my faculties intact. It wasn't easy being unbeaten, because there are land mines everywhere, and you might step on one. And if you do, you hope that it won't take you out. I've only been knocked down twice. I just wanted to get out of boxing whole, and the undefeated part was icing on the cake."

The sweetest part of that icing was Ward's entering a special class of fighters remembered for their greatness. Yet the majority of them, from Jack Johnson to Muhammad Ali, Sugar Ray Robinson to Sugar Ray Leonard, suffered defeat.

"Absolutely," Ward responded quickly when asked if he was pleased to join such fistic elitism, "even though I don't toot my own horn. If someone wants to call me great, it won't be me saying that. But I'm not naïve; I know what I accomplished. I don't know my place in boxing history, but in my era, I know who I was. What constitutes a great fighter is fighting the best competition, and that's what we did."

Ward includes himself and trainer/father figure Virgil Hunter, a perfect fighting team, achieving perfection together.

Ward named three fighters he modeled himself after: Bernard Hopkins, Mayweather, and Roy Jones Jr., whom Ward considers the greatest boxer of all time, even though Jones, unlike Ward, sullied his career by fighting beyond his prime.

"I watched them all, stole from them all," Ward said, immodestly, of that trifecta, "and it wasn't just their personalities. I wanted to know how they dealt with the big moment, even from their preparation."

Historically, well before Ward was born, boxers didn't denigrate opponents prior to a fight, or even afterward—nothing akin to the accusations Muhammad Ali mouthed at foes, which changed that entire dynamic. Ward was a throwback, regarding opponents with dignity, not disdain.

"I wasn't raised like that," he said of boxing's braggarts. "My dad raised me as a Christian. I had morals and faith, which some might see as a dichotomy in a sport like boxing. You don't have to be passive or a pushover as a man of faith, and I tried to toe that line as best I could. I wasn't going to attack you verbally, saying things about your family. I was going to attack you in the ring. So I wasn't going to start anything, but if my opponent did, I would finish it in the ring."

Unlike 95 percent of fighters, or something akin to that speculative figure, Ward didn't overstay his time in the ring, risking losing fights as an older boxer that he would have won easily in his prime. So he took off his gloves, for good.

"The core of it was knowing when that time came," Ward explained. "I asked my pastor, Napoleon Kauffman [the former Oakland Raiders running back], when he knew to retire. He told me, 'When it's time to do something else.' I had 32 fights, all those training sessions, all that running, and being away from my wife and kids. I also had several surgeries. All those things add up. I wanted to walk away from the sport, not limp away."

Many aging fighters have reconsidered retirement and returned to the ring, either for financial reasons or having found the post-boxing life unfulfilling. Ward protected himself against over-staying, and he's resisting coming back.

"I want to be a man of my word," he said, "though it would take a significant amount of money to make me change my mind. But not all of life is about money. I put my body through enough. I knew this day was going to come, so I prepared myself emotionally and spiritually. Boxing is what I did, but it wasn't meant to consume my life."

Ward intimates that he is financially secure. Could he, for instance, finance his five children's college educations?

"Absolutely," he assured.

Then all that is left for him is mind games, i.e., historians speculating how boxers would have fared against one another had their careers collided. Ward addressed a projected battle of the undefeateds, himself against Mayweather.

"Tough fight, tough fight," he said. "Slightly different styles, but it would be a very physical fight, a highly paced skillful chess match. I have a lot of respect for Floyd and those other fighters I mentioned, Roy Jones Jr. and Bernard Hopkins. They'd be tough fights, but I believe I would come out on top."

Doubters mustn't discount Ward's impressive combination of qualities—quickness, instincts, intellect, ring distance, patience, ferocity, recovery, and a stinging jab after switching from southpaw to right-handed.

"One of my intangibles," he said in adding to that list, "is I was insanely competitive. And, for some reason, opponents underestimated me. They'd say, 'He's good, but…' There was always that 'but.' Getting in the ring with me, they would see that competitiveness. I never wanted a fighter to outwork me. I hated to lose at anything. I'm still that same way today."

Two boxing writers, Jerry Izenberg and Lowell Cohn, separately linked the unbeaten Ward to greatness in the ring, though with some reservations on Izenberg's part.

"Ward was like a comet that didn't finish the full arc of his boxing responsibilities," Izenberg noted. "He didn't run the full course he could have, but maybe because he felt he couldn't. Unlike the typical fighter, 98 percent of whom come back, he didn't come back. One reason they come back is money; they're broke. The other reason is the sound of the crowd. For Muhammad Ali, it was his opiate.

"Maybe Ward doesn't need the money. The highlight of his career was the first [Sergey] Kovalev fight. Ward was losing, but he changed in the middle of the fight. He increased his movement and he made Kovalev come to him. Off that experience, he dominated the second Kovalev fight. Andre Ward was a thinking fighter."

Cohn once sat with Ward, during the latter's fistic heyday, before appearing together on a San Francisco television show.

"We got to talking about someone's big salary," said Cohn. "Andre looked at me, unenviously, and said, 'If I had made that kind of money, I could quit boxing.' So it didn't surprise me that he retired early. He was a brilliant defensive fighter, very hard to hit. He had all the offensive tools. He was a hard puncher, but not devastating. When he fought, he was the best fighter around, with the possible exception of Floyd Mayweather. But Andre was more exciting."

While others see Ward's two wins over Kovalev as the defining moments of his career, he believes that he assembled some convincing ring moments beforehand. He came out of the "Super Six" competition, for instance, to beat an undefeated light-heavyweight champion, Chad Dawson. Ward will admit, though, that Kovalev "cemented my boxing legacy."

So, then, how does a 33-year-old boxing retiree replace the spotlight, or ring lights, that shined down on him?

"My wife and I are in the ministry right now as youth pastors," he said in August 2020. "There's a lot of passion in that, plus we have a 19-year-old and a two-year old. And I'm doing [boxing] broadcasting, so I have a lot on my plate, different challenges that are keeping me motivated and busy."

Four of his five children are boys. Would he let them box?

"I probably would, but first, I'd have to see above-average talent and a good work ethic," he said. "I believe that they will find their way, and, besides, it's hard for them coming behind me, because they'd have big shoes to fill. Would I manage them? I have a couple of fighters I'm working with now. Like I said, it's about above-average talent and a work ethic. If it's there, and they want me to, then I'd manage them."

Ward needed someone to manage him, and to guide him, after his father, who was white, and his mother, who was Black, got heavily into drugs. Ward's godfather, Virgil Hunter, stepped into his life and provided vital direction when Ward was just a boy.

"I don't know what I would have done if I didn't have him in my life," Ward said of Hunter. "Me and an older brother, Jonathan, were displaced, and Virg and his wife took us in. Otherwise, I don't know what road in life I might have gone down. Because, at that point, I was done with boxing, and I was getting into trouble. But Virg got me back on the right road."

Ward recalled multiple instances in which Hunter advised him correctly—first as a godfather, then as his trainer and manager. Instilling self-confidence was paramount.

"Virg would always tell me that I could be a great fighter and a great man," he said. "Virg had a prophetic way about him. He predicted a lot of things—my Olympic gold medal and my [professional] championship. He also said that I would be a minister in the church one day. He told me that I would be a one-woman man and a family man, and I am that person."

Hunter was a huge influence for Ward outside the ring, but what was the main impact he had inside the ropes?

"He would always tell me a week before a fight, or the day of a fight, that God put me here for a reason," Ward said. "He just encouraged me, awakened things inside me. He told me that I wasn't an average fighter, that I had this purpose to become a great fighter, and he kept pushing me in that direction. Those constant reminders are what got me over the top."

During a fight, Hunter kept Ward on track, telling him "keep working, things are going good," and keeping him calm. "But when Kovalev knocked me down, Virg got in my grill, telling me that Ali got knocked down, Sugar Ray Leonard got knocked down, just get up and get it done," Ward said. "That's what you need, encouragement at a crucial moment. When Kovalev knocked me down, I was overthinking, and he was punching. That's when my competitiveness came out. I was embarrassed at being down, and it was a fight-or-flight situation. Kovalev put me in a hole, and I had to fight my way out of it. But I was a warrior, and that's what came out of me."

Great fighters do need great trainers—a Cus D'Amato, Ray Arcel, or Angelo Dundee. Ward places Hunter in that elite class.

"Virg is in his own lane," Ward said. "Some of those guys only show up four weeks before a fight, and they do a great job. But Virg is like a counselor at times, a father figure at other times. He has given me advice on relationships with girlfriends, with wives. He has a big heart, and he gives you a realistic approach. He's a great trainer, very knowledgeable. Sometimes, he'll tell you things you don't want to hear, but he never panics. I think he is one of the great trainers, because he didn't get me as an established fighter. He started me from scratch, from nothing, and he built me up to be a champion."

Hunter first saw Ward in a Hayward gym as a nine-year-old and was impressed by the boy's zeal in hitting a heavy bag. "He's got a little pop," Hunter told himself. Ward's father asked Hunter that same day if he could recommend a boxing teacher for his son. Hunter recommended himself and, after a two-week trial period, a beautiful relationship was born in 1994.

"He was so dedicated, so determined, that I knew we should be together," said Hunter.

He trained Ward for six months before entering him into Silver Gloves competition for kids aged nine through 15. Turning 10, Ward won a national championship at 90 pounds. Turning 12, he came to live with Virgil and Millicent Hunter, plus Jonathan, who also had ring skills, winning a national amateur title. But Jonathan gave up boxing because, unlike Andre, he didn't like to train.

"Andre was very athletic," Hunter recalled, "and he was intelligent. He picked up on instructions very well. I gave him the foundation, and he took it from there. He watched hours and hours of boxing film, a student of the game. He was very easy to coach, and he was competitive. He hated to lose."

Hunter, the sage, predicted correctly that Ward would rise from Olympic champion to professional champion. In between, Ward found faith and a wife, Tiffany, whom he married when they were teenagers. He then became a pro boxer at 19.

"We laid out a plan that when Andre won a title, he would keep the title, so he didn't fight for a championship until he was 24," Hunter said. "I knew he was a good boxer, but the last thing he needed to gain was an inside game."

Ward had a boxer's dual gifts: swiftness of hands and quickness of mind. "His anticipation was so good, he could pick up on your punches before you threw them," Hunter said. "He would time you, and he was accurate."

Ward left the middleweight ranks when "there was no one left to beat," said Hunter. So Ward became a light heavyweight, where ring purses grew. But there in the ring loomed Kovalev.

"Kovalev had a great jab, and he was a good boxer, so those two fights became Andre's greatest fights," said Hunter. "I told Andre beforehand that if he got knocked down, to get up and smile. After that happened, I appealed to his ferocious side in order to get back into the fight. And that's what took place, his winning round after round after losing the first two rounds. Andre had that grind in him."

Hunter is convinced Ward deserves the reputation as a great fighter. "He lost his last fight when he was 12 years old," Hunter pointed out. "He was an Olympic champion and two-time pro champion. He's a first ballot Hall of Famer for sure."

Hunter was 66 when he was interviewed in August 2020. "I'll never find another Andre," he mused, although he also trained Mario Barrios, a WBA super lightweight champion.

Ward's toughest fight, ironically, wasn't the first Kovalev fight, but an earlier match against Edison Miranda in Oakland.

"Miranda's the kind of fighter where it's going to be a long night—or a short night if you're not careful," Ward said. "He was a Colombian guy with long arms, he was fearless, and he punched like a mule. He had lived off the streets, so a guy like that has nothing to lose. Virg told me that no matter what he hit me with, it wouldn't be enough. I had to tell myself, 'Don't go down. Don't go down.' I won, but that was, physically, the worse I ever felt after a fight."

Ward was born in San Francisco and graduated from high school in Hayward, abutting Oakland. But Ward spent most of his young life in Oakland and considers it his hometown.

"Oakland embraced me," he said, "from the time I went off to the [2004] Olympics. I wasn't happy when the Warriors moved to San Francisco and when the Raiders moved to Las Vegas. I understand it's business, but I'm not happy about it."

Ward has studied boxing's past as far back as the early 20th century, when fighters fought 70- and 80-round marathon fights, even three fights a month.

"I have a lot of respect for the older generation," he said. "The current generation speaks the loudest, but has accomplished the least, which is unfortunate, yet that's what boxing has become. I do consider myself a boxing historian."

Thus has Ward pegged a fighter from the sport's distant past that he would have loved to square off against as champions?

"I would say all three of the fighters I mentioned earlier," he replied. "It's blasphemous to say how those fights would have turned out, because I have so much respect for them. But if I could add a fourth fighter, it would be Sugar Ray Robinson."

Now that's really touching greatness, because Robinson is regarded as pound-for-pound the greatest fighter ever. Ward then opined on his own legacy as an undefeated fighter.

"All of my peers show me respect for that," he said. "They comment that I fought the best, and that I was a champion for a long time. Turning it around, I had respect for my peers. Not all of the writers may like you, and not all of the fans either, but if your peers respect you, that's all you can ask for."

There are other world boxing champions who were also Olympic champions, but only Ward won gold at the Olympics and then went undefeated as a professional. (Mayweather was a bronze medalist at the 1996 Olympics.)

"The highlight of my career was winning the gold medal," Ward said, "because that was my first goal, and it wasn't a business at the time, so there was a purity about it. Also representing my country after we had just gone to war in the Middle East was special."

One sign that Ward left boxing at the right time is his physiognomy. His nose isn't smashed, he doesn't have cauliflower ears—he looks like he did when he began boxing.

"That was also a goal of mine, to get out of the ring without looking like a fighter," he said. "That's one of the greatest compliments, when people say, 'You don't look like a fighter.' When I hear that, I think to myself, 'Job well done.' I'm blessed."

Ward also avoided that often unspoken fear of boxers—dementia taking control of their minds, because of the many head blows absorbed during a bruising career.

"I would have more concerns of that happening if I failed to stop fighting when I stopped," he said. "I got out with a minimal amount of punishment. I like my chances of living a long life."

As a trivia question, who was the last fighter to defeat Ward, who wound up 115–5 as an amateur? That fighter is still etched in his mind: John Revish.

"It was in a tournament called Super Gloves. I was 14, he was 15," Ward said. "He was a little bigger, a little stronger, and I was intimidated because he was knocking guys out. I fought hard and thought I won the fight, which was held in Lenexa, Kansas. I felt so bad afterward that I never wanted to feel that way again. I saw Revish later on TV; he had one or two pro fights. I asked a coach who knew both of us what had happened to Revish. He said John had gotten on drugs and passed [away]."

Ward spoke openly about his parents and their own drug issues. "My mom was out there, man, and couldn't function because of the drugs, but she's doing good now," he said. "I was caught in the middle of that, and it's a miracle I came out of it the way that I did."

Spirituality helped too. "Son of God" was embroidered on his boxing robe. His religious acceptance at a young age gave him the direction he needed to live a virtuous life. He is grateful to his father, who died when Ward was in his teens.

"He gave me purpose," said Ward. "He was a good man who didn't believe in picking on people. He gave his jacket to a homeless person in San Francisco. My dad was a giver, and I'm a giver.

"But we're both the type of person that if you hit us, we'd hit you back. When I got up off the canvas against Kovalev, that was Frank Ward getting up."

Chapter 16

Tony La Russa: Calculating Manager

It was really amazing, his being 100 percent on top of every game. That was the most remarkable thing about his managing.

—Dave Duncan,
Tony LaRussa's longtime pitching coach

Tony La Russa already had an envious history of first-place finishes before outdoing even himself with a Baseball Hall of Fame first—becoming the only Cooperstown inductee to resume managing. The Chicago White Sox, La Russa's first managing job in 1979, hired him back in October 2020 after a nine-year retirement from dugout life. At 76, he was the game's oldest manager by five years over Dusty Baker in Houston. At 78, he retired again, for health reasons.

La Russa began the 2021 season with the third most career victories by a manager, trailing only Connie Mack and John McGraw, but only 36 wins away from surpassing McGraw. Halfway through the season, La Russa became No. 2 all-time. However, another factor motivated him to come back.

"When I retired from managing," he explained, "I took on these assignments from Commissioner [Bud] Selig [dealing with on-field issues]. Then I joined the Arizona Diamondbacks upstairs [overseeing their baseball operation]. I went on with Boston and Anaheim [the latter role in player development]."

And while he was still close to the baseball diamond, he discovered that it wasn't nearly close enough.

"I found that I missed working with a coaching staff, and being down on the field, where the action happened," he said. "In an advisory role, you don't really have a hammer on what's going on down there. I had some other [managing] opportunities, but to go back to the White Sox, where it all started, with a team ready to win, it was too good to pass up."

The White Sox then proceeded to win the American League Central by the widest margin of the six division races. La Russa, clearly, hadn't lost his managerial touch during his absence.

Baseball was in his heart all along, but his heart beat more naturally, he rediscovered, by filling out lineup cards rather than occupying an office desk. But as a 24–7 workaholic, and returning from that nine-year layoff, he would need a pacemaker by February 2022.

"My friend Jim Leyland reminded me that when I won my last World Series championship [with St. Louis in 2011], I was 67," he said in 2021. "Well, I feel the same now as I did then. I know the energy still is there, and I have no health concerns."

La Russa's family didn't want him to retire in 2011. They had urged him to overtake McGraw. But how did they actually respond when he brought up returning to the managing grind?

"They were surprised, but happy and excited," he said. "My wife, Elaine, our two daughters, and their husbands liked being a part of [his numerical spot in history], so they were pleased."

But 76 isn't 34, his age when he managed the White Sox the first time. Nonetheless, he began working with his same familiar pace—without thinking of a pacemaker and a second retirement ahead.

"I don't need much sleep," he said upon his return. "But if I didn't think I could manage the way I did before, I wouldn't have taken this job. I'm going about it the same way I always did, because it's the only way I know how to do it."

The White Sox had made the playoffs during the truncated 2019 season, but were eliminated in the first round by Oakland, causing the firing of manager Rich Renteria.

"I can't speculate why they made that change," La Russa said. "I just know they were close, and that they've been building a good club, and had an excellent chance of succeeding. I was always a White Sox fan, and I had stayed close to the organization. I guess they thought I would do a good job, and I'll do the best I can."

La Russa's best, career-wise, is about the best any manager has achieved. His first four seasons, with Chicago, produced a .506 winning percentage. His next 10 seasons, with Oakland, pushed that winning percentage to .542. His ensuing 16 seasons, in St. Louis, pushed it even higher, to .544. And his winning percentage his first year back was higher yet, .565. But on August 20, he stepped away to deal with a renewed heart issue and didn't return as the fading White Sox finished at .500 (81–81).

"His hiring was not based on friendship or on what happened years ago," team chairman Jerry Reinsdorf said in 2020, "but on the fact that we have the opportunity to have one of the greatest managers in the game's history in our dugout at a time when we believe our team is poised for great accomplishments."

White Sox general manager Rick Hahn echoed that the franchise was looking for someone who had "experience with a championship organization in recent years." Hahn, Reinsdorf, and executive vice president Kenny Williams agreed unanimously that La Russa was the obvious choice. Ironically, it was Reinsdorf who pushed hardest to get La Russa, even though the White Sox fired him as manager in 1986. But it was Ken Harrelson, then general manager, who made that call.

"Tony is the best man to help us win championships over the next several years," Hahn envisioned, "and to usher us into what we expect to be a very exciting place for White Sox baseball."

Thus the front office's highest expectations would be hardest on La Russa. Cooperstown notwithstanding, because of an additional factor.

The White Sox rehired La Russa within a year of his February 2020 drunk driving arrest in Arizona, his second DUI this century.

"The first one was 13 years ago," he said. "I made a mistake then, and the remorse over the second one is overwhelming, because of the stupidity, the lack of accountability, and the damage to family and friends. But the White Sox knew about those two incidents, and they said they'd support me. There's no excuse for it, but I will be accountable from here to the end."

La Russa didn't duck the DUI question, but his sobriety bore watching from management. As punishment for DUI No. 2, he was sentenced to one day of home detention, fined nearly $1,400, and was required to complete 20 hours of community service. He also underwent alcohol counseling.

On an unrelated sobering note, he addressed how much baseball has changed since he quit managing in 2011, focusing on the game's growing emphasis on analytics.

"There is really a critical place in baseball to use analytics, but I think they've gone too far in trying to scrutinize games, and the playing of percentages, because it's a game about men, not machines," he pointed out.

This critique, interestingly, came from the same creative individual who pioneered baseball analytics with his computerized strategy early on in his managerial baptism.

"The beauty of a coaching staff is to observe opponents every day," La Russa cautioned. "Baseball can change in the early innings of a game, or from game to game, and if you're not able to make adjustments, it makes winning more difficult.

"Secondly, crooked numbers are wonderful, and so is hitting the ball out of the park. But, if you're not going to do the little things necessary to win, like getting the guy over to the next base in a rally, then winning becomes more difficult. While the game includes power, it also includes the little game."

Such human analysis won't be found in a computer. La Russa inspired baseball-wide multitasking by winning three World Series combined in Oakland and St. Louis. At the same time, he rescued lost dogs and feral cats as founder of the Animal Rescue Foundation (ARF) in 1991. Mack and McGraw, unlike the ultrabusy La Russa, didn't couple playing and spaying.

In analyzing his managerial success, La Russa believes "some of that was circumstance. It begins and ends with love of the game. I started in the minor leagues at 17, and in winning those three world championships (as an A's player between 1971 and '73), I sat and watched how Dick Williams managed. He became one of my mentors. Dick was insistent that the game be played at your maximum effort, and with maximum attention to execution.

"Baseball is a hard game to play, but you've got to play it right. Dick also took notes during a game on lineup cards, and then reviewed them afterward. He taught me that, and I still have lineup cards from when I managed. I'm thinking of putting them out some day—they have my notes on them, too—in order to raise money for ARF."

La Russa embodies the logical mind of a courtroom attorney, which doesn't stray far from the truth. Graduating from the University of South Florida in 1969 with an industrial management degree, he next earned a law degree from Florida State University and was admitted to the Florida Bar in 1980. He hasn't ever practiced law, as sports kept him from torts.

"I thought I'd see what managing was about," he reflected, "and then I was named White Sox manager in 1979. I had the good fortune over the following three decades of seeing ownership, manager, coaches, and players working together. There wasn't one day where my coaches and I didn't have complete support from ownership and the front office. Communication was so good that we never were surprised.

"I don't know of any other manager who had it that good. There were no betrayals or having your authority questioned. It was a matter of the more you love the game, the more you learn. And the more you learn, the more you love the game."

His overall success has, indeed, been earned. For his managing debut practically coincided with the arrival of free agency, and the constant shifting of players who eyed bigger paydays, which Mack and McGraw didn't have to deal with.

"So you had to work harder to establish relationships between manager and player, building an intangible into a tangible," La Russa explained. "If you achieve that, players will buy in and want to compete. I never took that for granted."

Managing, like law school, focuses on "attention to detail and preparation." But managing against the successful likes of Billy Martin, Earl Weaver, and Gene Mauch provided La Russa with "a baseball education. The desire to learn and keep learning, together with the support around you, maximizes the potential you think you've got. And the more times you pull the trigger as a manager makes you a better decision-maker. And, then, with the metrics system…we were pro information, but metrics are separate from what the scouts might think."

That informative comment was La Russa's subtle dig at *Moneyball*, the baseball book-turned-movie about how computerized readings of a ballplayer's talent will offer more relevancy than what a scouting report might indicate.

"You need to balance this new era of information with the hard-earned approach to people," he said in defense of scouting. "We've always been aware of where our team's heads, hearts, and guts were. The game can't be totally formula driven."

Managers and coaches also must be informed, and consistent, or their players won't buy into the program, La Russa noted, before getting more specific about consistency.

"The leadership style we had in Chicago, Oakland, and St. Louis was described as personalization," he said. "A player has to make a commitment to your team by his contribution. But as a manager or coach, we had to present an image that we were the same people every day. We were into a total contribution to the game, every game. And we were a family. When players are doing good, you put them front and center, and when they're not doing good, you don't desert them. And if you say that you need to coach them better, they appreciate it.

"The more confusing it gets, the simpler you keep it, because it all comes down to scoring more runs than the other team. But we, literally, worked every half-inning from the first day of spring training until the end of the season."

And that describes the precise, human aspect to La Russa's managerial style, separate from his fascination with analytics. But he needed to further downplay his computerized persona.

"I actually spent more time watching how the game is played, analyzing players' strengths and weaknesses," he said. "So a lot of that calculating is what you learned today, and what you can expect to learn tomorrow. I am calculating, but it's more about making judgments."

For the record, Mack won 3,731 games and McGraw 2,763, while La Russa had 2,728 wins at the start of the 2021 season. He also had retired as the first MLB manager in history to vacate the same season he won a World Series.

"My family wanted me to go past McGraw back then," he said. "When I retired, they thought I was just worn out from the season. But I had put a lot of pressure on Elaine to run ARF, and a number [of victories] is just a number. In the end, the most important thing was the relationships we built in three baseball cities. Those relationships are the things that matter most, and they are relationships that continue to this day, with [physical] embraces whenever we see one another."

White Sox general manager Roland Hemond had the foresight to hire La Russa as a coach in 1985. Decades later, Hemond said, "Tony La Russa is one of the most brilliant managers I ever encountered in my baseball career. There were some managers who thought he was out of line with what he was trying to do, but, later on, they had to respect him because it was working. There's no question he changed the way the game was played."

One of La Russa's game-changing advents: his specialized bullpen. In Oakland, Todd Burns relieved in the sixth inning, Gene Nelson in the seventh, Rick Honeycutt in the eighth, and Dennis Eckersley in the ninth. Lights out!

La Russa's longtime pitching coach, Dave Duncan, was largely responsible for that modernized rotation. These two were manager and coach in Chicago, Oakland, and St. Louis from 1983 to 2011.

"Tremendous preparation," Duncan said in describing La Russa's managing skills. "There wasn't ever a game that he didn't do tedious preparation. That was a key, tremendous knowledge of the opposition, including the matchups with opposing hitters against our pitchers.

"I never remember Tony having a bad day, where things got away from him, or when he wasn't paying attention to what was going on in the game. Tony had philosophies. No. 1 was making it difficult for the opposition to score runs. He had great communication with his players, who knew where they stood with him, because he was honest with everybody, and even straight with his coaching staff. He listened to every coach, and he had great communication with the front office."

La Russa's and Duncan's lengthy relationship had roots as infielder and catcher in the A's organization, beginning in the late 1960s and continuing through Oakland's successful World Series run in the early 1970s. Though they've been a terrific twosome all along, did they ever get under each other's skin?

"I don't ever remember a major issue," Duncan replied, "but we had to work through things and talk them out. We were always able to work them out. Tony didn't want friction."

Duncan didn't accompany La Russa to Chicago this time around. "Dave doesn't move around like he used to," La Russa said. "If he were able to, he'd be with us." So La Russa named Ethan Katz as the White Sox pitching coach, with Duncan serving as a long-distance, unpaid phone advisor.

La Russa's and Duncan's two most significant player success stories involved Dennis Eckersley and Dave Stewart.

Eckersley, a fiuture Baseball Hall of Fame inductee, accepted the A's bullpen role reluctantly. He had been a 20-game winner in Boston, had thrown a no-hitter, and didn't view himself as a reliever. Was he reluctant? He was closer to defiant.

"When we got Eckersley, he was a mess. We lit him up in spring training when he was with the Cubs," said Duncan. "We decided to use him in long relief until we could work him into the rotation, and he was really pissed off. But he pitched competitively, and we started using him later in the game. He did well, but he still was pissed off. Jay Howell, our closer, was injured, so Tony and I decided on using Dennis there. He decided he liked finishing the game, and the rest is history."

Eckersley found his niche as a ninth-inning closer in Oakland. "We were in the forefront of that [historic advent]," Duncan noted.

Stewart hadn't known success before arriving in Oakland...and then won 20 games four straight seasons. What changed?

"His first game for us," Duncan remembered, "was against Boston, and he beat Roger Clemens by throwing hard, hard, hard. You could see he had a fierce competitiveness, but he needed an off-speed pitch. He had a split-finger that two other teams, the Dodgers and Texas, told him to stop using. I saw him throw it between starts and I got excited. The split became his biggest weapon, and that's why he had those successful years."

La Russa managed Oakland from 1986 to 1995, with a 798–673 regular season record and a 19–13 postseason mark. The A's played in three consecutive World Series, 1988–90, winning it all in 1989 by defeating cross-bay San Francisco in the only earthquake-interrupted World Series in history.

"I have regrets that haunt me from those three years," La Russa rued. "We should have gotten another world championship, maybe two. There were things I could have done better, like getting the team more ready to play."

Overall, in addition to the three World Series titles (two in St. Louis), six league championships, and 12 division titles, he also is the second manager or head coach in American sports history to reach 5,000 games. Plus, he is the first manager to win multiple pennants in both leagues, the second manager to win a World Series in both leagues, and one of four managers to be named Manager of the Year in both leagues.

Caring as a manager, he was ultra-protective of his players, with few exceptions, one being Jose Canseco. Teammate Mark McGwire played for La Russa in Oakland and St. Louis before his single-season home run record of 70 was besmirched by a steroids scandal. Clearly, La Russa's most humane managerial act was hiring a tainted McGwire as hitting coach in St. Louis.

"As a manager, you cannot afford to be sentimental in your decision-making," La Russa said. "You're responsible to too many people—the fans, your organization, your players. I watched the development of Mark McGwire as a really smart hitter. He had an amazing talent for contact and timing. He was asked to coach because he had so much to offer; it had nothing to do with trying to rehabilitate him. Mark gave batting tips to Albert Pujols. Mark tweaked David Freese's swing, and it helped us win a World Series in St. Louis.

"Here's something else that never gets printed: Mark has tremendous integrity. He dabbled with that [steroids] stuff; he admitted to me that he did a little bit. But most of what he became was because he really worked out [in conditioning]. Then in 2001, he hurt his back and could hardly play. But when the Cardinals offered him $15 million a year to play two more seasons, he said he couldn't play that way any more, and he retired. He walked away from $30 million. Isn't that integrity?"

Critics of McGwire also focused on La Russa, wondering how he could have looked away as Canseco and McGwire injected each other in clubhouse bathroom stalls before A's games, an unsettling image that Canseco described in his book *Juiced*.

"Those accusations from Jose about Mark were bullshit," La Russa insisted. "Jose has since reached out to Mark to apologize to him. Jose told me what he wrote about Mark was not true."

Why would Canseco lie?

"At that time," La Russa said, "Jose had wasted his talent and was bitter. His talent had betrayed him. At that point, [steroids] had gotten out of hand. So we reported it upstairs [to the A's hierarchy]. I know [general manager] Sandy [Alderson], and I also know the integrity of the Haas family, and they tried to do something with it."

Where that went, who knows. Baseball's summit, perhaps?

"One of the most unfair things about the steroids is that [former commissioner] Bud Selig has gotten blistered for lack of action," said La Russa. "But the [players'] union said no to any testing. So the media and everyone else blistered Selig. But the matter wasn't solved until some players went to the union to complain about not having a level playing field, and the union then agreed to have some testing.

"Hitters were doing it, pitchers were doing it, so were kids in the minor leagues, and then high school kids decided they wanted to do it. It was bad business. All I know is that Jose wants to apologize to Mark, and Mark wants no part of it."

After leaving St. Louis, and before returning to Chicago, La Russa was the graduation commencement speaker at Washington University in St. Louis in 2014. And during that same time frame, he continued managing—dogs and cats.

"I'm just a good volunteer," he said of ARF in 2021. "Charity Analyzer investigates every nonprofit in the country, and categorizes them, giving out stars on how you conduct your business. Four stars are the most you can get, and for the 13th year, ARF has gotten four stars."

A four-star field general, that's no surprise if it's La Russa. But baseball or bassets, issues do arise. Prior to his first spring training with the White Sox in his second go around with that franchise, his wife, Elaine, and daughter, Bianca, resigned from ARF's board of directors in protest of the foundation's "static leadership." Another ARF staffer put it more bluntly: "Toxic."

La Russa, who remained on the ARF board, called it a "mistake" for his wife and daughter to walk away, remaining hopeful that they might reconsider. "You can't accomplish what we've accomplish when you're toxic," he said. However, in March 2020, one-third of ARF's one-hundred-person staff reportedly was fired. Recharging ARF became a bigger challenge for La Russa than motivating his White Sox.

"It was never me," he said back in 2021. "I'll be as active [with ARF] as I have been through the years, because the work that's being done is vital. It always takes a staff, especially in baseball with young players learning how to play the game. I really like our coaching staff. The game is about players entertaining fans, and our staff will continue to develop the players' skills. It's always a challenge playing against good teams, but we aren't an easy team to play against either."

The old manager planned to show up younger managers.

"I know you can only get 100 percent excited," he said in 2021. "It isn't about career wins; it's about the next win. I have a chip on my shoulder hearing that I'm too old and out of touch. It's not age—it's the challenge of relating to your players. I still look forward to it."

Through it all, he maintained a sense of melancholy about the City of Oakland and felt badly that two of its three sports occupants have vacated, leaving a huge hole in Oaktown.

"When I think of Oakland, I think of the entire East Bay," he said. "The East Bay proved, even when the Warriors were struggling, that it could fill the Arena in Oakland. I'm not in a position to second-guess situations, because I'm a big fan of [Warriors general manager] Bob Myers and [former Raiders coach] Jon Gruden. The A's have a loyal group of fans; the team drew 2.9 million fans one year when I managed the team. I think East Bay fans have really turned out when they're excited about teams that compete. But I do know, almost without exception, that organizations know what's best for them."

Regretfully, though, in language La Russa can relate to, Oakland, sports wise, is no longer the cat's meow.

Thus, a manager whose heart was always into baseball stepped away from a big-league dugout for the last time in 2022, because that same damaged heart needed rest and cure.

"I was hired to provide difference-making leadership and support. Our record this year is proof I did not do my job," La Russa said, humbly.

His lifetime record as the second-winningest manager offers significant counterproof. To any detractors, woof!

Chapter 17

Billy Ball: Marketing Wizardry

No sir: there is nothing which has been contrived by man by which so much happiness is produced as by a good tavern.

—Dr. Samuel Johnson,
English critic and pub enthusiast

W hen new manager and tavern frequenter Billy Martin walked into the Oakland A's clubhouse at the beginning of spring training in 1980, he looked at his team and told them, soberly, "You are going to be winners. You're good enough to win, and I'm going to show you how."

Martin learned his hardscrabble baseball chops from oldtimers just outside Oakland in his Berkeley neighborhood. He attended baseball workouts, while still in high school, with players from the Triple A Oakland Oaks. Casey Stengel was the Oaks manager and, in time, would become Martin's baseball Yoda. When Casey went to the New York Yankees in 1949, he brought Martin to the team a year later. Martin's roommates with the Yankees were Yogi Berra, Phil Rizzuto, and budding superstar Mickey Mantle, another tavern regular who would imbibe with Martin over a lifetime.

Martin's time in Gotham City was highlighted with forays into the city's nightlife. His pugnacious nature always seemed to end up in some sort of extracurricular activities late at night, in the Big Apple and, really, across the big leagues. Like Dr. Johnson, Martin liked a good tavern, bar, whatever. But it didn't always produce happiness in his case. Instead of back-slapping, it turned into jaw-punching. Thus, headlines usually ensued which had nothing to do with baseball.

Finally, the fed-up Yankees traded Martin in 1957 after a brawl inside New York's famous Copacabana nightclub. He then kicked around with six teams in five years. In 1965, the Minnesota Twins hired him as a coach. He was on his way to becoming a marquee manager, and he managed five teams: the Twins, Detroit Tigers, Texas Rangers, the New York Yankees repeatedly, and Oakland.

There was one Martin constant besides his barhopping: His ballclubs always showed improvement. In 1980, when A's owner Charles O. Finley was in the middle of an on-again, off-again attempt to sell the team to Marvin Davis, he hired Billy to come back home. The Martin-Finley combination had as much swagger as any manager-owner combination in baseball, although the New York Yankees' George Steinbrenner, of course, would yell to differ.

When I, Andy Dolich, was hired in November 1980 as the A's vice president of business operations by the Haas family, I only knew Billy Martin through his reputation. And I had never heard of *Oakland Tribune* sportswriter Ralph Wiley or San Francisco advertising guru Hal Riney. As it turned out, the mix of these personalities, new team ownership, timing, an 11-game winning streak, dumb luck, and some dynamic DNA created "Billy Ball." Martin brought credibility and hope to the mess Finley had created in his swan song as A's owner.

There might never have been a Billy Ball advertising and marketing campaign without a column that Wiley wrote in the *Tribune* describing the unusual way in which the A's played the game after Martin took over in 1980. I remember a conversation with Ray Ratto, a San Francisco sports columnist and Wiley's Coliseum press box neighbor at

A's games. Ratto told me that "Ralph understood it that day in 1980" after watching the resurgent Athletics win yet another game with a steal of home, i.e., Billy Martin's burglar's baseball. Wiley then coined the phrase that launched a franchise: Billy Ball.

The phrase was perfect, and Wiley explained why—even, forcefully, to a *Tribune* copy desk editor, who found Billy Ball "corny" and was prepared to delete it. Wiley told him it would come to blows if he even tried. The copy editor acquiesced, and history was made.

Martin was hired to revitalize a team that had won only 54 games and drawn barely 300,000 customers in 1979. The A's were irrelevant both in the Bay Area and across Major League Baseball. Wiley, known among his contemporaries as "The Wiz," midwifed Billy Ball into the very lexicon of the game. The A's of 1980 and 1981 were Billy Ball, and Billy Ball was the A's.

Billy Ball was a concept the fans could identify with, fitting perfectly into what we—the Haas-run organization—were trying to do. We started off the 1981 season 11–0, and then were 17–1 and 24–6 right out of the gate. Brilliant marketing, hell no. Serendipity, hell yes!

Then Matt Levine, working with the club as a business consultant, and I created an introductory letter to the leading advertising agencies in the Bay Area. We wanted to make sure they were familiar with the philosophy, goals, and objectives we focused on in 1981.

Levine's objective: 'We asked fans to tell us what Billy Ball meant, and they described it as being unpredictable with the ability to get inside people's heads."

The fans translated that into a style of play they hadn't ever seen before, a risk-taking willingness under Billy's leadership that was anti-establishment. Billy's pugnacious personality was ingrained in the character of the way his team played.

Most of the time, advertising agencies just come and pitch a potential client on what they have done in the past. We heard back from four agencies interested in meeting with us, including Ogilvy & Mather, which had an impressive portfolio of clients: Rolls-Royce, American

Express, IBM, and General Foods. Ogilvy & Mather had just helped Marriott's Great America theme park open in Santa Clara.

The O&M team of Hal Riney, Jeff Goodby, Rich Silverstein, and John Crawford then created a presentation, focusing on Billy Martin challenging our fans to get into the action with this slogan: "Billy Ball. It's a different brand of baseball." We couldn't guarantee that people were going to witness wins, but, with Billy Ball, we were guaranteeing that our fans would have a good time at the Coliseum.

It's easy to see why we picked O&M, which spent a week at spring training in 1981, filming six different commercials built around the theme of Billy Ball. In a three-week period beginning April 1, the A's and Giants ran close to 500 30-second ad spots. It was the first time the two teams went toe-to-toe in Bay Area marketing.

It was no contest. Three Billy Ball commercials won prestigious Clio Awards—the Oscars of the advertising world. At the postseason baseball meetings, we won awards for advertising ticket sales and marketing. David Ogilvy, the agency's founder, awarded the San Francisco office a special award for its work on the Billy Ball campaign. The A's exploded on the national media scene through the exposure of Billy Ball, with stories appearing in the *New York Times, Boston Globe, Washington Post*, the covers of *Sports Illustrated* and *TIME Magazine, New York Post, Sporting News, Advertising Age*, plus exposure on the CBS Nightly News and ESPN.

Do you remember those ads?

A timid fan walks up to the ticket window and the seller is Billy Martin, who says, "I suppose you came out to sit on your hands?" He proceeds to give the fan some coaching on how to yell. Billy and the players who appeared in the ads all received actor's scale payments.

In another ad, pitcher Steve McCatty, catcher Mike Heath, and infielders Fred Stanley and Cliff Johnson stand on the mound, engaged in a serious conversation. "What's the matter?" asks Stanley. McCatty: "Who was Beaver's annoying friend on the TV show *Leave it to Beaver*?" The umpire comes on the scene to break it up. "Lumpy," he suggests. "Nah," the gaggle on the mound replies. Flash to Billy coming out of the dugout toward the mound. The announcer's voice: "Experts agree that Billy Martin has an uncanny ability to keep his team mentally sharp." Upon reaching the mound, Billy quickly sizes up the confusion and says, "Eddie Haskell," and then walks back to the dugout. Fred Stanley looks at his teammates and says, "That's why he is the manager!"

In a third ad, two senior citizens are sitting on their porch, reminiscing about what a well-behaved youngster Billy was growing up in West Berkeley. The grandmother remembers Billy as a "good boy who was polite to everyone." The grandfather touches his head a few times and adds, "Mother don't remember too good anymore."

Wait—there was a fourth ad, deploying even more advertising genius: a controversy taking place at home plate, with Billy talking to the umpire. TV viewers awaited an explosion of four-letter words and Billy being tossed out of the game. After listening to the umpire's explanation, Billy smiles and says, "Ron, I'm sure your vantage point was better than mine. My mistake, my mistake." He turns and walks away, leaving the home plate umpire gobsmacked.

Above and beyond the Billy Ball advertising campaign's smashing success, the A's business operations team had several marketing programs that took advantage of the daily upside of media kudos the team was receiving, right along with the wins they were piling up.

I came up with a promotional concept: Year of the Uniform. Instead of disjointed, un-exciting giveaways, I staged a hat, shirt, socks, shorts, visor, jacket, baseball, gym bags, and, ultimately, Adidas shoes giveaway for kids under age 14 to receive on weekend games. This power promotion lured decent crowds and injected more involvement in enhancing the total environment at the Coliseum. The young A's fans had to bring Mom, Dad, siblings, and friends of the family to those eight games. We'd have 20,000 walking billboards in A's gear around town, in schoolyards, and beyond.

Our radio jingle was based on the tune of "Charlie Brown," using the tagline: "Why is everybody always pickin' on me?" Our selection of Kool and the Gang's "Celebration" became our anthem after every

Coliseum win. We hired "Krazy George" Henderson as our official cheerleader for home games. He created "the Wave" during our ALCS playoff game with the Yankees on October 15, 1981.

Because the Bay Area is a hypercompetitive sports and entertainment marketplace, our plan was to go big. The local map that the A's ownership studied in developing their business strategy encompassed the entire East Bay. San Francisco already was overbuilt, but the I-680 corridor of Livermore, Pleasanton, San Ramon, and Danville was growing at a rapid rate. Our aim was to own those communities, a lost generation during Finley's dismantling of the team from 1975 to1980. Once we had placed the A's logo solidly, like a flag in East Bay ground, we expanded north to Sacramento, south to Salinas, and east to the Nevada state line.

The year 1981 was a Hollywood dream story come true. If I, Andy Dolich, had written the screenplay, people would have called me crazy. No one could have guessed how successful it would become.

Unfortunately, we knew the always combustible Billy Martin had a departure date. Hey, that was his history, the drinking and the infighting. Thus, his leaving came at the end of the 1982 season. Billy Ball was over, but the ascendancy of the A's as a quality franchise continued on the rocketship that Martin, brilliantly, helped the Haas family launch.

Here is a column I, Andy Dolich, wrote years later for the Ultimate Sports Guide, a weekly online publication, merging Billy Ball with more recent A's baseball:

> On August 6, 2016, the Oakland A's celebrated the 1981 Billy Ball playoff team by donning throwback uniforms in their day game with the Chicago Cubs at the Coliseum. As part of the promotion, the A's gave away Billy Ball retro T-shirts to the first 15,000 fans in attendance, along with showing Billy Ball commercials, and introducing a number of players from that unique time in A's history.
>
> Earlier this month, the team highlighted its giveaway policy by sending quality players to competing major league clubs, by

trading Josh Reddick and Rich Hill to the Los Angeles Dodgers for pitchers Jharel Cotton, Frankie Montas, and Grant Holmes.

Here's an idea for a promotion that would be an A's fan favorite: presenting the best team on the field in Oakland that money can buy, which is the goal of most franchises in professional sports. Oakland A's ownership has won the Revenue Sharing World Series for the past several seasons with $30-plus million dollars per year of redistributed revenue ending up in their bulging bank account. More importantly, they have seen a significant increase in team value from the purchase price of $180 million in March 2005 to $850 million or more today.

The A's have continually cited their inability to be a keeper or buyer of talent due to the lack of revenue generated from 'Roto Rooter Stadium,' although majority owner John Fisher was listed at No. 246 in the Forbes list of the 400 richest Americans in 2015, with a $2.7 billion dollar net worth. Perhaps a line of prospective new owners would put their money down to buy the team before the next Hello Kitty Bobblehead Night. If you owned the A's, would you have any interest in selling this cash elephant?

Here's a basic overview of how Oakland A's ownership is gaming the revenue sharing system. Major League Baseball teams participate in a system that redistributes income from the richest franchises to their less profitable partners in an attempt to improve competitive balance. Under the 2012–2016 Collective Bargaining Agreement (CBA), each team contributes 34 percent of its net local revenue into a pool that gets divided equally among every team. Higher-earning clubs put in more than they get back, while lower-earning clubs receive more than they put in.

A's ownership has been uncharacteristically quiet on their specific plans to build a new stadium on Coliseum property. No matter how hard Oakland Mayor Libby Schaaf pushes to gain some traction for a new A's new ballpark, the A's will bide their time since they have a guaranteed yearly profit whether

they win the World Series or finish last. The estimated revenue sharing check that the A's deposited from their brethren
in Major League Baseball was somewhere around $34 million
last season. Since 2012, according to published reports, the
A's have received $114 million to support a club that is always
swimming with the bottom feeders in payroll spending.

Over the past four years, the Marlins, Rays, Royals, Padres,
and A's are among teams receiving a combined $642 million.
The franchises that keep on giving are the Yankees, Red Sox,
Cubs, Phillies, and Giants. The mountain of cash deposited
since 2012 is a staggering $1.15 billion.

If your institutional sports memory is functional, there was a
former Major League Baseball commissioner, Bowie Kuhn, who
vetoed transactions by A's owner Charles O. Finley. In 1976,
Finley wanted to move pitcher Vida Blue to the Yankees for
$1.5 million, and outfielder Joe Rudi and reliever Rollie Fingers
to the Red Sox for $1 million each. Kuhn struck down the player
sales as 'not in the best interests of baseball.' Finley had traded
slugger Reggie Jackson and pitcher Ken Holtzman to the Orioles
earlier in the season. Finley called Kuhn a 'village idiot,' and the
legal battle was on. Ultimately the courts ruled against Finley
and upheld the commissioner's power. In 1977 the A's won
63 games, ushering in a decade with only one winning season.

And so a note to Commissioner Rob Manfred, who has
been publicly supportive of Oakland keeping its baseball team:
"The fans of this storied franchise are beyond patient in watching
their best talent traded away. It might be worthwhile for you,
Mister Commissioner, to look at the best interests of a baseball
clause, to make sure the A's keep some of the most talented
young players in baseball, instead of dismantling the franchise.'

"Financial victory," I say, "defined by making mountains
of money from a sports franchise is fine. The pursuit of victory
on the field is even better.

"Your move, commissioner."

Manfred is now less supportive of Oakland. Surprised,
anyone?

Chapter 18

Dan Siegel:
A Legal Outlook

When the Dodgers and Giants left New York, it felt like Walt Disney had bought the Statue of Liberty and moved it to Anaheim.

—Dan Siegel,
Oakland attorney, transplanted New Yorker

[Editor's note: the following chapter was written by Dan Siegel.]

Support for your community's competitive athletic teams is deeply rooted in human civilization, going back thousands of years.

As this book demonstrates, allowing unaccountable, self-interested businessmen like John Fisher, Joe Lacob, and Al and Mark Davis to exploit our emotions and loyalties is bad social policy and unacceptable. These business owners have no more concern for the health, happiness, and well-being of their customers than do the owners of oil companies and cigarette makers. Their model of sports ownership should be unlawful.

Humans have been playing sports and rooting for the home team for thousands of years. We have learned to think of the original Olympics, which date back to 776 B.C., as the first athletic competition. But the Irish staged track and field meets hundreds of years before the Olympics

207

started, and Berber tribesmen in Africa began playing "ta kurt om el mahag," a game very much like baseball, in the Stone Age, which ended around 3300 BC.

And in what is now known as Central America, indigenous Mesoamericans started playing "pokolpok," a form of racquetball, around 2000 BC. Their matches sometimes included human sacrifice, perhaps inspiring Raiders fans in the Black Hole at the Oakland Coliseum. Martial arts in China go back almost 3,000 years, and the ancestors of modern Iroquois tribes played lacrosse before Columbus arrived in America.

Amazingly, our ancestors enthusiastically supported their local teams despite the absence of electronic scoreboards, venues with flush toilets, and billionaire team owners. And they didn't have to worry about Russian oligarchs or Saudi oil sheiks buying their home teams and moving them to other cities, states, countries, or continents.

As a kid, I grew up a long walk or subway ride to Yankee Stadium in the Bronx, and I loved going to games with my father. He would buy a doubleheader ticket for $1.10 (60 cents for my brother and me), and we would sit in the bleachers all afternoon, cheering Mickey Mantle and Whitey Ford. Some of my friends, surprisingly, preferred the Dodgers (Jackie Robinson and Duke Snider) or the Giants (Willie Mays), but it was no joke when Major League Baseball owners voted in 1957 to allow Walter O'Malley to move "his" Dodgers to Los Angeles, and Horace Stoneham to move "his" Giants to San Francisco. If truth could be told, the Giants were also-rans compared to the Dodgers and Yankees in New York. But the Dodgers "owned" Brooklyn, and made lots of money for O'Malley.

Treating athletic teams as private property, indistinguishable from gas stations or apartment houses, undermines the public's ability to define and create models of what constitutes a great city. All cities need livable neighborhoods, schools, parks, sewers, and transportation. Great cities have more—music venues, public art, universities, a variety of restaurants, inspiring architecture, museums, and sports teams. People want, and deserve, more than the basics. Living in a great city—even a good one—adds so much to human satisfaction, happiness, and pride. Granted, not everyone cares about professional sports teams, but having a team like the Golden State Warriors competing for a championship creates a welcomed, even if partial, antidote to the daily dreariness of a world overwhelmed with war, COVID, gun violence, racism, and environmental destruction.

Joe Lacob was allowed to buy the Warriors and move them from Oakland to San Francisco because the laws that exist today enabled him to do so. He and his business partners bought the team for $450 million in 2010. Today, the Warriors are worth $6 billion. There's no doubt Lacob and his partners contributed to the 13-fold growth in the team's value. Mainly, what they did was to hire good management—general manager Bob Myers and coach Steve Kerr—and allow them to select, hire, and pay great players.

But it is not a stretch to point out that the Warriors' success is, at least, equally attributable to the tens or hundreds of thousands of Bay Area fans who buy the tickets and consume the products sold by the advertisers who pay for the broadcasts of the games on radio and television. And it's not only the team's fans who pay the taxes that built the roads and rapid transit that allow fans to get to the games, and to hire the police who maintain enough public order, to allow Lacob to make the obscene amount of money that he has accumulated.

John Fisher's approach with the Oakland A's has been a bit different. Lacob, at least, has been willing to invest in building a great team and spend his own money to build the arena in San Francisco. Despite being worth at least $2.3 billion, Fisher acts like the guy who says he can't afford to have his house painted or his lawn mowed while thumbing his nose at neighbors who complain about his impact on the neighborhood. Fisher refuses to pay his players or fix the bathrooms at the Coliseum, and he laughs at the dwindling number of fans willing to pay higher and higher prices for tickets. Fisher has seduced local politicians to the point that Oakland Mayor Libby Schaaf publicly justified the high ticket prices and lousy conditions at the Coliseum by saying that fans are just paying it forward for what will be a better experience when the new ballpark is built at Howard Terminal.

Fisher's game was to play Oakland and Las Vegas against each other to see which city will make him richer. He said he would keep the A's in Oakland and pay for that new ballpark at Howard Terminal in exchange for the whole city bending to his wishes about how to completely transform the Port of Oakland and a major chunk of West Oakland. He demanded that Oakland subvert its normal planning processes to gift him with the right to build 3,000 high-end residences, up to 1.5 million square feet of commercial space, 270,000 square feet for retail, an indoor performance center with 3,500 seats, and 400 hotel rooms. His plan gives no consideration to the impact of "Fishertown" on the Port of Oakland, with its businesses and workers and major impact on the region's economy. Nor does Fisher consider how his plan will impact the struggling businesses and real estate developments that already exist in other areas of Oakland's barely surviving economy.

American society runs, more or less, on the social contract model developed by philosophers John Locke and Thomas Hobbes in the 17th century. The laws that define people's rights and responsibilities are based on popular agreement, at least in theory. People accept a government and the burdens it imposes because it allows them a certain level of comfort and security. When the social contract breaks down, chaos, rebellion, and even revolution may result. Locke and Hobbes influenced Thomas Jefferson, Alexander Hamilton, and James Madison. For the U.S. Declaration of Independence, with its demand for "life, liberty, and the pursuit of happiness" and its emphasis on the equality of all people—at least, all people who were white, property-owning men—and their right to overthrow a tyrannical government reflects Locke's influence.

All of this leads to the question: What do the Lacobs, Fishers, and Davises owe the rest of us for allowing them to accumulate so much wealth, power, and property? Is this an area ripe for legislative reform? Until very recently, Congress seemed unwilling to impose any limits on Facebook, Twitter, and the other major social media companies.

Concern about the proliferation of fake news and hate speech, and their outsize influence on elections, has led many legislators to demand changes in what was previously considered to be the sacrosanct rights of the owners of those companies to decide what could be published on their sites.

The federal government regulates many industries and businesses to protect the public interest—banks, airlines, nuclear power plants, and telephone companies, to name just a few. State governments regulate public utilities such as electrical power companies and then decide where they can operate. City governments decide what companies are allowed to pick up the garbage. Under the commerce clause of the U.S. Constitution, the federal government has broad power to regulate industries that regulate interstate commerce.

The Supreme Court decided in 1922 that Major League Baseball could operate as a monopoly, based upon its rather quaint conclusion that a baseball "exhibition would not be called trade or commerce in the commonly accepted use of those words." Baseball's unique status as exempt from anti-trust laws has been maintained for a century, which means MLB can use its economic power to lawfully thwart the development of competitive leagues. Senator Bernie Sanders has attempted to remove the protection that gives MLB and its teams almost complete power over every decision, including where teams are established and where they can move.

MLB, the NFL, and the NBA already operate as near monopolies, with the unfettered discretion to decide where new teams—but not new leagues—can be established and where existing teams can be moved. The leagues establish salary schedules, create team salary caps, and determine which kinds of businesses can sponsor teams and buy ads during their games. Few would argue today that major league sports are not a business with substantial impacts on interstate commerce. Think of the gazillion-dollar television contracts and multi-million-dollar thirty-second ads during the Super Bowl. A business that impacts interstate commerce is subjective to congressional regulation under the commerce clause of the U.S. Constitution.

I propose a simple new regulation of major professional sports leagues that would prohibit a team from leaving the city where it is established without the approval of that city's government. No longer could John Fisher use the threat of leaving Oakland for Las Vegas to coerce the city into approving development plans that it would not otherwise accept. Instead, Oakland would be in a position to negotiate with the A's as equals, to develop plans for a new stadium that works well for both the city and the team.

Real partnership between Oakland and the A's would impact a number of decisions. The team and the city would have to agree on the location for the new ballpark. Without the threat of a team leaving, Oakland would be more willing to invest in the infrastructure and take on the regulatory work necessary to help make the project viable. In exchange for the city's support, Oakland could demand a share of the new stadium's revenue as well as improved pay and other benefits for team employees. If the team wants the right to develop the area adjacent to the new ballpark with housing and commercial uses, the city could insist—not beg—that the construction of housing includes a substantial number of affordable units.

Restricting the ability of a team to leave its city home would not prevent cities without teams from acquiring them. If a Major League Baseball team would be viable in Las Vegas, nothing would prevent it from partnering with a new ownership group and MLB to create one. Even better, Las Vegas could follow the example of Green Bay, Wisconsin, and establish a city-owned-and-operated team. Doing so might require an Act of Congress or a successful legal challenge to current MLB leadership if it were to adopt the NFL's ownership restrictions.

The Green Bay Packers are a publicly owned nonprofit organization that was created in 1919 to field a football team that has been one of the most successful franchises in NFL history. In 2021, it issued 300,000 new shares to be sold to the public at $300 each. No one is allowed to own more than four percent of the shares, and there are currently more than 300,000 stockholders.

The NFL apparently fears shareholder democracy. It amended its rules in the 1980s to mandate no more than 32 owners per team and requiring one of those owners to hold a minimum 30 percent stake. The Packers have been a success both on and off the field. The team's stock sales have financed improvements of its stadium, and the Packers are not going anywhere.

Is Oakland jealous?

Dan Siegel is an Oakland-based civil rights lawyer, political activist, and a fan of the Golden State Warriors, the San Francisco 49ers—ever since Raiders owner Al Davis abandoned Oakland the first time—and the New York Yankees. Siegel's law firm focuses on civil rights cases: fighting for the rights of workers, labor unions, victims of police abuse, prisoners, and the homeless. He has handled and won a number of high-profile cases on behalf of student-athletes and professional and university level athletic coaches.

Chapter 19

First National Champion: No-Helmet Football

If we had that 1969 team, we could have played in any first-division European league and been successful.
—Mirko Stojanović,
Oakland Clippers goaltender

Let's see; the first Oakland professional sports team to raise a major league championship flag, wasn't it the Raiders? No; this title team kicked, but didn't punt. So, was it the A's? No, this title team didn't pitch, but played on a pitch. OK, then, the Warriors? No, this title team had breakaways, but no dunks.

Soccer, anyone?

The Oakland Clippers are a forgotten entity in Oakland sports history, and not only because they lasted just three years. Soccer simply doesn't have the same foothold in America as football, baseball, and basketball. However, the Clippers paved the path to a stronger foundation for soccer before they disappeared from Oakland's landscape a half-century ago, a shooting star among sports titans.

They won the inaugural National Professional Soccer League championship in 1967, thus becoming Oakland's first major league sports champion. Even with the abundance of soccer league champions that have ensued, those Clippers still remain among the elite of American-based teams that played European football—or what we've defined in the USA as soccer.

"The New York Cosmos, with [Franz] Beckenbauer, Pele, and [Giorgio] Chinaglia, were a better team, but we would have given them a battle, because we beat the Russian and Italian champions," Derek Liecty, the Clippers general manager, noted in March 2020. "International experts said we could have held our own against the best teams around the world."

The Cosmos signed those three soccer legends in 1977, but that arrangement lasted about as long as the Clippers franchise, which, by comparison, was assembled more cheaply, without courting soccer's supernovas. The Clippers became heroes, nonetheless, to the small crowds they mostly attracted, although it was sparse attendance that sunk this ship.

The 1966 World Cup was the genesis of soccer coming to America as a professional entity, albeit in split form. The United Soccer Association (USA) began with 12 teams that same year as the NPSL, which started with nine teams, including the Clippers, owned by two oilmen, Toby Hilliard and Joe O'Neill, and attorney Bill Brinton. Their accumulated wealth proved vital as financial losses mounted early.

Liecty was a perfect hire as general manager, having played soccer at Stanford University and overseas in Germany, then qualifying as a referee in Chile before recruiting well-known European soccer clubs to participate in summer tournaments in the USA. He had the broad range of soccer experience necessary to run the day-to-day neophyte Clippers operation.

Liecty also helped assemble the Clippers coaching staff, for he knew Dan Tana, owner of the NPSL's Los Angeles Toros. As a youth in Belgrade, Yugoslavia, Tana played for the celebrated Red Star team. Through Tana, the Clippers ownership met the Red Star's successful manager, Dr. Aleksandar Obradovic, whose team had won the Yugoslavian league seven times since World War II, including in 1964.

Dr. Obradovic, or Dr. O as he became familiarized in Oakland, expressed interest in coming to America, but not by himself. So he brought along the Red Star's coach, Ivan Toplak, and trainer, Bora Babic, and a number of standout Yugoslavian players who formed the nucleus of those 1967 Clippers.

Goalkeeper Mirko Stojanović and center halfback Milan Cop were elite players from Yugoslavia's national team. Selimir "Sele" Milosevic and Ilija Mitic were scoring forwards, while Momcilo "Gabbo" Gavric was a rugged defensive fullback.

Stojanović, now 82 and living in San Jose, California, was a willing expatriate. "Some things were different in the United States, like the language barrier, but everything else was basic," he recalled. "At a Livermore picnic, a lady asked me if I was homesick. I didn't know what homesick meant."

The adaptable Stojanović adjusted well in English and on the soccer pitch. "We clicked very well," he said of the Clippers. "Our temperaments were similar. We joked with one another."

Dr. O scouted the globe in assembling the team. Edgar Marin and William Quiros came from Costa Rica, Mario Baesso from Brazil, Mel Scott and Barry Rowan from England, Trond Hoftvedt from Norway, and Ademar Saccone from Uruguay. Marin and Baesso were scoring threats, while Scott and Hoftvedt played solid defense. Rowan was a midfielder of average talent, but whose humor kept the team loose.

Herb Michelson, a club official, provided some of the Yugoslav players with American-sounding nicknames for the purpose of familiarity. Another important team addition was Dr. Leo Weinstein, a Stanford professor with an academic knowledge of soccer. He was hired to explain the intricacies of the game to unknowledgeable American sportswriters in the press box. Um, what's a free kick again, Dr. Weinstein?

Liecty recognized the arduous task ahead. "Our country saw soccer as an ethnic sport played in a feudalistic society," he recalled. "The Clippers started as a 9 on a 1-to-10 scale of difficulty in educating the public. But, in my young naïveté, it was the most exciting time of my life, the possibility of seeing my dream of soccer becoming famous in America. But I smoked a lot of cigarettes back then to calm my nerves."

Pulling out all the stops, the Clippers hired one of America's legendary football players—the kind who wear helmets—in Ernie Nevers, the Stanford and NFL fullback, to promote a sport he hadn't ever played. Nevers would be interviewed often, regardless, as he extolled soccer and the Clippers. But even this gridiron icon failed in boosting attendance.

An optimistic O'Neill projected an average gate of 15,000 as the break-even figure for the year. However, the Clippers drew below 5,000 much of the time. Their debut was dismal, blowing a 3–0 lead in a 3–3 tie with the visiting Pittsburgh Phantoms. The Clippers next appearance at home was a night game against the New York Generals, a 1–0 Oakland victory played before 2,600 in the cold and rain.

The blue-and-gold-clad Clippers lacked fire early, losing 3–0 to the Generals before 3,000 at Yankee Stadium. Oakland was winless in three matches before catching fire. They scored twice in the second half to overcome a 2–1 deficit and stun the Phantoms 3–2 in Pittsburgh. The Clippers then received goals from Saccone and Gavric to beat St. Louis 2–1 before 4,480 in Oakland. Dr. O grew confident: "I have seen all the teams in the East except Baltimore, and we can beat all of them, for sure."

Dr. O would see Baltimore again that season. But first he challenged the San Francisco–based Golden Gate Gales of the United Soccer Association to decide "the championship of Northern California." A Gales spokesman rejected the offer, saying the Clippers "know we can't play them, because it is against our rules as members of FIFA [soccer's international governing body]." The Gales were FIFA members; NPSL teams were not. Dr. O was blowing smoke but, then, he wasn't adverse to chain-smoking or a smokescreen story.

A curious airport traveler asked Dr. O if his team of average size and similar clothing was a band. The good doctor replied in the affirmative and told her that he played the tuba. Rowan, a continual cutup, then told a lady they were all Dr. O's sons. "How could that be?" she asked. "Oh," said Rowan, "he's been married eight times." Her reply: "Well, that beats everything."

The struggling Clippers, with a third of the season left, were stunned 3–1 in St. Louis. But when these same two teams met a week later in

Oakland, the Clippers dominated 9–0, comparable to a 63–0 win in American football. The suddenly on fire Clippers clinched the western division with three matches left, having, remarkably, built the league's best record. Four Oakland players were named all-league: Mitic, Scott, Stojanović, and Baesso, though one Bay Area journalist—I, Dave Newhouse—wrote that "Baesso" must mean "offside" in Spanish, as he was frequently just that. Gavric and Hoftvedt were chosen second-team All-League.

Late in the season, the Clippers had an exhibition match against Benfica of Portugal and its international star, Eusébio. Before 12,000 at Kezar Stadium, the home of the San Francisco 49ers, the Clippers and Benfica played to a 1–1 tie. That tie felt like a win to the Clippers against such a noteworthy opponent.

Then came a home-and-home championship series with the Baltimore Bays, the Eastern Division winner, for the NPSL title. But this is soccer, where games can end in ties. So after two games, if the teams were tied in goals, how would the championship be decided? As proposed by Liecty and Dr. O, and accepted reluctantly by the Bays, two 15-minute overtime periods would follow, and if the contest still was tied, a shootout would be held, six players per side.

Baltimore hosted the first game, a defensive battle with the only goal scored by the Bays. Dr. O said the 77-degree heat was "not good soccer weather. Oakland is much cooler, and we'll play better, I'm sure." The heat certainly didn't bother the Bays, but in order to decide the NPSL title at home, the Clippers needed to win the rematch by more than one goal.

Enter Dragan Djukic.

Dr. O had found an unlikely hero in Djukic, yet another Yugoslav, who was released by Los Angeles in midseason and picked up cheaply by the Clippers for $2,000. What a bargain! For the 28-year-old Djukic then scored a hat trick in the rematch, with all three of his goals coming in the first half. He headed in the first two before netting a penalty shot.

Who doesn't love the story of an unlikely hero? But his hat trick didn't receive the attention in non-soccer-oriented America it would have gotten in Europe, especially in Yugoslavia. Boldly, Dr. O had benched all-league Baesso to play Djukic. "We were undecided between Djukic and Baesso before the game," the good doctor said, "but we decided on Djukic because he is the only player besides Milosevic who can head the ball."

Smart thinking, Dr. O.

Baltimore proved a bad sport. Its captain, Juan Santisteban, kicked Djukic as he lined up his penalty shot, and then swore at referee Mike Askenazi, who later told the press, "He cussed me out in Spanish, which I understand, but you can't print what he said." Santisteban was banished, reducing Baltimore to 10 players. Though undermanned, the Bays scored to narrow the margin to 3–2. The Clippers still needed another goal, which the tiny Marin delivered in the 58th minute for a 4–2 victory and the league's first championship, played before a miniscule crowd of 9,037 gathered in the Oakland sunshine.

But the Clippers had become the Bay Area's first national pro sports titlist, two years ahead of the Oakland Oaks winning the American Basketball Association championship, seven years after the Raiders were launched, and one year prior to the A's relocating to Oakland from Kansas City.

But in facing a language barrier among various nationalities, how did the Clippers cohere so quickly as soccer champions?

"It was the fact that these players respected Toplak and Obradovic," said Liecty. "Toplak trained them to play together without their getting upset, and Obradovic wasn't threatening to the players, who grew into a group without rancor."

Talk about an anticlimax: the Clippers still had one game left to play in 1967, against St. Louis, which had defeated Philadelphia in the third-place playoff. Why can't a newly crowned champion simply put away its cleats until the following season? But the NPSL had the Commissioner's Cup, a strange pairing of first- and third-place teams. The Clippers won convincingly 6–3 to cement their superiority.

"You wait," Dr. O vowed afterward, "in two, three years, we will be good enough to play anywhere in the world."

Only the world, right then, was coming to America to play the Clippers, who would hold their own. Simultaneously, their world was coming apart. The NPSL filed an $18 million lawsuit against the United States Soccer-Football Federation, FIFA, and virtually every other soccer organization, contending they were driving the NPSL out of business. The end result was the formation of the North American Soccer League, temporarily stabilizing pro soccer in this country, but marking the end of the last unsanctioned league in world football.

Rest in peace, NPSL.

The Clippers remained positive despite the changing scene. "Next year, we will draw 8,000 to 10,000 a game, sure," said Dr. O. "In two years, it will be 20,000 a game, sure."

However, in 1968, Oakland would have four pro sports teams, not two. Besides the Raiders and Clippers, the Oaks and Athletics showed up, all four competing for local attendance.

Trond Hoftvedt didn't have Dr. O's rose-colored glasses to borrow. "Last year, we had the best field in America," said the Norwegian fullback. "Now we may have the worst."

The Clippers and A's shared the Coliseum—an uneasy working relationship, at best, because the A's would be the fans' favorite. Hey, it's baseball! A disheartened Hilliard projected that the Clippers' losses "would be well up in six figures." More bad news: some NPSL-founded clubs folded.

The Clippers did, however, achieve soccer independence in the Bay Area, as the Golden Gate Gales relocated to Vancouver, B.C. The Clippers envisioned a dynasty, but reality smacked them early as the defending NASL champion. Opening the 1968 season, they played to a 1–1 tie against the lowly Dallas Tornado. Then things worsened, with two wins in their next 11 matches. How the mighty had fallen so quickly, coupled with attendance figures of 3,000 maximum on their home turf. The Clippers' season needed an overall shot in the arm, and that booster injection, mercifully, arrived from abroad.

Manchester City, the English champion, came through Oakland on an American tour, playing its fourth contest in 11 days after leaving several of its best players home. Nevertheless, this was mighty Manchester City facing the Clippers, who were founded one year earlier.

And, rather miraculously, 25,237 showed up at the Coliseum to watch the Clippers deliver a 3–0 victory. Baesso scored twice, while Dimitrije "Dave" Davidovic, the team's latest Clipper import from Yugoslavia, added a final goal. Fullbacks Scott and Gavric held strong on defense, permitting only four shots by Manchester City, which hurt itself with stupidity. Mike Doyle swore at referee Eddie Pearson, himself an Englishman, and was banished. Then Tony Coleman slugged Gavric after a hard tackle, resulting in a second ejection. The Brits played short with nine men for two thirds of the match.

"Today we showed how good we are," said goalkeeper Stojanović. "We would have beaten them 11 against 11. In the English league… perhaps that's another story."

Dr. O was pleased, too, labeling it an "excellent game, one good for soccer." Good for the Clippers as well, though Joe Mercer, the Manchester City manager, said, "I don't think this will go down as a classic." English bitters.

Stojanović, now living an hour away from Oakland, relived the Clippers knocking off the likes of Manchester City. "I cherished those kinds of games, which were some of my best," he said. "And we clicked as a team, like a well-oiled machine."

Since the Clippers hadn't passed 10,000 in attendance beforehand, that game was, indeed, a milestone. But, then, only 2,527 showed up for their next outing, an overtime victory against St. Louis. The Clippers then slumped again, winning once over their next seven games. Team unity grew testy. "I can't play with Mirko; it's very difficult," Hoftvedt complained.

Why so difficult, Mirko?

"I can't remember that detail," Stojanović said a half-century later, "but we played with discipline in Yugoslavia, while Trond was taking it as it comes. Soccer isn't like playing in a church. Maybe I yelled at him, but that was nothing."

The Clippers then rediscovered themselves thanks to Sele Milosevic, who went on an absolute tear, scoring three goals against both Detroit and Dallas, and four goals against Vancouver. Saccone also scored in five straight games, and Mitic had a hat trick against Los Angeles. The Clippers were on fire, though ownership criticized lax fan support. "We're taking a terrible bath at the gate, and we're not worth that," Hilliard groaned. "We've got to make this thing pay for itself."

Right after Hilliard sang the box office blues, heroically, Pele came to town with Santos of Brazil. A Northern California record 29,162 fans showed up to see soccer's No. 1 legendary figure. He didn't disappoint, scoring twice in a 3–1 Santos victory. On one goal, he powered through two Clippers, somehow retaining the ball, then blasting it past a diving Stojanović. Oakland played well without two injured regulars, Milosevic and Quiros. "The whole difference tonight was Pele," said Dr. O. "If we had him, we would have won. He's fantastic."

After Pele left town, the Clippers were down to one remaining league game, needing a win at San Diego to qualify for the postseason. The score was 3–3 with five minutes left when Mitic headed a cross from Marin into the net. Teammates jumped and shouted, but Mitic was ruled offside. His goal was disallowed, and the game ended in a controversial tie. Thus ended the Clippers' brief league dominance. San Diego, instead, advanced to play Atlanta for the NASL championship.

Stojanović still is furious over that debated outcome. "They stole that second championship from us," he contended. "Ilija was one foot from the goal when he tapped the ball in, so how could he be offside? I put my life on the line in saying that."

At the same time, a number of NASL teams were closing shop, though the Clippers continued playing, scoring a 2–1 victory over Israel's national team before a crowd of 4,352 in Oakland. This would be the Clippers' final match as "Oakland," as Dr. O and Liecty devised a plan: Renaming the team the California Clippers, and playing strictly exhibitions in 1969, hoping that the NASL would reinvent itself in the interim.

The Clippers underwent a roster transformation. Milosevic went to Red Star of the French League, Scott went home to his construction business in England, and Ilija Lukic, yet another Yugoslav addition, joined a second-division club, Heracles, in the Netherlands. But, positively, Polish star Janusz "John" Kowalik of Chicago, the NASL's Most Valuable Player, and Cirilo "Pepe" Fernandez, a goal-scoring Uruguayan from San Diego, were signed to pair with Mitic, giving the Clippers the league's three highest scorers, just in time to tackle a toughened schedule against superb international competition.

The Clippers began 1969 by elevating themselves further in a three-match series against Dynamo Kiev, the first Soviet Union soccer team to visit the United States. Dynamo Kiev, from the Ukraine, had won its last three league championships. The first game was played February 23 in the rain and mud at Kezar Stadium. Dynamo Kiev prevailed 3–2, with Anatoliy Puzach scoring all three goals before 11,815 spectators. The San Francisco facility still had gridiron markings left over from the 49ers football season.

The second match was at the Los Angeles Coliseum on March 2 in front of 10,287. Stojanović was marvelous in making 18 saves, but he gave up a goal to Iosif Sabo with six seconds left in the match as the Soviets salvaged a 1–1 tie. Kowalik had scored earlier for the Clippers, while both teams finished with ten men as Fernandez and Ferents Medvid were banished from the physical contest for fighting.

Then it was back to Kezar on March 9, but this time the pockmarked field was dry as 11,223 fans showed up, a third straight attendance blow. Kowalik's header in the 72nd minute was the only scoring as the Clippers, behind Stojanović's latest demonstration of peerless goalkeeping, won 1-0. Holding their own for three games against a formidable power, the Clippers had reached their Mt. Everest moment. But where would they go from there, a steep descent?

Their next exhibition, in April, was against the United States' men's national team, an easy 4–0 triumph for Dr. O's side at Balboa Stadium in San Francisco. Matches were happening fast during the Clippers' slipping grasp on American soccer. In May, they played twice against Club America, a 3–1 loss before 3,666 at the Los Angeles Coliseum, and a 2–1 setback at Spartan Stadium in San Jose, with 5,112 in attendance.

The Clippers, meanwhile, organized an international tournament called The California Cup, involving themselves and three European clubs: West Bromwich Albion of England, Setubal of Portugal, and powerhouse Dukla of Czechoslovakia. The matches occurred at three sites: Stanford's football stadium, the Los Angeles Coliseum, and at a Fresno high school. Setubal won the opener, 2-0, in Fresno before 1,700 customers. The Clippers then tied West Bromwich, 2–2, in Los Angeles in front of 5,143 observers. Finally, at Stanford, 11,513 watched Dukla handle the Clippers, 3–1.

The end was in sight for the Clippers, and that farewell process began in Los Angeles with a 2–1 loss to Italian champion Fiorentina. On June 1, the Clippers retaliated with a 4–2 win over Fiorentina, which absorbed its first defeat in thirty matches as 7,356 watched at Kezar Stadium. The Clippers now had a 7–6–2 record in exhibitions. Mitic, Kowalik, Fernandez, and newcomer Johnny Moore scored for the Clippers against the Italians in a glorious, but saddened, exit.

"The owners told the players that [the two Fiorentina matches] would be the last," said Dr. O, "and would they try to play these with heart."

Mitic's mind was made up beforehand. "When the Clippers die," he said, "they die like men." Words to make a fitting epitaph on the Clippers' tombstone.

Three days later, the Clippers suspended operations, announcing that they were contemplating a suit against the United States Soccer-Football Association, blaming most of their problems against USSFA's control of soccer in this country. The Clippers lost $1.5 million in three years. Only Hilliard's and O'Neill's deep pockets could handle such a loss.

"It was fun, also terribly expensive," Hilliard said, good-naturedly. "Joe and I are strictly back in the oil business—with both feet."

Scottish-born Johnny Moore came to America in 1965 at 17, becoming the leading scorer in a San Francisco semi-pro league. The Clippers signed him strictly as a bench player, but he scored a goal in his first game, and then scored the franchise's last goal ever, against Fiorentina.

"The Clippers were the best team in the country, and that's a fact," Moore, 72, recalled in the spring of 2020. "They won the league championship [in 1967] and would have won many more. When they broke up, their players went to some of the best teams in the world."

The Clippers were loaded with stars, but Moore's favorite was fullback Gabbo Gavric: "He was the No. 1 guy, the cornerstone of the team, even though he was unheralded. He was a tough guy, the hardest worker on the team, and he had the hardest shot—it was frightening. He was in such good condition; he was bionic."

The gentlemanly Gavric, who later kicked briefly for the San Francisco 49ers, was the first Clipper to welcome Moore on the team. Moore later played on the United States national team, 1972 to 1975, and then starred for the San Jose Earthquakes before becoming their general manager.

"But the Clippers gave me my chance, even though the exhibition season was short-lived," he said. "I do remember the owner [Hilliard] coming into the locker room and saying to us, 'We're going to have to fold up our tent.'"

Liecty, now 90, gave up tobacco after the Clippers' tent folding. Would he do it all over again, even with further chain-smoking endangering his health?

"Yes," he said, immediately. "It was a high that became a low, but until it failed, I was on top of the world."

The Clippers' franchise farewell was played out at San Francisco International Airport. Dr. Aleksandar Obradovic, the irrepressible Dr. O, stood alongside his wife, Mara, daughter Biana, 14, and son Dragomir, 12, waiting to catch a plane to Yugoslavia. Team officials and friends were there to see them off, knowing they wouldn't be coming back.

"I still can get into the hotel business," Dr. O envisioned. "I have friends. I don't know about soccer. Possibly I could get a position on the board of directors of Belgrade Red Star, the team I used to manage."

Then it was time to board. There were hugs and handshakes as goodbyes were made with smiles and tears. It didn't work out in America the way Dr. O imagined, except for the league championship. But what he and other pioneers started in this country would lead eventually to a USA soccer explosion for men and women, topped by the latter's World Cup domination.

And there is still men's professional soccer played in the Bay Area, by those very same San Jose Earthquakes, with their very own stadium and with capacity crowds supporting them.

The Earthquakes do owe a measure of gratitude to a team called the Clippers for laying the groundwork. But what of two recent teams abandoning Oakland, the Raiders and Warriors, though, unlike the Clippers, wealthier for the experience?

Don't get Liecty started.

"That snake Al Davis, taking the Raiders to Los Angeles, then invited back—don't get me going on Al Davis," he said, suddenly steaming. "And the Warriors could have built their arena in Oakland, not San Francisco. It's ridiculous, of course."

But that sadness is Oakland's to endure, certainly not felt by its greedy sports owners.

Chapter 20

Jethro McIntyre:
The Eternal Coach

I owe baseball a lot, though I don't ask for much.
—Jethro McIntyre,
baseball scout, youth clinic creator

Some coaches teach baseball strictly for the satisfaction of watching youngsters mature under their guidance—free of charge. The ultimate reward for these committed coaches is having one of their youngsters drafted by Major League Baseball, the only "compensation" a selfless coach would need.

Jethro McIntyre is one of those giving coaches. He has worked with countless young ballplayers who dream of playing in the big leagues, even if their potential stops at the high school level. However, if they possess even an ounce of ability, McIntyre will draw it out of them—without a fee.

"The bottom line is that baseball people try to scare these kids into thinking that they have to go to these academies to make it in professional baseball, and then charge them an arm and a leg," said McIntyre. "The kids who come from humble backgrounds, they can't pay that kind of money.

"So I've tried to create a vehicle where these kids can learn baseball and better their craft. The problem is getting exposed, because those academies are for the laziest scouts. When I was growing up, scouts brought gloves, bats, and balls and worked you out. You hardly ever see that kind of scout anymore, because today's scout wants to go see 'the best.' That's easy scouting. I want to see a kid who's a 'late bloomer.' But you've got to beat the bushes to find that kind of kid."

Beating the bushes is what McIntyre, who was 75 when he was interviewed for this book in August 2020, has been doing most his life, and without remuneration, all because he loves helping kids to discover something in them they didn't know existed. And then, he brings it out of them at his Sunday clinics.

"I do it," he explained, "because people did it for me when I was a kid in Oakland. There was a man, Robert Mason, who owned a cleaning shop. He was pressing clothes one day when I walked by, and he said, 'I want to put you on my Little League team.' He followed me home and got my mom's permission. Mr. Mason taught me discipline, and how to be a man, sticking by my decisions. That's how I started playing baseball, and those things he taught me have stayed with me."

Right then as a boy, baseball became McIntyre's life: professional player, coach, manager, and scout. And so he, naturally, started these free Sunday clinics, taking schoolkids and teaching them the intricacies of baseball. He helped develop shortstop Jimmy Rollins, a future National League Most Valuable Player, and big-league pitcher Dontrelle Willis, both on Oakland-area diamonds.

Those clinics lasted 24 years. McIntyre now works with smaller groups, whenever he is asked. "I'm just available for people who want to see their kids get some help," he said. "I've been doing this kind of work since 2007. As long as I can hit fungoes to the outfield, and grounders to the infield, and work with kids on their mechanics, I'm OK. My doctor told me not to be a couch potato, to stay active."

What tells him that he is shaping a potential big leaguer?

"You look for athleticism," he said. "I can go to a ballpark, and you could put all 18 players [from both teams] on the field, and nine out of 10 times, I can point to the best guys, just by the way they walk.

They have a certain swag, and then they'll do something the other players can't do."

Finding the best players, sometimes, is easier than finding the best ball fields for one of his moveable clinics. That became a constant problem for McIntyre in Oakland, his hometown, because some of those fields were grossly maintained.

"You worried that a kid might get all his teeth knocked out on a bad hop, because they didn't drag the infield," he sighed.

He experienced better field situations in the Pittsburg area, where he lives, and where he was given a key to unlock any ballpark gate he needed.

But Oakland, Pittsburg…it's the same, hopeful, outcome.

"To see the smile on their faces after having some success," he said, smiling at the thought.

McIntyre's been a giver, not a taker, as a baseball lifer.

He cited the case of Alonzo Powell, whom McIntyre managed professionally in San Jose in the 1980s. Powell was taking too many pitches and getting himself out. McIntyre made him more aggressive, getting him to swing the bat as soon as he stepped into the box. Suddenly, pitches he once watched go by, he started knocking out of the park. Powell made it to the majors in Montreal, and then won three batting titles in Japan.

McIntyre also developed Rowland Office, Jerry Manuel, and Tyson Ross among his list of major leaguers. "Rowland once saw me sitting in the stands with some other scouts. He came over and, in front of everyone, said, 'If it wasn't for this man,' he pointed at me, 'I wouldn't have made it to the big leagues.'"

McIntyre, too, benefitted from the assistance of others as a youngster. At that time, he played with kids of all ethnicities, who got along with one another—a communal love of playing baseball. Equally important, adults in his West Oakland neighborhood "were good people who wanted you to do well."

McIntyre carried those kindnesses into adulthood, helping young ballplayers to become, if at all possible, professionals.

Breaking scouting down further, what are the skills McIntyre looks for in a pitcher?

"With a young guy, you look to see if he has a good arm," he said, "and the aptitude to throw breaking stuff at different speeds. But if he has a good arm, I can teach him how to throw a breaking ball or a changeup. However, I can't teach him how to throw hard. Nobody can do that."

What skill identifies an everyday player? "Hand-eye coordination," McIntyre replied, "and the quality of his swing. Can he hit better pitching?

"Look, talent is talent, whether you find it in Piedmont, Montclair Village, West Oakland, or San Lorenzo," he said. "Dennis Eckersley came out of San Lorenzo, while Frank Robinson and Vada Pinson came out of West Oakland."

Thus, there are no boundaries, physical or geographical, on talent, which McIntyre identified over 30 years of scouting, two years of managing, and coaching in the minors. Adding kids' clinics, which of these levels was the most challenging?

He responded by citing a past incident. A player he managed in San Jose, an unruly prospect, had come to blows with previous managers. Needing to set ground rules, McIntyre called the player in for a meeting. Reaching into his briefcase, he took out a .38 revolver and put it on the desk between himself and the player. That was, um, a rather bold talking point, but they got along smoothly afterward.

What keeps McIntyre going in baseball? "Good health and a good wife," he answered. Plus he is grateful for longtime clinic assistants Bert Strane, Ken Faulkner, Crawford Johnson, Sonny Rodgers and George Aubrey—who also work for free.

McIntyre took on these gratsis baseball clinics without much prodding. "That's true," he said, "but don't forget how much baseball has given me."

It's giving individuals, just like Jethro McIntyre, who become vital links inside a city, working unselfishly in its underbelly, grooming kids who might one day call themselves big leaguers, but, at least, responsible adults. Yet for those like McIntyre, public recognition ranges from scant to nonexistent.

"The best compliment I've ever gotten is 'thank you' for helping someone develop his baseball skills," he said.

A mere "thank you" for a devoted scout is all the payment he needs or even expects. What would baseball be like without the Jethro McIntyres of this world? A lot less giving, that's for sure.

And as an Oakland native, what are McIntyre's feelings about his hometown possibly losing all three of its teams?

"It would be a kick in the teeth. Oakland would be a ghost town," he predicted. "What's wrong with the Coliseum? It's the easiest location for ball clubs who fly into Oakland, for it's very simple to get to the ballpark, and there are hotels to stay in en route. So what would be the advantage of putting a ballpark at the Port of Oakland at Jack London Square?

"And I would hate to see the workers at the Coliseum lose their jobs. There are 25 players on a ball club, but there are hundreds of support people at the Coliseum. That's an important element to a city, but they never talk about the support people in any sport. The bottom line is you don't want to be held hostage by a major league club."

McIntyre then got to "the truth:" Oakland's crime problem.

"Oakland has a bad element," he said, "and that's why its teams want out, just like the Braves wanted out of downtown Atlanta. So they moved to Cobb County, which is like Danville."

Danville is an Oakland suburb that is white, wealthy and, largely, crime-free. But despite Oakland's crime numbers, it is on the rise economically, even experiencing a business boom.

"Oakland will figure it out," McIntyre said, optimistically. "Would Oakland survive if all three teams left? Sure, Oakland is doing great commercially, really growing.

"The A's want a new stadium, but it would be cheaper to renovate the one it has. It's sad, really sad."

Chapter 21

Matt Levine, Dan Rascher: Economic Eyes

> *It seems to me that Oakland and Alameda County*
> *have no appetite for stadium- and empire-building. The*
> *Coliseum site has…everything!*
>
> —Matt Levine, sports strategist

In an Economics 101 discussion, the shifting of a sports franchise would possibly portend a financial boom for the welcoming city and a financial dagger for the forsaken city.

Those would be logical assumptions, though Oakland can't ever be deemed logical, not with the Raiders leaving for Los Angeles, then returning to Oakland and, finally, leaving for Las Vegas. All right, students, we'll need your analysis in an hour.

Oakland has evolved into an airport gate for the well-traveled Raiders and a bus stop for the bridge-hopping Golden State Warriors. With two of its three sports franchises sporting new zip codes, Oakland has given desertion a new definition.

But after factoring in the $750 million price tag costing Nevadans to recruit the Raiders, plus steeper ticket prices, and a seismic forfeiture of attendance revenue in 2020 during a pandemic, who really came out ahead, the acquiring city or the abandoned city?

Such a question required serious financial analysis, which Matt Levine and Dan Rascher were qualified to provide after decades of immersion in sports analytics. Rascher's email address is sports economist, while Levine's business card says sports strategist.

Their astute opinions on Oakland's broken sports image, though, need to be heard separately to digest their full value. So, without filling out a lineup card, Levine bats leadoff.

"Oakland's soft underbelly and the romance with San Francisco has long existed with sports franchise owners," he said. "It is ownership ego, which is a major factor [in determining] where teams play. It's amazing how many owners care what their friends think about where they are playing, and how these friends will react when they become the owners' guests in the front row or in a suite."

Levine [pronounced Leh-VIN] stated further that acquiring a sports team feeds an owner's ego in a more satisfying manner than do their other businesses, for they now get to show off.

"The owners will react to this [sports] ownership as an accomplishment in their professional career lives, which they hadn't found previously," he said. "But the owners don't want to play in an area where their friends don't circulate."

Does that mean Warriors co-owner Joe Lacob wouldn't dare keep his team in Oakland, because his wealthy friends on the San Francisco Peninsula wouldn't come there to watch it play?

"I didn't want to imply that, but yes," Levine said. "And the Warriors' other owner, Peter Guber, is a Los Angeles [movie-entertainment] guy, and L.A. is more [West Bay] San Francisco than Oakland, Emeryville, and Berkeley, let alone Concord and Walnut Creek [all located in the Oakland East Bay]."

Levine offered another example of ownership ego: Donald Sterling. Former NBA commissioner David Stern "tried for multiple years," Levine recalled, "to get Sterling to move his Los Angeles Clippers to Anaheim, which would have given the NBA a team in Anaheim and a team [the Lakers] in Los Angeles. Sterling refused because he could never get his Hollywood Hills friends to go to Anaheim. So he stayed in L.A., playing in the same building as the [eminently more successful] Lakers."

Does Levine's analogy also suggest that Oakland, regardless of its abundant success on the national sports landscape, always will be regarded as San Francisco's ugly stepsister?

"Yep," he responded quickly. "And with the Raiders' success in Oakland, and the image Al Davis cultivated with all his fans in the end zone wearing their Halloween regalia, that became a metaphor for Oakland, which translated into merchandise [sold]. But major sponsors didn't want to be associated with hooligans."

Hooligans? Such an unflattering image, Levine continued, evoked an ongoing negative reaction in terms of how outsiders perceived Oakland, including, additionally, its very location.

Oakland where?

"People across the country don't know generally where San Jose and Oakland are," Levine noted. "They think San Jose is somewhere near Santa Barbara, and Oakland is somewhere near Sacramento."

Levine speaks from a half-century of business experience in the San Francisco Bay Area. Originally from Philadelphia, and having established a food and beverage industry background, he relocated in 1971 to the West Coast, shifting into sports consultancy with offices in San Francisco and Los Angeles.

His first client, in 1974, was the NBA franchise in Oakland. From the Warriors, and proceeding into a new century, he has worked with 60 teams in all major sports, plus dealings with commissioners and stadium managements. Horse racing, wrestling, and even polo, he has consulted them all. His latest project: three-on-three basketball, this time as an investor.

The No. 1 revenue producer at the Oakland sports complex in those early days, Levine pointed out, wasn't the Raiders, A's, or Warriors. It was Bill Graham Presents—music concerts that accounted for one-third of Coliseum revenue.

"When you looked at the Bay Area back then, it wasn't an east-west market," he said referring to Oakland and San Francisco and the Bay in between, "but a north-south market [the Bay Area to San Jose]. The advent of the [hockey] Sharks and the new arena in San Jose changed all that."

Thus, folks in Santa Clara County no longer needed to travel to San Francisco and Oakland for their sports or entertainment fixes; it was right there in San Jose. The Rolling Stones, Luciano Pavarotti, and other mega-entertainers who performed in Oakland now sold out in San Jose. With Davis [Raiders] and Charles O. Finley [A's] refusing to market their teams, Oakland suffered financially over time. But when the Warriors moved to Oakland, and the 49ers to Santa Clara, San Francisco suffered, too, for that east-west dynamic shifted to north-south.

Levine encouraged the A's to market San Jose as a revenue source. The outcome? "A modicum of success," he said. "The A's always have had a problem establishing their base, except with the Haas family and Andy Dolich's marketing at the same time, when they drew nearly three million fans one year.

"The Warriors were a sick pup with the Joe Barry Carroll teams owned by Franklin Mieuli, an image which changed under the ownership of Dan Finnane and Jim Fitzgerald, who realized that the north-south relationship was important."

Applying that same directional theme in a larger, revised context, Davis moved his Raiders from Oakland south to Los Angeles, with all that perceived glitter and celebrity status awaiting him. But then he moved the team back north to un-Hollywood Oakland. So what did all that travelling imply?

"The Raiders' marketing was as bad in Los Angeles as it was in Oakland," Levine replied. "Los Angeles is a very big market, so if you're not L.A.'s team, like the Lakers and Dodgers are, you've got to really work at it. Davis had a skeleton front office, and he left the marketing to the league to protect him."

But the National Football League deeply resented the Raiders over the Davis–Pete Rozelle rift and also because the Raiders were the only franchise that refused to contribute to NFL Properties and other league causes. So, what protection?

"Then Davis sued the league," Levine added, "for not supporting him in L.A. when the league was against his moving there in the first place. But Davis knew that Oakland loved him so much, with a fever that had no parallel, and he could get the stadium he wanted there."

Therefore, Davis returned to Oakland, where his Raiders then mostly stunk on the field. After he passed away, his son Mark, a black sheep, got control of the franchise and moved it to Las Vegas. And, once again, the NFL wouldn't put a team in Oakland, as it had done in vacated Cleveland and Baltimore. Oakland is victimized in almost every imaginable way.

"This is a north-south thing, too," Levine continued. "The NFL feels the 49ers will build a following [in Santa Clara] and [Oakland fans] will treat the Raiders as if they still were there."

The NFL is replete with such illogical thinking, including its stadium roulette policy. The league believes that if you build it, they will come, whoever they are. But don't build a new stadium, and franchises will be gone, not only in Oakland but in San Diego, from which the Chargers moved to Los Angeles. Despite a feverish following in Bordertown, the Chargers were instant orphans in L.A., which didn't care a fig about them, not after the Rams returned from St. Louis. Those two now share a new facility, further NFL stadium roulette. But the Rams, not the Chargers, immediately won a Super Bowl. Good luck, Bolts!

"Teams need pillar sponsors: six to eight sponsors who pay billions of dollars a year," Levine said. "The Chargers couldn't get a new stadium built in San Diego, and [owner Dean Spanos] didn't want to build it out of his pocket. But I think he will regret leaving San Diego by doubling up with the Rams. After being there five years, the Chargers might get antsy about moving."

So why move in the first place? Further evidence that some of America's dumbest people are wealthy sports owners? Another franchise given: sports cycles. Nobody stays on top forever. Outside of the New England Patriots, no franchise in any North American sport is competitive longer than a five-to–10-year cycle, though the NBA's Warriors come close. There are too many teams, and too much free agency, to emulate the long past ultradominant New York Yankees of Babe Ruth, Lou Gehrig, Joe DiMaggio, and Mickey Mantle. But if sports owners don't get a new stadium or arena inside an eclipse, watch out!

"What drives the value of sports franchises, and what drives revenue-building?" Levine asked. "Owners will put up with operating losses while playing the game of franchise value. But one thing hasn't changed: franchise success comes and goes. The Warriors may not get back to [in San Francisco] where they were before [in Oakland], winning multiple championships. I agree there are cycles in sports, yet even with all the comings and goings in success, a team's worth continues to soar, from the millions into the billions, regardless."

With sports franchises balancing these varying obstacles, Levine noted, "teams can withstand periods of losing if they represent competence, capital, and commitment, a three-legged stool. But miss one leg and the stool collapses."

Oakland sat on that same three-legged stool and watched it crumble without commitment and capital. So what happens to Oakland, economically, if the A's also move? Does the apocalypse descend upon Oaktown? That's the big question.

The answer, according to Levine: an A's relocation to Las Vegas doesn't seem feasible, even with an Oakland football expatriate, the Raiders, calling Roulette City home.

"Baseball requires much more population than any other sport," Levine pointed out. "Football requires the least—the number of games to be played, the number of seats to be sold. Basketball and hockey are in the middle. I don't think the baseball owners are interested in Las Vegas, because it isn't big enough to support a Major League Baseball team. And so what place, then, is left in the country to support a baseball team? Maybe Oklahoma City, but it isn't much bigger than Las Vegas."

In that case, can a desperate Oakland hold onto the A's? Levine paused 10 seconds before he responded.

"The county has sold its stadium rights to the city, which can build what its wants there, a shopping complex or whatever," he projected. "Does the city want to do that, while still carrying debt from when the stadium and arena were renovated or enlarged? I don't know, legally, if the city can eat that debt."

Major League Baseball, agreeing with its pro football and basketball counterparts, holds Oakland accountable for its teams leaving town instead of seeing the greed involved in their leaving. The contrast: Oakland feels it couldn't have done more to retain its teams; the departed feel it didn't do enough.

"There's work to do on the Oakland side," offered MLB Commissioner Rob Manfred. "I think the A's, most prudently, have have continued to pursue the Las Vegas alternative. We like Las Vegas as a market."

Those weren't comforting words in Oaktown, though Manfred added, "There is really significant political activity in Oakland. Mayor [Libby] Schaaf has done a really good job of moving the process forward in Oakland. But as you all know, California political processes are their own sort of animal."

A's team officials first visited Las Vegas in May 2021, and then made repeated trips to the Nevada desert. A's president Dave Kaval contended Oakland and Las Vegas were on "parallel paths," but Oaklanders saw his Pinocchio nose lengthening.

Although Manfred complimented Schaaf, that didn't mean she had changed her thinking on Howard Terminal being the best ballpark outcome for Oakland. But Levine doesn't blame the mayor or the city for its shriveled sports scene.

"Davis II [Mark Davis] is looking for a reason for being, in getting out from underneath his father's giant shadow," he said. "That had nothing to do with Oakland, which busted its hump in rebuilding the stadium for Al Davis. Oakland also helped in the expansion of the arena, in keeping the Warriors satisfied. Oakland must get credit for building the Coliseum Complex in the first place, and Oakland's economy, currently, has turned around positively.

"Oakland isn't fully appreciated, but you can't blame Oakland, because this goes back to what we were talking about earlier: Ownership's motivations, which are ego-driven."

Next up: Dan Rascher, who commented on Oakland's losing two sports franchises "in such a short time frame. But the financial impact on Oakland isn't that huge. Having a sports team is more of a cultural impact. So it's more of a moral issue than an economic issue."

But, he added, Oakland must decide what to do with its arena now that the Warriors no longer play there.

"That's a big chunk of land," he said, "that needs to be turned into something else. Does the city try to get another franchise, which then might require an upgrade [of the arena]? The A's, I believe, are willing to stay."

What's that again?

"Maybe the A's would like to redevelop the [Coliseum and Arena] property into a huge development, a fascination spot," Rascher envisioned. "That's probably the best outcome, and that way, the city doesn't have to pay a lot [of the existing Coliseum renovation debt], because it's a real estate spinoff."

Strictly speculative, he noted, but no one really knows how this philosophical, financial ballgame will end. Extra innings?

Rascher, a St. Louis native, migrated as a youth to Walnut Creek, a half-hour drive from the Coliseum Complex. He earned a doctorate in economics at U.C. Berkeley, and then actually consulted for the Raiders, before working against them in anti-trust cases, while representing the City of Oakland.

"Oakland is a good football market; the issue is the stadium, which everyone knows," he said. "Everything was there [economically] to make the Raiders successful, and their fan base was excited."

The Raiders moved to Las Vegas, regardless. Rascher also, successfully, represented Oakland against the Warriors, who owed the city money. He has taught at the college level, including a class on sports economics at Stanford along with this book's co-author, Andy Dolich, and is currently the academic director of the University of San Francisco Sport Management department. Rascher's evaluation of sports franchises fed into a sports consulting business. He works out of his Orinda home, just over the hill from Oakland.

Speaking of the Warriors, their relocating from Oakland back to San Francisco produced an NBA championship within three years. But if they don't win there with the same stunning regularity of their farewell, five-year NBA finals run in Oakland, could the reverse move across the Bay somehow blow up?

"Absolutely," stressed Rascher. "Especially on the West Coast, where [fans] back winners or they do something else. And the Warriors not only have to win, they have to bring in something else to pay off the debt of a really expensive building. The Warriors will have to hit on all cylinders."

He referred to the Coliseum site as "the perfect spot" logistically for a sports complex, much more ideal than the "downtown imprint" in San Francisco. But what does all that mean if Oakland isn't viewed as a desirable sports destination?

"My research shows that Oakland is the No. 1 city for an NFL franchise," Rascher countered. "Oakland is the highest-rated market in the United States without an NFL team."

He placed Oakland above St. Louis and San Diego, two other abandoned NFL cities, and Portland, yet another possibility.

"I don't think Oakland should be blamed for the Raiders leaving [twice]," Rascher said. "Part of it is the Al Davis thing, fighting the NFL. But if an ownership group wanted to put a new stadium in Oakland, I think the NFL would take that [offer] seriously. If you look at the true economics that make an NFL city successful, Oakland has it."

San Diego, like Oakland, was also abandoned, although just once. But Rascher believes, like Levine, that "the Chargers will wish in five years that they had stayed in San Diego" instead of moving to Los Angeles, "where they are the second tenant [to the Rams]. That was such a crazy decision. The NFL should have pushed back on that."

Rascher is convinced that NFL cities should step back from assuming the entire cost of stadium building, because if a team then decides to leave, the city "isn't put out that much financially. Oakland has gotten stuck owing a lot of money."

Professional sports have reached a selfish juncture where if team owners aren't gifted a new stadium whenever they want, they threaten to leave—and then, often, they do.

"Cities will pay 30 to 50 percent of the cost of a new stadium," Rascher reasoned. "But in the Bay Area, the 49ers', Warriors', and Giants' new facilities were privately financed.

"People are sort of tired of paying, and the costs keep going up. It all comes down to supply and demand, because the leagues run themselves that way. We allow our sports leagues to have that kind of power. The capital gains that cities achieve are beyond what they can get anyplace else. If you can build a development around a stadium, then it would be wise for a city to put some money into it."

But only under those development conditions, Rascher emphasized. The wisest current investment, he noted, either by a sports owner or a sports fan is Major League Soccer, "which is less expensive. I hope that continues, because it's nice to see another sport having a chance to grow. And it doesn't cost that much to build a soccer stadium, nothing like building a baseball stadium with luxury boxes. By building a new baseball stadium, you do double your revenue. That's why owners want new stadiums."

That way, he added, owners gouge the fans more deeply; a further demonstration of disloyalty by callous billionaires toward those minions who've continuously fed their wealth.

"The cities and counties have to stand up [to owners] more," Rascher insists. "That's because it's franchise free agency; they can go wherever they want. To make loyalty happen, it has to be forced upon the owner. What I mean by that: before you decide to leave, Mr. Owner, you must sign a long-term lease, and then you will have to pay off any debt.

"That's the only way you'll get loyalty from the owner, unless you find something like the Haas family, where the money wasn't as big as the deal, because they have money elsewhere. But the Haases wanted to be loyal to their community. Otherwise, what did [President Ronald] Reagan say—'Trust and verify'? That's the sports world we live in today, so you have to make that loyalty expensive."

But what will that loyalty, or lack thereof, appear like in the future in regards to sports owners' relationships with their communities? Could there be an entirely new legal business relationship between the two, somehow protecting communities from being abandoned by greedy owners?

"That's a great question," Rascher reacted. "Some day, perhaps because of antitrust considerations, owners won't have as much power to move. I don't know exactly how it will play out, but leagues will have more teams with more communities, and that way it will become easier to negotiate deals. Cities will wind up not having to spend as much money on their teams.

"That's my hope of what the future might hold."

But when does that future begin? Or if? Perhaps not soon enough, or ever, for a victimized Oakland, possibly damaged beyond repair, marking the death of a once great sports city.

Postscript

I'm an Arkansas native, but in looking for opportunity, I moved to California, eventually settling in Oakland in 1953. The great African American migration from the South at the time assured that Oakland would be the centerpiece for the Black population, the place to live because Oakland was thriving. There were jobs, entertainment, a vibrant downtown, and a bustling Seventh Street, which was similar to Harlem with its music and togetherness.

I immediately merged into the city and began meeting citizens from all over the world. Oakland was more than 40 percent Black at the time, but with whites, Asians, Filipinos, Latinos, Native Americans, Portuguese, Italians, and other ethnicities also living there, Oakland became one of the most diverse cities in America. Although there was discrimination, those nationalities were living together and interacting.

Oakland was considered a cultural city, and downtown Oakland was exciting 24 hours a day. Broadway was the main street with various businesses and movie theaters. Oakland had a Triple A baseball team, the Oaks, in the Pacific Coast League, led by a future Hall of Famer in manager Casey Stengel, and a pesky second baseman–turned–manager in Billy Martin. And I was in awe watching umpire Emmett Ashford on his way to becoming the major leagues' first Black umpire.

Oakland was about to become big league itself. And when the Oakland Coliseum Complex opened in 1966, I became an usher there.

I got to see the baseball A's when they moved to Oakland in 1968, and I also saw my first hockey game with the Oakland Seals. That was the beginning of something good, and it only got better. I was overjoyed to see the "Swinging A's" of the 1970s win three straight World Series, and I watched the Oakland Raiders amp up the intensity for sports in the city. Then came the Warriors, which amped things up even more. Oakland now was ethnically and athletically diverse.

But when the Raiders moved to Los Angeles, it broke the hearts of many, including mine, while confirming that the rich are different from you and I. And Oakland politicians, in failing to govern in the manner we had come to expect, then were questioned. Many people I've spoken to say Oakland's inability to keep the Raiders and Warriors from leaving is abhorrent.

For a city that has the propensity for giving up its sports teams, Oakland still is a beautiful city, with rapid growth and a strong economic base. Oakland has great parks and the beautiful Lake Merritt, with its circle of lights right there in the middle of the city. Oakland has great shopping, many hiking trails, and an excellent view of San Francisco from its hills. Oakland also has ideal weather, averaging 68 degrees year-round. Oakland's population is forecast to increase to 500,000 people by 2031. Anyway, to look at it, Oakland is on the rise.

I had the distinct honor of being one of two people to name Candlestick Park, which became the San Francisco home for the baseball Giants and the football 49ers. However, my biggest Bay Area influence occurred in 1998 when I established the African American Sports Hall of Fame, located in Oakland. I later changed that name to the Multi-Ethnic Sports Hall of Fame, recognizing Oakland's diverse sports culture. I've inducted more than 200 professional athletes and honored over 250 community leaders.

Though I've been approached by other American cities to launch similar halls of fame, and while I've also honored other notables worldwide, my main focus is Oakland, which has an athletic history second to none. In 2018, I appointed a female president to run the Oakland hall, relinquishing my day-to-day responsibilities. But I'm very proud of my creation, which Oakland richly deserved.

I'm so glad my life's journey brought me to Oakland, where the journey ended. I live in Oakland, where else, while witnessing its development into a technological hub. Oakland's social and political histories are well documented, and though we may disagree about Oakland's attributes, or have different philosophical and ideological viewpoints about Oakland, or question Oakland's inability to save its sports teams, Oakland remains a great city.

I love Oakland.

Arif Khatib has a diverse business background, establishing a record label, a publishing company, a production company, an African American sports magazine, an entertainment newspaper, and a boxing promotion company. His consultancy also developed and implemented minority and women's business enterprises. He produced the documentary Because They Believed *in 2021.*

Acknowledgments

The authors are grateful to the following contributors to this book for providing background, foresight, and substance:

Matt Millen, Art Thoms, Fred Biletnikoff, Tom Flores, Jim Otto, Vida Blue, Billy North, Joe Rudi, Roy Eisenhardt, Wally Haas, Jethro McIntyre, Dave Stewart, Tony La Russa, Dave Duncan, Andre Ward, Virgil Hunter, Dan Siegel, Rick Barry, Lynn Norenberg Barry, Scooter Barry, Joe Roberts, Jerry West, Jeff Mullins, Butch Beard, Clifford Ray, Tom Meschery, Charles Dudley, Dick D'Oliva, Shirley Figgins, Blake Green, Ken Flower, Paul Cobb, Bill Patterson, John Simmonds, Art Spander, Matt Levine, Dan Rascher, Joe Starkey, John and Sue Brodie, Barbara Lee, Alex Katz, Jerry Izenberg, Dick Spees, Ignacio De La Fuente, John Beam, Lowell Cohn, Tina Ricardo, Jim Zelinski, Russell Rivera, Kenny Mellor, Chris Dobbins, Derek Liecty, Mirko Stojanović, Johnny Moore, Casey Newhouse, Wayne Deboe, Joe Audelo, Mark Acasio, Barry Gifford, John Porter, Len Shapiro, Corey Busch, Dale Tafoya, Mike Jacob, Dennis Mannion, Michael C. Healy, Mark Macrae, Chris Berman, Steve Lopez, Ted Robinson, Arif Khatib, Mark Purdy, Pete Wevurski, Lawrence Ludgus, Dennis Eckersley, Steven Vogt, Delvin Williams, Eric Bjornson, Chris and Barbara Westover, Scott Ostler, Martin Snapp, Christopher Weills, and Oakland Mayor Libby Schaaf.

Also quoted in the book *Jim Otto: The Pain of Glory*: Bill Walsh, Hank Stram, Joe Greene, John Madden, Tom Yelich, Edwin Pope, Chuck Allen, Willie Lanier, and Phil Villapiano.

And thanks to Diane Curry of the Hayward Area Historical Society, home of the Oakland Tribune's library/photo files since the *Tribune*'s closing—yet another move out of Oakland.

Bibliography

Barry, Rick, with Bill Libby. *Confessions of a Basketball Gypsy: The Rick Barry Story.* Englewood Cliffs, New Jersey: Prentice-Hall, Inc., 1972.

The Official NBA Basketball Encyclopedia. New York City, New York: Villard Books, 1989.

Otto, Jim, with Dave Newhouse. *Jim Otto, The Pain of Glory.* New York City, New York: Sports Publishing, Inc., 2000.

Ribowsky, Mark. *Slick: The Silver and Black Life of Al Davis.* New York City, New York: Macmillan Publishing, 1991.

Seese, Dennis J. *The Rebirth of Professional Soccer in America.* Lanham, Maryland: Rowman & Littlefield, 2015.

Wangerin, David. Distant Corners: *American Soccer's History of Missed Opportunities and Lost Causes.* Philadelphia, Pennsylvania: Temple University Press, 2011.

About the Authors

Andy Dolich has five decades of experience in the sports industry, including executive positions in professional baseball, football, basketball, and hockey, all at the highest level. He owns Dolich and Associates, a sports consultancy, teaches at Stanford University, and is commissioner of Fan Controlled Baseball. He lives in Los Altos, California.

Dave Newhouse, a Bay Area sports observer since the 1940s, was an award-winning sportswriter and columnist at the *Oakland Tribune* before retiring from a half-century of journalism in 2011. He then became a full-time author, and this is his 19th book. He lives in Oakland, California.